# PROFESSIONAL ETHICS

"Society in the future may become progressively intolerant of voluntary professional institutions especially if they are the bulwark of private practice, and yet be oblivious to the truth that in these institutions resides a most precious liberty essential to the health of a civilised society."

Lord Butler of Saffron Walden

"These are my politics: to change what we can; to better what we can; but still to bear in mind that man is but a devil weakly fettered by some generous beliefs and impositions; and for no word however sounding, and no cause however just and pious to relax the stricture of these bonds."

Robert Louis Stevenson,
*The Dynamiter*

# PROFESSIONAL
# ETHICS

THE CONSULTANT PROFESSIONS AND THEIR CODE
*by*
F. A. R. BENNION

CHARLES KNIGHT & CO. LTD.
LONDON
1969

CHARLES KNIGHT & CO. LTD.
11/12 Bury Street, St. Mary Axe, London, E.C.3


Copyright © 1969
F. A. R. BENNION


Printed in Great Britain by
William Lewis (Printers) Ltd., Cardiff
A member of the Brown Knight and Truscott Group


SBN 85314 037 5

*To*

CHARLIE DENNIS PILCHER

*a professional man*

# CONTENTS

vii

## PART II: WHAT THE CLIENT LOOKS FOR

## PART IV: TODAY AND TOMORROW

# CONTENTS

# INTRODUCTORY

The professions, particularly those based on private practice, have been under close scrutiny during the past few years; many would say they have been under attack. They have been dissected by sociologists and criticised by economists. They have been referred to public inquisitorial bodies like the Monopolies Commission and the Prices and Incomes Board. They have been told that they have no business to fix their own scales of charges, but should let someone else do it for them. They have been accused of inefficiency, complacency and worse. They have been subjected to a novel form of taxation, the Selective Employment Tax, based on the proposition that the services they provide are in the nature of a luxury which people should learn to do without, or to do with less of. In much public comment they are regarded, indulgently or not, as anachronisms in need of radical overhaul. Phrases like "closed shop", "monopoly" and "restrictive practices" are freely bandied about.

Little has been done to combat these attacks. Many professional people disdain to answer them, shrinking from self-praise and the statement of what to them is the obvious. Outsiders know little and care less for the traditional values and rules of the professions. Their code, as it applies in Britain, has not been extensively examined in any published work. The terrain, as one commentator has said, is virgin and difficult.

In this situation and climate of opinion the present book has been written. It attempts to show in detail how the various rules of the professional code fit into an ordered pattern and embody a coherent philosophy. From this philosophy springs the peculiar value to the community of professional services, particularly those undertaken by private practitioners. Being human institutions, the professions have their imperfections. They exhibit, however, virtues of humanity, independence and incorruptibility which are much needed in the world today. Those who appreciate them should spring to their defence. Otherwise there may well, in a few years, be nothing left to defend. Private practice will have been blotted out by economic and other pressures and the citizen will go for advice to one source only — an all-beneficent state.

# PART I: PROFESSIONALISM

## CHAPTER 1

# ELEMENTS OF PROFESSIONALISM

Anyone writing about the professions inevitably has to begin by discussing what is meant by the term "profession". Admittedly, it is nowadays used without explanation or definition even by the highest authorities. For example, the President of the Board of Trade directed the Monopolies Commission in 1967 to report on certain practices prevailing in relation to the supply of "professional services", including restrictions on entry into a "profession", without deigning to explain what he meant. No outcry followed from the Commission or anyone else, it being generally assumed that these terms were sufficiently precise to enable the Commission to get on with its job. Again, when in 1965 the Governments of the Commonwealth decided to set up the Commonwealth Foundation and subscribe a quarter of a million pounds a year for the purpose of promoting links between the professions throughout the Commonwealth they did not think it necessary to explain precisely what activities they had in mind.

Yet this is one of the least precise terms in the English language. Quite apart from obvious difficulties such as those posed by the contrast between a professional and an amateur (a distinction which happily is rapidly becoming of little importance), there is the persistent inclination of people to use the term profession as more or less synonymous with calling, vocation or indeed any daily activity whereby bread and butter may be earned. This meaning is as old as Johnson's dictionary and has often led to qualifications of the term by prefixes such as "learned" and "liberal". Further difficulty is caused by the implication that to do any job in a professional way is to do it skilfully, with an expert finish.

It is unnecessary to labour the point, or to duplicate such full length discussions as are to be found in, for example, Geoffrey Millerson's book *The Qualifying Associations* (1). Where, however, a term is hopelessly imprecise if reference is made to dictionaries, but is yet currently used in official references and other important documents in a way which indicates that it has an unmistakable core of meaning, it is worth spending a little time trying to ferret out what that core of meaning is.

In other words, while a mere semantic exercise may be arid and profitless, a search for the quintessential attributes of a profession can yield a fruitful result. Indeed it is the thesis of this book that it is important to the wellbeing of the citizen that these attributes should be isolated and fully known.

Until comparatively recent times the professions have been taken to be limited to the church, the law and medicine, with possible claims from the army and the navy. This was the position at least up till the time of the census of 1841, but such an approach finds little favour in the twentieth century. The Oxford English Dictionary offers as a definition of "profession": "a vocation in which a professed knowledge of some department of learning or science is used in its application to the affairs of others or in the practice of an art founded upon it". While Carr-Saunders and Wilson eschewed a definition in their famous book *The Professions,* the Carr-Saunders report on Education for Commerce regarded as a profession "any body of persons using a common technique who form an association the purpose of which is to test competence in the technique by means of examination". (2) Millerson suggests: "a type of higher-grade, non-manual occupation, with both subjectively and objectively recognised occupational status, possessing a well-defined area of study or concern and providing a definite service, after advanced training and education". (3) Finally there is the definition put forward by the Royal Institute of British Architects in its submission to the Monopolies Commission: "A professional is a person expert in some field of activity who shares the responsibility for decisions, and gives a service to others in that part of their affairs to which the professional expertise applies, bringing to bear in this participation wider values than those whom he is advising may necessarily themselves consider relevant". (4)

These definitions would not be regarded even by their authors as satisfactory, though they clearly represent the product of much thought. The alternative to an all-embracing definition is a list of occupations regarded as professional; indeed such a list may almost amount to a definition in itself. Thus, while Carr-Saunders and Wilson put forward no definition they nevertheless, by the occupations they discuss in their book, indicate where they consider the dividing line to be. This classic work goes very wide and embraces activities which few would accept without question as professional. At all events if the same concept includes midwives, opticians, masseurs, merchant navy officers, mine managers, secretaries, civil servants, teachers, journalists and artists it must be a very broad concept indeed. Are there in fact any common threads which unite all these people except that they are earning their daily bread in a number of different ways? It may help to answer this question if we take some of the activities about which there has been much debate as to whether they are or are not professional and briefly analyse the arguments.

## Are They Professions?

*1. The Church.* The Church is the mother of the professions in the sense that until the end of the middle ages membership of the priesthood was virtually synonymous with professionalism. But is the Church a profession within the modern meaning? Lewis and Maude say "we cannot doubt that the clergy form a true profession". (5) yet Carr-Saunders and Wilson omit the Church from their wide-ranging discussion of the professions. Their reason for doing so is "because all those functions relating to the ordinary business of life, education among them, which used to fall to the Church, have been taken over by other vocations. The functions remaining to the Church are spiritual, and we are only concerned with the professions in their relation to the ordinary business of life." (6) Although the clergyman's role seems to fit neatly within each of the definitions cited above, many will share the view of Carr-Saunders and Wilson that in a meaningful modern use of the word profession the clergy should be omitted. Nowadays, led by Professor D.S. Lees, people tend to think of the professions in terms of economics, and the supply of services in return for a fee or other reward.

This hardly accords with the spiritual role of the clergy; and their hierachial organisation also places them apart.

*2. The Armed Services.* Historically, the Army has been looked on as a profession. W.J. Reader gives a clue to the reason: "But the most gentlemanly occupation of all, really, was fighting, particularly on land. Warfare, like Government, had founded many a family fortune, and in the eighteenth century the industry had only recently been nationalised: a strong flavour of private enterprise remained." (7) Up till that time regiments were very often raised on a private enterprise basis, and were regarded as the private property of their Colonels. The Navy operated similarly, and Reader cites the Earl of Bristol who in the middle of the eighteenth century "followed the usual practice of carrying treasure and charging one per cent. on the value of the cargo for doing so." (8)

Again, however, Carr-Saunders and Wilson exclude the Army, giving the curious reason that "the service which soldiers are trained to render is one which it is hoped they will never be called upon to

B

perform". (9) Whatever the reason, most people would exclude the armed forces from any but the most general meaning of the term profession. Their having been for a very long period completely under the control of the State is probably conclusive in itself, though perhaps an exception might be made for those fighting men who still hire themselves out as mercenaries in overseas wars.

*3. The Civil Service.* Carr-Saunders and Wilson take the Civil Service as having been a profession since the middle of the nineteenth century, which witnessed the end of patronage and the introduction of the examination system. It may be assumed however that the Monopolies Commission, in conducting their enquiry into the so-called restrictive practices of "the professions", did not take evidence from the Joint Permanent Secretary to the Treasury, the Civil Service Department or any other representatives from Government service. This is not because their terms of reference expressly excluded the Civil Service, but because the Civil Service is not nowadays regarded as being in a meaningful sense "professional". There are of course professional civil servants, represented by the Society of Professional Civil Servants. These, however, are persons employed within the Civil Service after having achieved a professional qualification elsewhere. The administrative civil servant, or the ordinary member of the executive or clerical classes, is not generally regarded as a professional person either because he has no training in a particular expertise or because his employment is entirely public in nature. Similar considerations apply to the local government service.

*4. Brokers.* The function of a broker is to bring together the owner of property who wishes to sell or let it and prospective purchasers or lessees. He does this without himself becoming the owner, thus differing from the "middle-man" in the sale of merchandise. Many would say that the services he provides are not professional.

These services cover a wide range. There are estate agents acting as brokers in the case of land and property, ship brokers, produce brokers, stockbrokers, insurance brokers and mortgage brokers. Their difficulty in being accepted as professional is illustrated by the remarks of Lewis and Maude: "It is arguable, however, that since commercial buying-and-selling of an entrepreneurial kind makes it impossible to regard the stock jobber as professional, the broker ought not to qualify either, even though he is remunerated solely by commission for fiduciary services". (10) The jobber is thus excluded because he is regarded as purely commercial in function, presumably because he actually becomes the owner of the stocks and shares he deals in. Others would disqualify brokers of various kinds on the grounds that they do not require to master an intellectual expertise.

*5. Teachers.* In the past teaching was often regarded as a profession, perhaps because it derived from the church. In ordinary usage it would still be referred to as such, though its having very largely entered the public sector at levels below that of the university and its lack of a representative body (apart from trade union aspects) clearly remove it from the narrow meaning of the term.

*6. Nurses, Midwives, etc.* Carr-Saunders and Wilson show some hesitation about the status of nurses. Their tentative conclusion is shown in the following passage: "At all times the direct personal relation of nurse to patient is a foundation upon which a sense of responsibility can be built. Until lately, however, the nurse worked under the direction of the doctor, and there was little element of co-operation. While the nurse must continue to work under direction, the tendency is to work towards co-operation which is made possible by the higher training. The vocation of nursing is becoming professionalised." (11)

Midwives, masseurs and other medical auxiliaries may be expected to continue to act under the supervision of a doctor or as his assistants. While no clear-cut judgment can be made about whether or not they constitute professions in their own right, these attributes of dependence clearly militate against this status. Since Carr-Saunders and Wilson wrote, the position has been modified by the passing of the Professions Supplementary to Medicine Act, 1960.

*7. Pharmacists and Opticians.* Doubt as to professional status in the case of pharmacists and opticians has arisen from the fact that they couple their advisory services with retail selling. In the eighteenth century "the physicians could always point to the fact that the apothecaries lived not by charging for attendance and advice, like proper professional men, but by selling drugs like the tradesmen they were. This gave them a direct interest in the quantity of drugs they sold and cut across developing notions of professional ethics". (12)

The modern view is that the ordinary pharmacist carries on two activities, one professional and the other commercial. This applies to about three-quarters of the 29,000 members of the Pharmaceutical Society. As Lord Upjohn put it in the 1968 case of *Dickson* v. *Pharmaceutical Society of Great Britain,* "a pharmacist's life consists of two parts: first, carrying on the profession of a pharmacist by dispensing and supplying medicines, surgical appliances and so on, and, secondly, carrying on a retail trade in what are called traditional goods, perfumes, cosmetics and the like, cameras and photographic materials. In recent years to meet increasing competition the range of goods sold by pharmacists has extended to non-traditional goods such as . . .

handbags, beachwear, souvenirs, pottery, jewellery, books and wines and spirits". (13) The Society's attempt to check the practice of selling such non-traditional goods as being unprofessional was quashed by the courts on the ground that it constituted an unreasonable restraint of trade in a sphere where commercial activity had long been accepted.

8. *"Creative" Vocations.* W.J. Reader refers to actors, authors, artists and musicians as the "creative" group of professions. These would include journalists, often regarded as a separate profession.

Harold Nicolson, himself no mean journalist, wrote of a dinner of the Arts Council: "The heads of all the professions are there. Tom Eliot for literature, the Oliviers for the theatre, Margot Fonteyn for the ballet, William Walton for music, Graham Sutherland for art, and Lord and Lady Waverley for the Port of London Authority". (13A)

Carr-Saunders and Wilson also regard these creative artists as belonging to the class of intellectual workers and therefore as coming within the professional field. They go on, however, somewhat surprisingly, to say that they differ from the architect (who also uses his aesthetic sense) in not possessing an intellectual technique, which can be learnt and tested. The technique of the musician certainly has an intellectual element which can be, and frequently is, learnt and tested. Admittedly the craft of authorship or use of words, where it goes beyond mere literacy, is less susceptible to academic instruction − though the attempt is often made to instruct people in the skills of novel writing, play writing and so on. But while freely conceding professionalism in the wider sense to these activities, many would feel uneasy at treating them as including those characteristics which we are coming to think of as the essence of professionalism. They lack developed professional societies and specialised codes of conduct. They do not provide advice, and are essentially individualists, whereas the type of professional we are beginning to identify tends to believe in the virtues of fraternal intercourse.

9. *Banking and Insurance.* Lewis and Maude express doubt about banking as a profession: "Banking, for example, is generally thought of as a profession − and so perhaps it was when bankers were individuals or small firms of partners, comparable to legal firms. But is it possible to regard a vast joint stock entity like one of the 'Big Five' as a professional entity?" (14) They take a similar view of insurance companies, but allow insurance brokers a professional role. In these fields it is not the nature of the activity undertaken but the way it is organised, namely in the form of large commercial companies, which raises difficulties in treating banking and insurance as professional.

The occupations just dealt with have been picked out as indicating various factors which cause difficulty in accepting a vocation or occupation as professional in the fullest sense. We have surely taken the discussion far enough to indicate that as a description of an occupation the term professional has at least two meanings, one wide and one narrow. The wider meaning is indicated by Carr-Saunders and Wilson's assumption mentioned above, namely that any intellectual activity is professional. The narrower meaning, with which this book is chiefly concerned, is shaped by the factors which have caused difficulty in the full acceptance of particular occupations as professional. Before attempting to pin down this narrower meaning, we pause to examine three matters which have bedevilled discussion on what is and is not a profession.

**Crucial Factors**

*1. "Trade".* It has long been an obsession with professional men, and still is today, that if they indulge in any activity which is "commercial" they are to that extent less "professional". The two are seen as opposites and the true professional man is obliged to refrain from all acts bearing the taint of commerce or run the risk of losing his professional status. The brokerage activities, such as estate agency, are particularly suspect. This is well illustrated by the fact that the Bill introduced into Parliament by Arthur Jones in 1965 with the object of setting up a statutory registration system for estate agents included a provision requiring that "account shall be taken of the fact that estate agency has both professional and commercial attributes". (15) This provision found its way into the articles of association of the Estate Agents Council set up voluntarily on the failure of the Jones Bill.

Probably most people in the property field would agree that the professional aspects of an estate agent's work are concerned with valuations, structural surveys and matters of that kind, whereas the commercial aspect is the purely brokerage function of bringing together buyer and seller and negotiating on the seller's behalf. This may be an over-simplification, however. The Royal Institution of Chartered Surveyors, the Chartered Auctioneers' and Estate Agents' Institute and other leading professional bodies in the property field take the view that the ordinary house agent's practice in the south of England is less "professional" than it is in the north. This is because in the south it is common for the vendor of house property to put it in the hands of a number of different agents, so that they each compete with the others in trying to find a purchaser. The societies accept with resignation the fact that in these circumstances there will be strong competition between agents in the seeking of instructions, but it is felt to be somewhat unprofessional. In the north, on the other hand, it is usual for the estate agent to be given a sole agency. This strengthens the relationship of trust between client and agent and enables the agent to offer advice on delicate questions, such as the right moment to close a transaction, without being harassed by the thought that he is by no means the only adviser in the field.

On balance, however, these societies believe estate agency, at least as practised by their members, to be basically professional. As they said in their submission to the Monopolies Commission: "The services of a professional estate agent are devoted to the best interests of the public as represented from time to time by the client who retains him, and this involves him in a fiduciary relationship with that client. The best interests of that client must be served in preference to the interests of other members of the public (provided that the latter are treated openly and fairly) and always in preference to any private interest of the estate agent, such as a quick sale to make sure of commission when some patience would have achieved a better result for the client." (16) Norman J. Hodgkinson, an experienced chartered surveyor, felt it was not strictly professional where the agent was one of those "who merely obtain particulars from an owner, and hand out those particulars to all and sundry, rather like groceries over the counter, often without inspecting or advising the owners as to value, nor, in fact, negotiating but merely putting a possible buyer in touch with the owner, hoping that business will result . . ." He contrasted this with the agent who inspected the property, took his own particulars, and advised on price and the best method of sale. This was "very much professional work". (17)

"Trade" has been used as a term of opprobium throughout the modern history of the profession. Thus when a representative of the Royal College of Physicians was asked by the select committee on medical education of 1834 what he thought of the idea of reducing the three branches of the profession, medicine, pharmacy and surgery, to one faculty he answered, "It would be the downfall of all three . . . it would reduce those which are professions now to a mere trade". (18) As late as 1878 the British Medical Journal expressed the view that "Medicine is a profession, dentistry is largely a business." (19) In 1927 the British Medical Journal was again stigmatising as commercialism the taking out of a patent by a doctor and his wife covering the results of their research into the prevention and treatment of scarlet fever. The view was expressed that they had their full and sufficient reward in having made the discovery, and that to ask money for it "would be revolting in the extreme". (20) Opticians, mentioned above, are dismissed by Carr-Saunders and Wilson as shop-keepers whose financial interest is to prescribe spectacles rather than diagnose disease. (21) The ·inescapable links between pharmacists and retail trading are mentioned above (page 5).

Why are professional people so anxious to be dissociated from trade? Carr-Saunders and Wilson say, "If a professional man were asked to explain the grounds of this objection to commercial activity, it is not unlikely that he would be unable to formulate them with any definiteness. At bottom they would appear to be the same as those which render it improper for a civil servant to speculate in foreign currency. No one engages in commerce who does not expect to make a profit out of fluctuations in prices, and the mental attitude associated with speculative profit-seeking is felt to be incompatible with single-minded devotion to a professional calling." Although the distinction has often been criticised, as by Matthew Arnold in his attack on English education as producing snobbery, neglecting science and perpetuating and reinforcing the damaging division between "professions" and "trade" (22), nevertheless it is very deeply ingrained – not least among writers on the professions. Thus Reader labels auctioneering "an undoubted trade" (23), although a case can be made out for saying that some types of auctioneering at least require a considerable degree of intellectual knowledge for their proper performance. There is after all more to the practice of the auctioneer than a run of patter on the rostrum and the ability to wield a gavel. Reader himself says that, "it is in depth of theoretical knowledge, as much as in anything else, that a professional man differs, or ought to differ from a tradesman." (24) A considerable amount of theoretical knowledge is required of a man before he is permitted to mount the rostrum at a sale at Christie's or Sotheby's.

Dicey took the view that the chief difference between a profession and a trade or business was, that in the case of a profession its members sacrificed a certain amount of individual liberty in order to ensure certain professional objects. In a trade or business the conduct of each individual was avowedly regulated simply by the general rules of honesty and regard to his own interest. (25) This suggests that a grocer could turn himself into a professional man by adopting a code of conduct similar to that of a chartered accountant.

It is indeed absurd for a nation dependent on trade as this nation has been since the sixteenth century to look down on those who earn their living in that field. Surely a more sensible ground for the distinction lies in the functions involved. There is a difference in kind between the supply of furniture or groceries and the supply of skilled advice on a basis of trust and confidence. One need not be better than the other; they are simply different.

2. *Manual Effort.* Commentators in search of marks distinguishing professions from other activities have seized thankfully on the concept of manual work. Here surely is a disqualifying i..,redient, at least where it plays any substantial part in the activity. Yet is a land surveyor any less a professional man because he uses a ranging rod and theodolite? Does a surgeon cease to be professional if he spends a great deal of his time carrying out operations? The physicians formerly looked down on surgeons "as mere manual operators", (26) but the time has long passed when their function was equated with that of the barber. Yet barbers also have obtained a professional-type regulating council, so in one respect are no different from surgeons. (27)

Despite the fact that they have completed the circle and rejoined company with the surgeons in this respect at least, few would consider the barber's essentially manual operations to be consonant with professional status. John Hunter advanced the prestige of surgery by applying scientific method to it; perhaps one day someone will do the same for hairdressers. Most people would feel that more than this is required, and that the function of cutting hair is not one which ever could be equated with true professionalism, perhaps because it lacks the advisory element which is an important feature of the surgeon's role. One does not "consult" a barber, even if one suffers from alopecia or any other disease of the scalp. It cannot be denied that manual work, or at least physical activity, is a concomitant of many occupations generally treated as professions, at least in the wider sense. From the dentist carrying out an extraction to the commercial artist drawing a poster; from the chemist analysing a specimen to the architect at the drawing board, most professional people use manual and other physical techniques. Clearly manual effort is not a disqualifying factor, though if little or no intellectual effort accompanies it the activity will rank with trades rather than professions.

3. *Employee Status.* Until the middle of the nineteenth century activities now regarded as professional (in the wider sense of the word) were seldom carried on by persons in salaried employment. Where such work was not done by independent practitioners, it was the responsibility of quasi-independent office holders appointed under the extensive system of patronage which prevailed, and remunerated by fees and other perquisites rather than salaries. Very often of course such posts were in themselves sinecures and the actual work was done by low-grade clerks, supervised or not as the case might be.

In the older professions today members in private practice are often regarded within the profession as having a higher status than salaried employees. Employees rather bitterly regard the professional institution as an employers' club and themselves as excluded from a fair share of the senior offices. Some professional bodies openly prefer the private practitioner, and regret any diminution in his numerical strength and influence. Indeed some, notably the Bar, do not regard a salaried employee as a practising member of the profession at all. Yet a barrister employed as a legal adviser in a company is handicapped by rules of etiquette of the Bar which prevent him from instructing counsel without the intervention of a solicitor or acting as an advocate for his employer in the Courts. He is not even allowed to use in correspondence, for example in his employer's letter heading, the appellation "Barrister-at-law". These restrictions undoubtedly limit the usefulness of salaried barristers, and lead to a preference among employers generally for solicitors (who are not subject to such stringent restrictions) to manage all work in legal departments of companies.

The Institute of Chartered Accountants on the other hand does not regard the profession of accountancy as being restricted to those of its members who are in private practice. The Institute specifically regards all its members as being within the profession, including those engaged as employees of members in private practice or as directors or employees of limited companies or public corporations, or as employees within the Civil Service or local government service.

In a recent study of British medical practice, the American Samuel Mencher recognises that the medical profession in Britain has maintained "an image or ideal of professional performance identified with independent practice". (28) Millerson notes that over the last hundred years, the tendency has been for independent professionals to decline in number and proportion, even in the older professions. (29) In 1964 about half the architects in the United Kingdom were in private practice, a little over a quarter being principals and a little under a quarter assistants. At the end of 1966 about 40% of the 50,000 members of the British Medical Association in the United Kingdom were principals in private practice. In 1967 about half the 18,000 qualified members of the Royal Institution of Chartered Surveyors were engaged in private practice either as principals or employees of firms. The Pilkington Commission found that in 1958 the proportion of members of various professions who were principals in private practice were as follows:

| | |
|---|---|
| Accountants | 33% |
| Actuaries | 4% |
| Architects | 25% |
| Engineers | 2% |

|  | |
|---|---|
| Solicitors | 62% |
| Surveyors | 27% |

In 1968 nearly 23,000 solicitors held practising certificates, of whom 15,000 were principals in private practice; 1,750 solicitors were employed in local government, 750 in commerce and industry, and 350 in the Civil Service. (31)

The following are sometimes given as reasons why salaried employment is less "professional" than independent practice: the employer, and not the client, comes first; the client cannot choose between employees of one employer; the standards applied by professional bodies are less strict; the relationship tends to be impersonal.

The argument that the employer comes first is applied particularly to large public employers, notably the Civil Service. Many professional people in the Civil Service tend to think of themselves as Civil Servants first and barristers, valuers or accountants second. Membership of their professional body is regarded only as a necessary qualification which enables the Civil Servant or local government officer to obtain his appointment. Thereafter his interest in the activities of his professional body is often non-existent. Employers must take their share of the blame for this; they often discourage, and seldom encourage, service by their employees on committees or working parties of the professional body. Employees find difficulty in obtaining leave of absence to attend meetings and conferences – sometimes being made to feel that they are thereby throwing an unfair burden on their colleagues. It is difficult for an employee to act as an official of a professional institute or its branches since he is not free to use his employer's stationery, telephones, etc. The public employee often has to pay his own fare to attend meetings, while colleagues in private practice are able to treat such outgoings as deductible from the profits of the firm for tax purposes.

Another point tending to make the employed member of a professional institute feel that he is regarded as an outsider is that most professional bodies either are not empowered to act, or decline to act, as trade unions in defence of the salaries and conditions of work of their members in employment. This contrasts with the fact that many of them do act in this way in the private sector, laying down scales of fees for members in practice. This is seen, particularly by employees of members' firms, as an example of the institute acting as an "employers' club".

An aspect of the tendency for the employer to come first is noted by Millerson when he says that loyalty to strictly professional values may be replaced by observance of those emanating from the employer:

"Any code of professional conduct, imposed by an external organisation, may not coincide with the aims and methods of bureaucracy. Instead of being an independent, fee-paid principal, the professional is a salaried employee, who has to superimpose a duty to his association upon any obligation to his employer." (32)

The point about the client's freedom of choice being restricted assumes great importance where there is only one employer, as in the case within the field of the nationalised industries. By the client here of course is meant the individual citizen or corporate body seeking to make use of the services provided by the employer through his employees. Millerson confuses the matter by applying the term "client" to the employer as well, as where he says that the teacher serves the child, the parents, the school authorities and the community – all as "clients" in one sense or another. (33) In truth the term "client" is inappropriate when speaking of employees, who do not have clients of their own though they may assist the principal to serve his clients. The work of the professional when serving as a salaried employee may of course be different in kind from work carried out by an independent practitioner. Thus accountants employed by local authorities do work for which there is no direct parallel in private practice. The techniques of the draftsmen of public Parliamentary bills are exercised only within the Civil Service, though in former times they were part of the multifarious expertise of the Chancery Bar.

The British Medical Association attaches great importance to the principle of free choice of doctor and recognises that this principle may be interfered with where employing authorities seek to impose restrictive conditions of service, which the Association resists wherever possible.

Britain has had a National Health Service for twenty years. It was organised by the Health Minister, Aneurin Bevan, in a way which permitted private practice to continue, and remains thus. On this, Mencher comments:

> "The doctors were particularly sensitive to losing their freedom in a state-administered service, and it may have been literally true, as one physician and Labour Member of Parliament observed, that if it had not been for Bevan there would have been no opportunity for private practice in the Health Service." (34)

The point that rules of professional conduct are applied less strictly to employed members has some foundation in fact. The Institute of Chartered Accountants, for example, does not object to a member not in practice being connected with a management consultancy organisation which does not follow the strict code of ethics expected of members in practice. Similarly, a member not in practice may work for a merchant bank or similar institution which advertises its services in a way not permitted to accountants in private practice. Many of the strict rules of etiquette of the Bar do not apply to barristers who, even though they are carrying out legal work, are not in practice as barristers within the meaning applied to that term by the Bar Council.

The criticism that salaried service leads to an impersonal relationship with the client can be reduced in importance by appropriate organisation on the employer's part. The joint stock banks for instance have been successful in preserving personal relationships with their customers through their branch organisation and the tradition by which the branch manager in most cases makes himself readily available to any of the bank's customers who may seek his advice. Other large organisations, such as some insurance companies and local authorities, have not been so successful.

The foregoing brief account is enough to show that there is no unanimity of view on the question whether entering salaried employment makes a qualified member of a profession lose his professional status. This is probably because the proposition is virtually meaningless in view of the uncertainty as to what "professional" really signifies. It is clear however that some at least of the qualities often associated with professionalism can be displayed less easily, or not at all, outside the direct relationship which exists between the independent practitioner and his client. Where the activities being considered are predominantly, or even exclusively, carried out by persons in salaried employment, as in the case of teachers and secretaries, there is perhaps to be gathered from this discussion the conclusion that the activities are not really professional — at least in the narrower sense of the term.

## Conclusions

The time has now come to try and identify more precisely the characteristics which distinguish a profession or professional in the narrower sense from the wider meaning which extends these terms to virtually any occupation where some degree of intellectual discipline is required. We are looking for characteristics such that when all or most are present in the case of a particular occupation we can say with the prospect of general acceptance that the occupation falls within a definite category unequivocally labelled "professional". On the basis of the foregoing discussion we can say that if the following factors are present the activity will be professional in the strictest sense, while acknowledging that the absence of any of them will not necessarily rule out professionalism, at least in the wider sense:

*1. Intellectual Basis.* An intellectual discipline, capable of formulation on theoretical, if not academic, lines, requiring a good educational background, and tested by examination.

*2. Private Practice.* A foundation in private practice, so that the essential expertise and standards of the profession derive from meeting the needs of individual clients on a person-to-person basis, with remuneration by fees from individual clients rather than a salary or stipend from one source.

*3. Advisory Function.* An advisory function, often coupled with an executive function in carrying out what has been advised or doing ancillary work such as supervising, negotiating or managing; in the exercise of both functions full responsibility is taken by the person exercising them.

*4. Tradition of Service.* An outlook which is essentially objective and disinterested, where the motive of making money is subordinated to serving the client in a manner not inconsistent with the public good.

*5. Representative Institute.* One or more societies or institutes representing members of the profession, particularly those in private practice, and having the function of safeguarding and developing the expertise and standards of the profession.

*6. Code of Conduct.* A code of professional ethics, laid down and enforced by the professional institute or institutes.

It is the thesis of this book that these six characteristics, taken together, identify a group of vocations or callings essentially different from others and of particular value and importance to the community, which we may call the consultant professions. This is not to say that other callings are of less worth; only that they are different in nature. Since these excluded callings comprise those, for example, of the senior civil servant, the artist, author or composer, the business executive and the pure scientist it is obvious that no slur is intended by their exclusion.

It is also contended that while historical developments have played a large part in determining what occupations are currently included among the consultant professions, there is a theoretical basis for this category. In other words there are sound reasons why the public good requires certain services to be provided on a basis conforming to the six points given above. With the help given by observing the occupations which, actually or potentially, conform to these six points we can put forward the following basic proposition:

**Advisory services (including concomitant executive functions) on**

matters requiring expert intellectual knowledge and concerning the physical or mental health of an individual, or the protection or advancement of the rights or property of an individual or body corporate, are best provided by a private practitioner whose competence and integrity are vouched for by an independent body representative of such practitioners.

If this basic proposition is correct it follows that any opposing development, such as the introduction of a scheme whereby professional services are provided by a salaried staff employed by the state, is bad and should be resisted. It also follows that public policy should be directed to providing conditions in which the consultant professions may flourish, with the removal of factors militating against their successful operation. It is not intended to denigrate in any way members of a consultant profession who have chosen to enter salaried employment. The qualities developed over the years by private practitioners and absorbed by each new generation of students are of great value to employers. A profession does not cease to be a consultant profession because a proportion of its members enter full-time employment, nor do they thereby cease to belong to the profession. If the basic proposision is accepted however it does involve that the best type of private practice has advantages over employment as a medium for rendering the professional services in question.

It is not the object of the present work to offer formal proof of the validity of the basic proposition, if indeed such a thing is possible. The core of the proposition is that problems of health, rights or property call for a personal relationship with a trusted adviser, whose discretion is absolute, who serves no master but his client, and whose competence is assured. The codes and traditions of the professions who supply these services support the basic proposition. They also display the uniformity that its truth would lead one to expect.

## CHAPTER 2

# CONSULTANT PROFESSIONS

Having in the previous chapter arrived at the conclusion that there is a distinct group of activities within the wider professional sphere which may appropriately be called the consultant professions, we proceed to consider these activities, and their field of operation, in more detail. The field is that laid down in the basic proposition given on page 15, and may be more briefly described as 'health, rights and property'. The following table shows the main consultant professions operating in this field* —

| | |
|---|---|
| HEALTH | Dentist |
| | Optician |
| | Pharmacist |
| | Physician |
| | Surgeon |
| | |
| RIGHTS | Barrister |
| | Notary |
| | Parliamentary agent |
| | Patent agent |
| | Solicitor |
| | |
| PROPERTY | |
| (A) LAND AND BUILDINGS | Architect |
| | Auctioneer |
| | Building Surveyor |
| | Civil engineer |
| | Estate agent |
| | Heating and ventilating engineer |

* Names of professions are those current in England. Similar activities elsewhere may have different names, e.g. Writer to the Signet (a solicitor) in Scotland.

Land agent
Land surveyor
Landscape architect
Mining engineer
Quantity surveyor
Structural engineer
Town planner
Valuer

(B) MONEY AND SECURITIES

Accountant
Actuary
Insurance broker
Loss adjuster
Mortgage broker
Stockbroker

(C) CHATTELS

Auctioneer
Chemical engineer
Electrical engineer
Mechanical engineer
Naval architect
Ship broker
Valuer
Veterinary surgeon

Compiling a table like this is a rash exercise, since it cannot fail to offend some people — from the advertising agent or public relations consultant, who finds himself omitted, to the animal lover who objects to veterinary surgeons being regarded as dealing with chattels. Such is the fate of the classifier. The reader may amuse himself by compiling his own table but it will not come out all that different. The important point is that the table given here relates only to the basic proposition, which is the core of the importance of professionalism. Other activities may qualify as consultant professions too, if they substantially satisfy the six tests given in Chapter 1 (see page 15). Activities within the field (health, rights, property) of the basic proposition may fail to qualify if they do not satisfy the six tests, and some will argue that this applies to occupations included in the above table, such as those of the stockbroker, auctioneer or estate agent.

### The Consultant in Practice

One of the essential characteristics identifying the consultant professions is a foundation in private practice, which exists where the professional man holds himself out as prepared to offer professional services on his own account, and sets up whatever may be necessary in the way of an office, consulting room, clerical staff and so on. He may do this on his own, or with partners on an equal footing with himself. His firm may have one office or several, but it will have a number of clients no one of which provides a majority of the work. Thus independence is secured.

The antithesis of private practice is salaried employment. It is possible for the conditions of employment to be such that there is little practical difference in the day-to-day work of the employed man and his professional brother in private practice. This is by no means always the case however, and nothing can remove the ultimate power of the employer to insist on his will being obeyed, with the sanction of dismissal in the background. As will appear in the course of this book, the essential qualities of the consultant professions – those which make them of peculiar value to society – can only be fully deployed in the conditions prevailing in private practice. The qualities came into being because the freedom and independence of private practice encouraged their growth. Once brought into being, these qualities of independence, impartiality, discretion and so on may flourish in employed service if the conditions are right, the employees concerned are alive to their responsibilities and their professional institutes are vigilant in support. Employed service can only be a second best however, at least within the consultancy field. The present tendency of most sizable organisations, from Government departments, local authorities and other public bodies to private commercial and industrial undertakings, towards setting up their own professional departments is regrettable. Many of these employees have no experience of private practice or the values it inculcates. The spread of this kind of salaried employment can only lead to the ultimate decay of qualities and attributes which are of great value to the public.

The origins of private practice are multifarious and often obscure. Many callings now ranking as separate professions originated with the Church. Under the parochial system established after the Norman conquest and continued ever since, the English churchman has enjoyed a large degree of independence. The priests, many of them of Norman origin, who held themselves out as legal advisers in the twelfth and thirteenth century often did so as independent practitioners. The same is true of physicians, architects and others who, holding ecclesiastical preferment as securely as any property could be held in those turbulent days, held thereby the means of independence. Some it is true were

C

members of the household of a lord or magnate, and were dependent on his pleasure, but this only reflects the origin of many professions as helping the individual to do what, if he were able, he would do for himself. Thus the advocate arose to do what, under our Norman kings, a man was obliged to do for himself unless he had express permission to appoint a deputy or "attorney". Similarly the predecessor of the modern surveyor, the land steward or seneschal, acted in relation to his master's estates as the master would himself have done if he had had the time and ability, and was accordingly required to be "prudent, faithful and profitable". (1)

While the "professional" member of a great medieval household, such as the priest or steward, might plausibly be equated with the salaried employee of today, it is clear that the prized professional qualities did not develop in this milieu but, nourished by the growth of representative institutions, grew up later in the independence of private practice. The nature of these qualities, and the way they are upheld by the professional code, will be discussed in Part II. Meanwhile we need to take a brief look at the representative bodies responsible for administering the code.

### A Band of Brothers

The codes of conduct were all drawn up, and are administered, by bodies consisting wholly or mainly of members of the profession in question. This is of crucial importance. The reason is indicated in the opening words of *Medical Ethics,* published by the British Medical Association: "The entrant to the profession of medicine joins a fraternity . . . " In 1947 the World Medical Association was formed "to unite the profession throughout the world in a single brotherhood" and one of the articles in the modern restatement of the Hippocratic oath produced by that Association states simply: "My colleagues will be my brothers."

Other professions are not always so explicit about this concept of brotherhood, though it is there in greater or lesser degree. It explains rules such as those forbidding undercutting of fees, the poaching of clients and the extremer forms of self-advertisement. It produces the helping hand for the raw beginner, the benevolent fund for brethren who have fallen on hard times, the practice of not charging a fellow-practitioner for professional services, and many other features. It encourages professional bodies to arbitrate informally in disputes between members, and otherwise preserve harmony within the brotherhood. Most people gain strength from indentification with a group, and the public benefit derived from the existence of strong professional groups, with pride in their calling, is, or should be, obvious.

Many different types of organisation exist to give expression to the concept of professional brotherhood. Some cover all aspects of the regulation of the profession, while others concentrate on particular features such as conduct and discipline. Some include all, or nearly all, members of the profession; others have only a small minority. A few are set up by Act of Parliament, but most are voluntary. The leading bodies have all however received some form of recognition by the State, whether by the grant of a Royal charter, or by the conferment of certain statutory powers, or at least by the inclusion of references to the body in legal provisions. There is one universal characteristic: the initiative in setting up the body and the guidance of its policy come from members of the profession and not from outside. A typical statement of the essential functions of the representative body of a consultant profession is provided by the Association of Consulting Engineers:

"The Association is a ready medium through which its members can consult with each other on all matters of professional interest, and affords a means by which the procedure of the consulting profession may be co-ordinated and handed on to those entering its ranks. Experience has shown that matters are constantly arising on which it is an advantage to Consulting Engineers to obtain the opinion of their colleagues in the profession. The Association provides this opportunity through its Council which keeps in touch with all matters affecting the profession, and puts its advice and assistance at the disposal of members in any matters of difficulty arising in the course of their practice. The Association is also a medium through which the public can be informed as to the standing, experience and qualification of its members. If any person requiring professional advice and assistance is in doubt as to whom to approach the Association is always willing to nominate one or more members specially qualified for the purpose." (2)

It is not necessary for the purpose of this book to pursue the details of the ramifications of professional organisation. This task has recently been exhaustively tackled by Geoffrey Millerson in his book *The Qualifying Associations* and no attempt will here be made to duplicate his valuable work. All that we need do is to consider some of the leading organisations so far as is necessary to understand the philosophy and practical working out of consultant professionalism and its code.

The most fully-developed example of an all-purpose professional organisation is the Law Society, founded in 1826 as successor to a body dating from the early eighteenth century. Membership is voluntary, though almost all solicitors belong. The Law Society handles every aspect of the training, examination, practice and conduct of solicitors, operating through a council and numerous committees all manned by solicitors. Although enforcement of the standards of the profession is in the hands of what is technically a separate body, the Disciplinary Committee, its members are all past or present members of the Law Society's Council and co-operation between the two bodies is extremely close. It is a general duty of the Council to see that no solicitor remains on the Roll if guilty of conduct which renders him unfit to do so, but 'the function of the Council like that of an auditor is to be a watchdog and not a bloodhound'. (3)

The Law Society was incorporated by Royal Charter and has many statutory functions. Its objects are defined in the charter as 'promoting professional improvement and facilitating the acquisition of legal knowledge'. Apart from its strictly professional role, it plays an important part in advising the Government on legislative proposals and in operating the legal aid and advice scheme. It has a large and skilful staff, and is looked upon as the leader in the field of inter-professional politics. Nevertheless the difficulty of sustaining such an all-embracing role is evidenced by the rise in recent years of the British Legal Association, founded to supply what a minority of solicitors felt was a lack of vigour by the Law Society in pressing its members's claims.

The homogeneity enjoyed by solicitors is not shown by the other branch of the legal profession, the Bar. Here regulation of the profession is divided between the fourteenth-century Inns of Court, the General Council of the Bar, the Senate, the circuit messes and the Council of Legal Education. As one might expect from their antiquity, the four Inns of Court display features not characteristic of the usual run of professional institutes. They are unincorporated societies whose governing bodies, the benchers, are self-appointing and beyond any control by the ordinary members. Individualistic in origin, the Inns now act together on professional matters. The Bar Council was set up in 1895 to consider and take action on all matters affecting the barrister's profession, including conduct, etiquette and discipline. It took over the duty, formerly exercised by the Attorney-General as head of the Bar, of drawing up rules of conduct. It has no disciplinary powers itself, but investigates complaints against members of the Bar and where necessary refers them to the benchers of the appropriate Inn. Since 1966 the Inns' powers of examination and discipline have been delegated to the Senate, which consists of practising barristers (as to about two-thirds) and judges. The Senate normally gives effect to the rulings of the Bar Council, but is not obliged to do so. There is a right of appeal from the Senate to the judges sitting as a special tribunal.

The seven circuit messes, convivial in origin, supervise the conduct of their members while on circuit. Membership of one of the Inns of Court is compulsory for a barrister, but the Inn provides no professional service to (and demands no subscription from) its qualified members. It does however offer the hospitality of its Hall, at an economic price, and so maintains the ancient tradition that professional fellowship is best sustained over a meal. It also affords the use of a well-stocked library. The organisation of the Bar is substained, not by recent Parliamentary enactments, as in the case of solicitors, but by immemorial usage upheld by the courts. It has aroused the wrath of commentators such as Professor D.S. Lees, who stigmatises it as an intolerable private monopoly. (4) Nevertheless it works in practice, and produces a uniform set of rules to govern conduct at the Bar. Some would say, with Professor Lees that the Bar is "riddled with restrictive practices". (5) Others would argue that the unparalleled standards of probity and ability of the English Bar testify to the value of their institutional framework, illogical though it may seem to be. The small number of practising barristers (a little over two thousand) perhaps justifies the somewhat informal professional structure.

Yet another type of professional organisation is illustrated by the medical profession. Here a voluntary representative body of recent date, the British Medical Association, is coupled with a statutory disciplinary authority, the General Medical Council. Round the periphery are older learned societies concerned with particular aspects of medical science, but occasionally superimposing their own, stricter, rules of conduct,

The B.M.A. has a remarkable history. It was founded in 1832 at Worcester as a merely provincial body. A hundred years later it had grown into what Carr-Saunders and Wilson described as "the most ably conducted and most powerful voluntary professional association that this country has ever known." (6) To this its unique constitution, with a representative body or "Parliament" of several hundred members, contributed. Its main object, "the maintenance of the honour and respectability of the profession", has been widely construed, and it has amassed a vast store of knowledge and experience which is freely available to its members. Though not directly concerned with ethics and discipline, it has a powerful influence on the General Medical Council's handling of these matters. Its membership of 70,000, of whom 50,000 live in the United Kingdom, gives it a strong voice in the development of national policy.

The statutory counterpart of the B.M.A., the General Medical Council, was set up under the Medical Act of 1858. It keeps a register of qualified practitioners, prescribes educational requirements, lays down standards for drugs and medicines in its publication the British Pharmacopoeia, and administers the code of medical ethics. While entry on the medical register is not compulsory for practitioners its absence involves important disabilities. Fees cannot be sued for, certain medical appointments cannot be held, and possession of dangerous drugs is made unlawful. The Council is composed of forty-seven members, twenty-eight of whom are nominated by universities and professional bodies. Of the remainder, eleven are elected by the individual members of the profession and eight are Government nominees. Three out of the forty-seven are laymen.

A similar pattern of a powerful all-embracing voluntary association coupled with a statutory council enforcing discipline prevails in the architects' profession. The Royal Institute of British Architects was founded in 1834 and received a Royal Charter three years later. This recited the objects as being "for the general advancement of Civil Architecture and for promoting and facilitating the acquirement of the knowledge of the various Arts and Sciences connected therewith." The R.I.B.A. sees its activities as falling into two groups:

"The first is the promotion of scholarship, the encouragement of architecture by awards and competitions, meetings and discussion; as well as public presentation of the importance of architectural values to social wellbeing. But, since the practice of architecture requires practitioners, and since most building design requires a professional service, the R.I.B.A. has always been the headquarters of the profession, concerned to promote those qualities of efficiency and integrity in its members which society requires . . . " (7)

In 1931, at the instigation of the R.I.B.A., Parliament set up the Architects Registration Council of the United Kingdom. The Council maintains a register of qualified persons, and only those on the register may describe themselves as architects. There is no other consequence of registration. The Council is a large body. Of the sixty members thirty-three are appointed by the R.I.B.A. itself and the remainder respectively represent other professional organisations, bodies connected with the building trade, and the public. The Council lays down and enforces a code of conduct binding upon all registered architects.

So far in this section we have been discussing areas of the professional field where the organisation of the profession, and the intervention of the State, are at their most developed. In other areas the position is different. The multifarious surveyors' profession embraces land survey and mapping, valuation or appraisal of real estate, estate agency and land agency, auctioneering, quantity surveying, farm management, mining surveying, hydrographic surveying and aspects of town planning. It is scarcely surprising that there is no one professional body with claims to blanket coverage, and the State has so far refrained from interference. The leading body is the Royal Institution of Chartered Surveyors, whose membership comprises all the above-mentioned specialties but at around 20,000 covers less than half the practitioners in the field.

The Institution was founded in 1868 by practitioners who in the main were valuers in private practice. Their chief activity was as advisers to promoters of railway Acts and landowners affected by them. This resulted in the Institution's being located a stone's throw from the Houses of Parliament, on a site it still occupies today. The objects of the Institution are "to secure the advancement and facilitate the acquisition of that knowledge which constitutes the profession of a surveyor" and "to promote the general interests of the profession and to maintain and extend its usefulness for the public advantage." (8) Although some attempts have been made by the profession to obtain the setting up of a statutory register of surveyors these were not resolutely pursued and were unsuccessful. More serious efforts were made to provide for compulsory registration of estate agents, and a number of Bills have been introduced in the House of Commons, so far without success. After the failure of the latest effort in 1966 a registration council was set up voluntarily as a company limited by guarantee. Although it began as a body having possibilities of welding together the ten different representative organisations which set it up, and thus creating a unified estate agency profession, the Estate Agents Council seems likely to do no more than act as a registration body without power to compel any agent to register — if indeed it survives at all.

Within the wide field of surveying the greatest prestige is enjoyed by the three bodies possessing Royal Charters. In addition to the R.I.C.S. these are the Chartered Auctioneers' and Estate Agents' Institute and the Chartered Land Agents Society. These, together with a fourth body, the Incorporated Society of Valuers and Auctioneers, operate a uniform code of conduct, though it is individually enforced by each body.

A similar pattern of numerous specialties, equally numerous representative bodies, and lack of state intervention is displayed by the engineers. Different institutions respectively represent civil engineers, mechanical engineers, structural engineers, electrical engineers and many others. An attempt has recently been made to introduce a uniform approach in matters of common interest with the establishment of the Federation of Engineering Institutions. A feature of the engineering scene is that most bodies aim above all to be learned societies, discussing and developing the techniques of the profession. The problems and interests of engineers as private practitioners are handled by yet another body, the Association of Consulting Engineers, incorporated in 1913. This is the sole example of a professional body formed to represent only those qualified members of other institutions within the same field who practise as consultants. Consulting engineers form only a small proportion of the membership of the major engineering institutions, and in the view of the Association "it is obvious that the rules of professional conduct, as formulated by the Association, would not be applicable to the majority of the members of these Institutions." (9) Like the surveyors, the engineers have toyed with the idea of obtaining an Act to provide for compulsory registration. The idea was not pursued, for the reasons usual in such cases — namely, lack of unity in the profession as to the contents of a Bill and unwillingness to face the necessary initial stage of allowing all practitioners to register whether qualified members of a professional body or not.

Within the field of accountancy there is less diversification and a closer approach to the kind of uniform structure displayed by the architects and solicitors. The leading body is the Institute of Chartered Accountants in England and Wales, formed by Royal Charter in 1880. In 1957 the Institute absorbed the second most important body, the Society of Incorporated Accountants and Auditors. Further amalgamations are contemplated which would give the combined body nearly as complete a coverage of the profession as that enjoyed by the R.I.B.A. in the case of architects.

The main aim of the Institute is to secure that its members provide the best possible accountancy service to the public. For this purpose it arranges for education and training, conducts examinations, encourages and develops new techniques in accountancy and lays down and enforces rules of professional conduct. It also advises the Government and other public authorities on accounting matters and pending legislation. The total membership is over 40,000; parallel bodies in Scotland and Ireland have approximate memberships of 8,000 and 2,000 respectively. The only other sizable body representing accountants in private practice is the Association of Certified and Corporate Accountants, with nearly 12,000 members.

There is no system of statutory registration for accountants, but persons undertaking certain types of accountancy work are required by law to be members of the Institute or one of the other bodies mentioned above. These include auditing of accounts of public bodies, joint-stock companies, building societies, etc., and reporting in connection with the observance by solicitors of rules as to keeping of accounts.

We have in this brief survey looked at the main professional bodies within the field of the consultant professions. A more complete list will be found in Millerson's book (10) and a more exhaustive description in Carr-Saunders and Wilson. (11) Enough has perhaps been said here to indicate the outlines of the way the consultant professions are organised to combine the brotherhood of their calling with service to the public.

## The Code

The code of the consultant professions, so far as it forms a consistent corpus, embodies numerous individual rules or traditions, which can be arranged in a number of different ways. What is its essential nature? It clearly stands apart from the ordinary law, both criminal and civil, though there is a certain overlapping. A conviction for a serious criminal offence will lead to expulsion from the professional society, even though not arising out of the practice of the profession. A finding of negligence or misrepresentation by a civil court may well be held relevant in domestic proceedings for professional misconduct. Nevertheless, even though Parliament may have stepped in to regulate disciplinary procedures, as with solicitors and medical practitioners, and even though the courts will in all cases ensure that the rules of natural justice are observed, the professional code has up to now been distinct and separate. In essence it is the judgment of the profession on how members should conduct themselves, and this judgment has prevailed over different views from outside. Many, if not most, of its precepts are unknown to the general law, breach of them constituting neither crime nor tort. It binds the professional man because, in voluntarily joining the profession, he is taken to have agreed to be governed by its code as currently in force. Where, however, the professional organisation comes into existence *after* he has begun to practise, its code will not bind him unless he agrees. So in the case of *Hughes* v *ARCUK*, where Hughes had been in practice as an architect and house agent for some ten years before the passing of the Architects Registration Act, it was held he could not be struck off the register for refusing to give up his house agency work; "His case differs *toto coelo* from that of the new entrant who is admitted on terms, written or unwritten." (12)

Some professional people, misunderstanding its true nature, describe the code of conduct as "the club rules". This equates it to something quite different, the body of rules of a private society or club, where a member who dislikes the rules will free himself from them by resigning, and be none the worse. This cannot apply to the codes of the great professional institutions, whose members have studied for years to gain their qualifications, and depend for their livelihood on continued membership. The public have an interest in rules of this importance, and will not easily suffer them to remain operative where they cannot be shown to be beneficial. Differing from ordinary law in being laid down by the profession itself rather than the state, the professional code has a force akin to law in its effect on the members of the professions, and through them on the public generally. This justifies public concern with its details, though not some of the current manifestations of this concern.

Professional rules approximate most nearly to law when the profession is, by law, a closed one. It may be appropriate or not that, as we have seen, the only really closed profession in England has for long been the law itself, though the dentists have recently achieved this position. A barrister with a High Court practice who transgresses his professional code and is disbarred has absolutely no opportunity of continuing to practise. An architect on the other hand, although his professional appellation is protected by statute, will find himself removed from the register but not prevented from practising. A chartered accountant will not even be removed from the register, because none exists, but will be disqualified from carrying out certain functions such as the audit of limited companies' accounts. A chartered surveyor will suffer virtually no restriction of this sort, but will lose the prestige and authority which derives from membership of the leading body in his field; a surveyor still, he will no longer be "chartered".

One way of subdividing professional rules is to separate those which are explicitly laid down in some detail and enforced by formal disciplinary proceedings from those which form the unwritten etiquette of the profession. Breach of the latter may be visited by nothing more than coldness and frowns from professional brethren, and loss of that mysterious thing called "face". Many professionals, especially those with ambitions to rise in the hierarchy of their institute, dread this displeasure of their colleagues nearly as much as formal proceedings. Others, especially the sort who never attend a branch meeting or open their "journal", are indifferent. Just as it is a question how far disciplinary sanctions should be backed by law, so it is debatable whether a particular rule should be enforced by penalties or left as mere "etiquette". Since the latter is largely beyond the reach of reforming busybodies it has its attractions for those who like to see a profession with pride in governing itself.

A more elaborate sub-division of the code reflects the four different aspects of consultant professionalism:

1. *Rules arising from the fact that an expertise is involved.*

(a) Rules regulating admission. These include restrictions on admission as a student (e.g. to those having at least two Advanced Level passes in the General Certificate of Education); requirements of entry into articles; control of syllabuses, either in examinations held by the institute itself or in those held by universities and colleges and carrying exemption from the institute's examinations; and of course control of the level of competence considered adequate for admission. Rules may admit members in stages, full membership (usually that of a "fellow") being deferred sometimes for years.

(b) Rules securing continued competence after admission. Little developed as yet, these rules would require periodical refresher courses, instruction in new techniques and possibly re-examination at intervals. They penalise acts of incompetence.

(c) Rules governing the method of obtaining advice. Examples are rules precluding advertising of specialties and those requiring access to a specialist to be sought only through a general practitioner.

(d) Demarcation rules, laying down the boundaries between different professions.

2. *Rules arising from frequent concern with intimate personal matters.*

(a) Rules requiring a personal relationship between practitioner and client. The chief rules are those prohibiting practice as a limited company or (in the case of barristers and medical specialists) even prohibiting partnerships.

(b) Rules imposing strict confidence and discretion as to clients' affairs.

(c) Rules requiring courtesy and dignity to be displayed at all times.

(d) Rules preserving the client's freedom to chose a practitioner, and, so far as the public interest allows, enabling the practitioner to be equally free to reject a client.

3. *Rules arising from frequent concern with property of great value.*

(a) Unimpeachable integrity and honesty, usually required to be vouched for before admission and supported by numerous practice rules, such as those requiring separate bank accounts to be kept for clients' monies or payments to be made into a compensation fund.

(b) Independence and impartiality. The practitioner must avoid any position where his own interests, or those of a person connected with him, may conceivably conflict with those of his client. Indeed he must *subordinate* his own interests to those of the client, who must come first in all things except where this would injure the public.

(c) Responsibility. The advice given must be that of the practitioner himself and he must take full responsibility for it. On matters beyond his competence he must procure another practitioner to give direct advice to the client on the same basis. The practitioner must back his advice with whole personal fortune, without limitation of liability.

4. *Rules arising from the fact that the profession is a brotherhood of long standing.*

(a) The standing and repute of the profession must not be prejudiced.

(b) Fellow-practitioners must be treated with courtesy.

(c) Poaching of clients is discouraged.

(d) Advertisements exalting one's own abilities at the expense of one's colleagues' are prohibited.

(e) Competition on the level of fees ("undercutting") is restricted.

This classification distinguishes rules directed to safeguarding the standard of service offered to the public (categories 1 to 3) from those more concerned with relationships within the profession (category 4). It is on this distinction that the succeeding chapters of this book are based, Part II dealing in turn with the six essential qualities of the consultant, namely competence, humanity, discretion, impartiality, responsibility and integrity, while Part III discusses matters more within the realm of internal professional relations.

## Enforcing the Code

The ultimate sanction for breach of the professional code is expulsion from the profession, or at least from that portion of it represented by the institution whose code has been infringed. The professions vary in their description of the offence. Many merely refer to "professional misconduct". The Medical Act of 1858 introduced the formula, still current, "infamous conduct in a professional respect". Other examples are: "Conduct disgraceful to him in his capacity as an architect", "conduct unbefitting a solicitor of the Supreme Court", and, "any act or default discreditable to a public accountant". Whatever the precise form of words the effect is usually the same. It was defined in 1894 by Lord Justice Lopes as covering an act done by a professional man in the pursuit of his profession which "would be reasonably regarded as disgraceful or dishonourable by his professional brethren of good repute and competency". (13) Another judge expressed it as "no more than serious misconduct judged according to the rules, written or unwritten, governing the profession". (14) Where a term such as "disgraceful" is used in the code of conduct the law will give it its natural and popular meaning, and will not uphold a finding of guilt based on giving it an artificial meaning condemning conduct which the ordinary person would not think disgraceful. (15) It will not be limited to acts done in the course of the profession, even if required to be "in a professional respect". A veterinary surgeon who also farmed was fined by magistrates for leaving eleven carcases lying about the farm unburied. A finding of conduct disgraceful to him in a professional respect was upheld although the animals had been his own property. (16) Apart from actions falling within the general heading of professional misconduct, criminal acts of a serious nature, even though not committed in the practice of the profession, may result in expulsion. So too may breaches of specific rules of the profession such as those governing the keeping of accounts by solicitors.

Disciplinary proceedings are usually initiated as the result of complaints either by clients or fellow-members of the profession. The Law Society receives two hundred complaints a week about the conduct of solicitors; the vast majority are without foundation. (17) Most professional institutions will take pains to satisfy a complainant even if his complaint is unfounded. As Sir Thomas Lund, Secretary-General of the Law Society, has said: "It is far better for us to enquire into a complaint, even if it does mean that some solicitor has to turn up the papers and write a letter in explanation – it is far better that we should write a reasoned letter to the complainant than that a person should go round amongst his friends as a dissatisfied client, airing his misconceived grievances up and down the country, as used to be done." (18)

Professional bodies are also concerned, where this is legitimate, to avoid the institution of a formal disciplinary enquiry. Most bodies have established as part of their disciplinary machinery an investigating committee which looks into complaints not obviously groundless, invites the observations of the person against whom the complaint is made, and makes such other informal enquiries as are necessary. Only if the matter cannot be satisfactorily disposed of in this way will formal proceedings be initiated by referring the matter to the disciplinary committee. The medical profession has a Penal Cases Committee which sits in private to investigate complaints and also to look into convictions of medical practitioners for any offence. These convictions are in the normal course reported to the General Medical Council by the court concerned. If the Penal Cases Committee is satisfied that the matter is one of substance, but not sufficiently grave for the institution of full disciplinary proceedings, it will send a letter of warning to the doctor concerned. This may be done for example where he has been convicted of driving while under the influence of drink for the first time or has failed to visit or treat a patient or has issued a misleading professional certificate. (19)

A matter will not be referred to a disciplinary committee unless a prima facie case has been established against the accused. Indeed in the case of solicitors the accused is not even notified of the complaint unless a prima facie case is established. (20) This is a salutory rule since it prevents a professional man being alarmed by the possibility of disciplinary proceedings where in fact no sufficient evidence has been disclosed.

Disciplinary committees vary in their composition but are usually independent of the governing bodies of the profession in question. The disciplinary committee of the General Medical Council is typical of those constituted under Act of Parliament. Its full membership is nineteen, including two lay members. The majority of cases are however heard by nine members only. The committee normally sits in public and its procedure closely resembles that of a court of law. Witnesses may be subpoenaed and evidence given on oath. Accused practitioners are usually legally represented. (21) The disciplinary committee of the solicitors' profession is appointed by the Master of the Rolls from among present or past members of the Council of the Law Society. There is a maximum of twelve members, but normally the committee sits in divisions of three. Again, the proceedings resemble those in a High Court action, and parties may be represented by a solicitor or Counsel. The two tribunals differ however in that whereas the disciplinary committee of the General Medical Council normally sits in public that of the solicitors' profession invariably sits in private. Sir Thomas Lund gives as the reason for this privacy that "even if a case is thrown out it might do great damage to the solicitor against whom the complaint is made". (22) These statutory committee are masters of their own proceedure, and of how they require facts to be proved. (23) They are not bound by strict rules of evidence, and the prior decision of a civil or criminal court on the same facts may be treated as proof; but any challenge to that decision must be heard. (24)

An example of a different form of disciplinary committee not established by Act of Parliament, is furnished by the chartered accountants. Under a Royal Charter of 1948 their disciplinary committee consists of twelve members of the Institute and each complaint is heard by a panel of five. The case is put forward on behalf of the investigation committee by a solicitor, Counsel only being employed in very complicated cases. A legal assessor sits with the disciplinary committee to advise on questions of law. The accused may present his own case or be represented by Counsel or solicitor as he wishes. Alternatively he may be represented by another member of the Institute. There is no power to take evidence on oath.

Most disciplinary committees have power to order the expulsion of the member found guilty of misconduct, or to impose a lesser penalty such as suspension for a period or reprimand or admonition. Before deciding on the punishment they will usually invite the accused or his representative to call attention to any mitigating circumstances, and to produce testimonials or other evidence as to character. The typical approach of the committee to the question of punishment is indicated in the B.M.A.'s publication *Medical Ethics:*

> "Under the Act the disciplinary committee are not called
> upon to punish, in any retributive sense. Their primary
> duty is to protect the public. 'Is it in the public interest to
> leave this doctor on the register?' must be the first question
> in their minds in difficult cases. Subject however to their
> overriding duty to the public, members of the committee
> may and do constantly ask themselves, 'What is in the best
> interest of the doctor himself?' " (25)

It may be added that such committees are, rightly, not unmindful of the best interests of the profession also.

An appeal usually lies from the decision of a disciplinary committee. In the case of disciplinary committees set up by statute the appeal is to the court. For solicitors an appeal lies to the Divisional Court and from there to the Court of Appeal and thereafter to the House of Lords. In the case of the Architects Registration Council disciplinary penalties are imposed by the Council itself, and an appeal lies to the High Court or (in Scotland) the Court of Session, whose decision is final. Disbarred barristers may appeal to a special committee of High Court judges, and in the case of doctors appeal lies to the judicial committee of the Privy Council. The appellate court can go fully into the merits, and in fact rehear the case. (26)

Where the disciplinary procedure is not laid down by law an appeal, if it lies at all, will usually lie to a further body of persons drawn from the profession itself. Thus in the case of chartered accountants the charter of 1948 provides for an appeal committee consisting of the President and Vice-President of the Institute, if available, and three other members of the Council none of whom may have taken part in the previous proceedings. (27)

How far does the disciplinary procedure of the professions operate effectively to safeguard the public? It cannot be denied that the professions vary in the readiness with which complaints of professional misconduct are investigated and offenders brought to book. There is rarely any encouragement to the public to report misdemeanours to the professional body concerned, and often a reluctance to intervene between the professional man and his client. Naturally enough the staff of a professional body, who are usually the first to read letters of complaint, are inclined to be more sympathetic to the members whose servants they are than to outside persons. There is among members too a natural reluctance to contemplate that any colleague of theirs may have fallen short of the standards expected of him. Nor is very much done to remind members of their obligations by publishing details of disciplinary cases. There is a tendency to feel, that publicity given to members' shortcomings tends to lower the reputation of the profession generally. Nevertheless this argument scarcely justifies reluctance to publish details in the profession's own journal or in other media not likely to be read outside it.

Where the profession is closely regulated by statute, and the public has a major interest, publicity cannot be avoided. It is most intense in the case of doctors, whose disciplinary tribunals sit in public. Figures are thus easily obtainable, and in fact 316 doctors were erased from the medical register during the period from 1900 to 1963 on disciplinary grounds. Of these cases 83 were concerned with adultery or other improper relations with a patient, 57 with illegal abortion or miscarriage, 52 with drink or drugs, 29 with advertising or canvassing, 28 with fraud, false pretences or other dishonesty, and 67 with various other grounds. (28) In the case of chartered accountants during the period from 1962 to 1966 the number of complaints dealt with by the disciplinary committee other than in relation to overdue subscriptions was 109, of which 98 were found proved and 45 led to expulsion. 19 of the findings of guilt were in respect of convictions for larceny, fraud or other dishonesty and 27 were in respect of delay in attending to professional business. (29)

## CHAPTER 3

# COMPETENCE: THE GIVING OF THE HALLMARK

"We know a few secrets of nature in our profession, Sir.", said Dr Jobling in *Martin Chuzzlewit*, "Of course we do. We study for that; we pass the Hall and the College for that; and we take our station in society *by* that. It's extraordinary how little is known on these subjects generally."

The idea of certain callings being "mysteries", whose lore is available only to the initiated, is an ancient one. It is a concept not confined to the professions and has been the source of much unnecessary mumbo-jumbo and self-importance. Nevertheless the complexity and obscurity of many occupations has grown with the increase in scientific knowledge, the development of inventions and the general sophistication of industrial societies. Because of the personal and vitally important areas within which the consultant professions operate the need of the layman for competent advice is crucial. As has been stated by the British Medical Association, "The nature of medical advice and treatment is such that the patient cannot effectively assess the quality of the services he is receiving and he must therefore repose considerable trust in the doctor . . . The successful treatment of many, and to some extent of all, medical conditions depends upon a high degree of confidence by the patient in the professional competence of his doctor." (1)

The state has long recognised that the public interest requires competence to be enforced by law in certain instances. As long ago as 1522 an Act was passed laying down that it was "expedient and necessary to provide that no person . . . be suffered to exercise and practise physic but only those persons that be profound, sad and discreet, groundedly learned and deeply studied". (2) Similarly, Acts were passed to ensure the proper training of lawyers, e.g. an Act of 1729 "for the better regulation of attorneys and solicitors" enforced training under articles.

The need to ensure competence in financial matters has been recognised by many Acts of Parliament. The most notable is the Companies Act, 1948, s.161, which requires that the accounts of all companies be

35

D

audited by persons who are members of a recognised body of accountants. Similar rules apply to the audit of accounts of building societies, friendly societies, industrial and provident societies, nationalised industries and numerous public corporations.

Although the state has thus frequently recognised the need to legislate to ensure competence, it has looked to the professional bodies themselves to provide a sufficient supply of practitioners of the necessary level of ability. By and large the professional bodies have accepted this role. The Royal Institute of British Architects for example has regarded itself as obliged to raise the standards of competence in the profession. In its submission to the Monopolies Commission in 1967, the Institute said: "The need to equip architects for the tasks of twenty to forty years ahead was the mainspring of the Institute's determination to raise standards. Human needs, building materials, the inter-relation of different parts of the man-made environment, methods of control and organisation of industrial processes, are changing fast and becoming increasingly complex. The quality of entrance to, and of training in, most schools of architecture in the 1950s seemed unlikely to yield a profession able to cope with the tasks of the future. Since 1958 a whole series of steps has been taken and more are projected to raise the standards." (3) Even such an unsympathetic body as the Prices and Incomes Board recognises that the quality of professional work ultimately depends on the standards of the profession, as enforced by its representative institutions. (4) The Board in its report on architects in 1968 welcomed the R.I.B.A's initiative in producing a code of good performance.

The institutions see their main function as maintaining standards. Thus the Association of Consulting Engineers states that one of the primary objects of the Association is to secure that persons undertaking to advise as consultants on engineering matters shall be fully qualified in their respective fields. (5)

### The Hallmark

The public looks for a hallmark bestowed by a trusted professional body, and evidenced by entry on a register or members' list. Few people will employ an architect, unless they have other assurances of his quality, if he is not a member of the R.I.B.A. Similarly those needing to employ an accountant or surveyor will feel happier if he is "chartered". Often, however, the public is confused by the number of differing qualifications within the same field. When the Estate Agents Council was set up in 1967 to compile a standard register, there were about a dozen different professional bodies operating within the field of estate agency and each giving their own professional qualification with accompanying designatory letters. Confusion in this field has been so great that very few members of the public are aware when consulting an estate agent whether he has any professional qualifications, and if so what they are. This problem is made more serious by the fact that the differing qualifications are of very variable standard. At one end of the spectrum stands the Royal Institution of Chartered Surveyors, requiring a five-year training and the passing of very difficult examinations, while at the other is the so-called "English Association of Estate Agents", which once enrolled on its register a domestic cat named Oliver Greenhalgh, whose owner sent in a form giving particulars in no way departing from the facts and describing its occupation as "rodent operative". (6)

The standards of a professional body tend to rise with the passage of time. Many bodies owe their origin to the desire of practitioners excluded from an existing body by standards they could not meet to find some society which would accept them, even if they had to form it themselves. Thus the Incorporated Society of Valuers and Auctioneers was formed in 1924 (as the Incorporated Society of Auctioneers and Landed Property Agents) to accommodate estate agents whose connection with a furniture store or other "commercial" concern excluded them from membership of the senior estate agency bodies at a time when those bodies were seeking to persuade Parliament to take away the right to practise from those not among their own members. The Incorporated Society today enjoys a high reputation for its standards of competence, and shares to the full the code of conduct of the senior bodies. Nevertheless a man who sports the initials F.S.V.A. may well have obtained his membership in the early days when the standard of competence imposed was far lower. Even the senior body in the land profession, the R.I.C.S. itself, has considerably increased the level of its examinations since they were first set in 1881. The public therefore needs advice on the relative standing of different qualifications. It can scarcely expect impartial advice as to the relative value of their qualifications from the institutes concerned (though it may very well get it). This kind of advisory service might well be offered by a body representing the consultant professions collectively. The establishment of such a body is suggested below (page 235).

Another problem arising from the "hallmark" concept of a professional qualification relates to regional variations in the expertise of the profession. A man in trouble with the law will not very happily consult a "qualified" lawyer unless he is satisfied that the qualification was gained from a study of the law of the country where the problem arises.

For this reason most professional bodies give a qualification related to the particular country in which they operate. Chartered accountants, solicitors and barristers are qualified for their own country only, though their qualification may gain them partial exemption from the examinations of their profession in Commonwealth countries having similar systems. A chartered surveyor on the other hand has a qualification without territorial limitation. This does not mean that the examinations are everywhere the same; for example, a quantity surveyor qualifying in Scotland will take papers some of which differ from those set in England to take account of differences in the methods of measurement and building construction in the two countries. The R.I.C.S. holds examinations in many countries, but except in Scotland and Ireland does not attempt to equate them generally to local conditions: many a Chinese youth sitting an examination in Hong Kong has grumbled at being tested in the intricacies of the London Building Acts.

This problem of how far a "hallmark" should be given a territorial limitation caused much difficulty to the Estate Agents Council. The Council was set up to give the public an assurance that estate agents recognised by the Council had at least the minimum degree of competence requisite for proper practice as an estate agent. Estate agents are, however, closely involved with the law of land and property, and the legal systems of Scotland and England differ considerably. Should an agent who has qualified in England be allowed to practise in Scotland under the seal of recognition by the Council? When this question was under debate it was pointed out that it was not only the law of the two countries that differed, but the practice of estate agency as well; indeed it could be said with justification that practice was very different in the North of England and in the South. Where then should the line be drawn? In the end the Council decided that a registered agent should not be prevented from practising anywhere in Great Britain.

The professions naturally set much store by the concept of the "hallmark". That they are not alone in this view is shown by the submission made to the Monopolies Commission by the Consumer Council, not a body noted for rushing to the support of the professions. The Council considers it an admirable policy that professional advisers should be competently trained and the public protected from charlatans by a controlled entry system. The Council's submission continues: "It is clear that minimum standards of achievement ... should be required of practitioners of at least those professions where the client seeks specialised advice. Those who seek advice are almost by definition little capable of assessing its value and the customer seeking advice, cannot, unlike the buyer of consumer goods, inspect what he is buying before committing himself."

Professional bodies are sometimes accused of artificially restricting entry to the profession by setting the level of competence required too high. Even worse, they are suspected of raising and lowering the level in order to secure that a predetermined number of entrants should be admitted each year. This complaint is often heard from unsuccessful examination candidates; it is almost certainly unfounded. Carr-Saunders and Wilson reported that the only case of limitation of the number of entrants they had encountered was in the case of stockbrokers, which they defended on the grounds that without such a limitation a private market could not be preserved and the absence of such a market would endanger discipline. (7) Although the Prices and Incomes Board has shown a tendency to regard the professions it has examined as over-supplied with manpower, evidence of this is very difficult to substantiate. It would be a dangerous thing for anybody to presume to know several years in advance how many new entrants a profession needed, and to govern the entry accordingly. Quite apart from the fact that surplus practitioners will tend to be weeded out by economic forces, there are often people who seek a qualification without intending to practise in that profession. The best known example of this is the Bar, where a large proportion of those who qualify are not in practice as barristers five years later.

The form in which the "hallmark" is given varies, sometimes being simple and at others very complicated. With some professions, such as solicitors, the hallmark simply consists in the right to call oneself a solicitor or whatever it may be. Other professions have developed a bewildering variety of designations. We are not here concerned to explore the complexities of different grades of membership of professional organisations, but only to see how far these are useful indications of competence. In this respect the designations are significant where they indicate the attainment of a certain seniority or level of responsibility in the profession, or where they denote entry by examination rather than on the basis of a number of years' experience in practising the profession. In certain cases designations may have a further purpose of distinguishing between the members of an institute who have qualified in one type of expertise rather than another. For example, corporate members of the R.I.C.S., which embraces a number of different techniques, will not have qualified in all of them. While any such member may describe himself as a chartered surveyor, this is not as informative as it might be, and many members also employ the more precise description of "chartered quantity surveyor" or "chartered land surveyor".

The most usual way of indicating seniority is by dividing full members into associates and fellows. Admission to fellowship is only granted on the attainment of a certain age, such as 30, with, in addition, a fixed number of years of experience in the profession. Attainment of a responsible position, such as a principal in a private firm or head of a department, is also sometimes required. An indication that examinations have not been passed is sometimes given by having a licentiate grade of membership. It is said that many members of the R.I.B.A. are reluctant to proceed to the fellowship because this is open both to licentiates (who have not taken the examination) and associates (who have). A member who remains an associate demonstrates that he has qualified by examination.

The value of many of the indications of seniority, and the corresponding initials affixed to the member's name, may be doubted — at least as far as the public is concerned. The public rightly assumes that the hallmark will not be given to one below years of discretion. The usual age limit is twenty-one; and the necessary lengthy training period would make any lower age limit impracticable as well as unwise. A member may carry greater prestige among his colleagues if he is seen to bear the senior rank of a fellow; the general public are likely to remain unimpressed because unaware of its significance. Since the rules governing the different grades in the various professions are so diverse, there seems little hope of evolving a system which can have general utility. As it is the public may even be misled by assuming that an apparently senior status indicates long experience which is in fact lacking. The most notorious example of this is the rank of Queen's Counsel. Most people assume that if a barrister has taken silk that is a sign of advancement in the profession. Such indeed is often the case, since appointments are made by the Queen on the recommendation of the Lord Chancellor and many of those who apply are not appointed. The number to whom silk is granted in any year is fixed by the Lord Chancellor in accordance with the advice he receives as to the number necessary to do the work available, the appointments being related to the needs of London, of each circuit and of each specialty within the profession. What many members of the public do not realise however is that some barristers are made Q.C.s not through their experience at the Bar but because the title is treated as an honour to reward the man who reaches the head of a Civil Service legal department or is elected to Parliament. On the other hand many ordinary practitioners who would be regarded as having ample experience do not apply for appointment as Queen's Counsel, preferring to remain juniors. Similarly many architects who would be eligible for fellowship do not apply, not only for the reason stated above but because, as the R.I.B.A. puts it, "the test for admission is not so severe as to create sufficient sense of great professional distinction for the fellowship class". Another deterrent to proceeding to the fellowship is that the subscription rates are usually considerably higher.

It seems therefore that the tendency for these distinctions to die out need not be regretted. Indeed the less there is to mystify the public, and the simpler it is to identify a competent practitioner, the more effective will be the service provided by the professions. The Privy Council has requested the professional bodies to keep down the number of designations to a minimum. In conformity with this the Institute of Chartered Accountants has drawn the attention of its members to the "desirability of adopting and using without additional words the title chartered accountant. It is comprehensive in its meaning and is now well understood as covering all branches of work entrusted to members. Any addition to it is apt to depreciate its character and value . . . " (8) Thus chartered accountants, unlike chartered surveyors, are not permitted to use designations such as "valuer and arbitrator", "financial, property and insurance agent", or "cost specialist". Fellows of the Royal College of Physicians are not permitted to use designations implying the adoption of special modes of treatment, since these are opposed to the "freedom and dignity of the profession". (9) Dentists are not allowed to describe themselves as "orthodontic specialists" or "specialists in children's dentistry", and commit a criminal offence if they do. (10) Does the public lose by the lack of this information? The professional philosophy says no, since information about such specialties should come by word of mouth from personal recommendations.

## Admission for Training

In its submission to the Monopolies Commission, the R.I.B.A. remarked: "The recruitment of the right human material, and its education, is obviously a major task in promoting the efficiency of a profession. Society will not give its confidence to a profession whose practitioners are of inadequate calibre or expertise." (11) The consultant professions are attaching more and more importance to the quality of the initial intake. Only young people of relatively high intellectual endowment and a good general education can, it is felt, tackle the professional examinations with a good chance of success.

This is all very well provided a sufficient number of young people of this standard are prepared to enter on a course of professional training. It is vital for the professions to continue to present a sufficiently attractive picture to the young to encourage them to come forward in sufficient numbers. Otherwise the consequences to the public could be serious, though not perhaps so serious as those depicted in the evidence of the President of the Royal College of Surgeons to a select committee in 1834. Army surgeons had been desperately needed in the Peninsular war, and the only tests that were required were one course of anatomy and another of surgery. There were too many failures to enable a sufficient number of surgeons to be recruited. The Government was obliged to give warrants to persons lacking even this simple qualification and, said the President (who had himself served in Spain): "Some of those men who came out to us in Spain committed such destruction in consequence of their ignorance as to render it most deplorable." (12)

Most professional institutes have traditionally been examining, though not teaching, bodies. Some, such as the Accountants and Surveyors, have relied on the teaching of new entrants by correspondence courses combined with practical training under articles. Almost all the leading professional bodies now however are moving over, if they have not already done so, to an entry standard requiring the student to have obtained a level of general education entitling him to university entrance. In England this is taken to be two passes at the advanced level of the General Certificate of Education. In this way the professions hope to avoid the waste of training pupils not equipped to master the course, and to obtain their fair share of the schools' higher-quality output. This is an advance from the days when the only qualification needed for entry as a student was attainment of the age of 16 or 18.

### Practical Training

The traditional method of training for the professions is by the attachment of the new entrant to an established practitioner under articles of apprenticeship or clerkship. The concept is of learning by being in close proximity to those who are actually doing the job. Instead of poring over books in a remote university, the novice drinks in the atmosphere of his profession and makes himself useful into the bargain. Formerly a substantial premium was paid to the master for this privilege; nowadays where the system survives it is the student who is paid, though not at the market rate for those doing similar work without tuition by the master.* The system often gave rise to the abuse of using the articled pupil as cheap labour or, even worse, pocketing the premium and then treating the pupil as if he were nothing but a salaried clerk. These abuses are illustrated in *Martin Chuzzlewit*, where the eponymous hero was articled to Mr Pecksniff, who described himself as "Architect

---

* The Prices and Incomes Board found in 1968 that 5 per cent of solicitors' firms charged premiums – usually about £250 (Cmnd. 3529, p.5).

and Land Surveyor", but betrayed little evidence of competence in either capacity.

The effectiveness of the system of articled pupilage largely depends on the quality and conscientiousness of the master. Where the system works well it provides the best training for a professional man. Indeed there is no other way in which the ideals as well as the expertise of the profession can be satisfactorily learnt. For this reason credit is due to the Institute of Chartered Accountants, who stand out against the tide which is tending to sweep away articles as a system of training and still insist on them as the only means of entry to the profession. The features to which the Institute attaches particular importance are:

1. The creation of a quasi-parental relationship between the principal and his students, allowing for the development in the student of the necessary professional qualities of character and personal behaviour, with the ability to handle relations with clients.

2. The effect in bringing the ordinary senior member of the profession into contact with new entrants, giving him a share in the teaching role of the profession.

3. The inducing of an added sense of responsibility in the pupil because he is learning through the medium of actual cases rather than theoretical or hypothetical situations.

Unfortunately this last stronghold of compulsory articles is likely to disappear soon, since the Institute is contemplating amalgamation with other accountancy bodies which do not insist on articles and draw their members largely from industry, commerce and the public service. In line with modern tendencies therefore it may be expected that the peculiar value of training the young in the atmosphere of individual service and professionalism found at its best in private offices will gradually disappear.

Since the Chartered Accountants' Institute so far retains the fullest system of articles of any profession except the solicitors, it is of interest to consider its requirements in some detail. The period of articled service is generally five years. A member is not allowed to take an articled clerk unless he is in private practice as an accountant in the United Kingdom. Before taking an articled clerk for the first time a prospective principal must obtain the consent of a special committee of the Institute. This is designed to ensure that the member is aware of his obligations as a principal and able to fulfil them. Approval is only given after an investigation by a sub-committee, which interviews the member. Most applications are successful; out of about 400 applications a year only one or two are rejected. To ensure that a member does not accept more articled clerks than he is able to look after properly a limit of four per member is imposed; until 1957 the limit was two. The lower age limit for entry upon articles is at present 16, though this is likely to be raised shortly to 18. An articled clerk is not allowed to follow any other occupation without the consent of the Council of the Institute, which is only given where the time spent in other occupations will not affect training or studies. There is a compulsory probationary period at the beginning of articles, allowing either party to cancel their contract if on closer acquaintanceship they do not wish to continue it.

The institutes do not as a rule lay down the content or method of practical training, even where it is to be given under articles. This reliance on the principal's discretion may not always be justified, though it fits the basic idea that the pupil takes the office as he finds it. The range of work in particular offices varies widely and it would be unworkable to demand of a principal practical training in fields to which his practice does not extend. Nevertheless entrants for the examinations of the R.I.C.S., for example, have been refused permission to sit, on the ground that their practical training was in an unsuitable office. Principals can and should ensure, however, that pupils are really trained in professional work, and not employed in pettifogging tasks which as qualified men or women they will never have occasion to perform.

The breakdown in the apprenticeship system was attributed by Carr-Saunders and Wilson to the increased theoretical content of the courses of training, which nowadays necessitates full-time education at a university or similar establishment. (13) That this is not altogether incompatible with practical training is demonstrated by the R.I.C.S., who continue to require two years' practical training with a practising member of the Institution even after the necessary theoretical training has been completed. The Bar Council also considers practical experience to be an essential part of the barrister's training. It has for many years been the practice for a barrister to do a year's pupilage in a barrister's chambers before accepting briefs on his own account. The positive rule was introduced in 1965 that a pupil may not accept instructions or conduct a case until six months of his pupilage have elapsed.

The importance of practical training with a practising member of the profession in private practice cannot be over-emphasised. While practical training in the expertise of the profession may be effectively given by practitioners not in private practice but, for example, employed in a public department, such practitioners are rarely able to implant those aspects of professionalism which spring from dealing with private clients. The code of the professions essentially originates from situations where a private client, often an individual, needs to be protected by the integrity of his personal consultant. These ideals cannot be learnt thoroughly except in an office where they are put into effect daily. If the professions value their code and standards they should hold on at all costs to the prime importance of educating their young entrants in the essence of professionalism. The failure to give full effect to this need is already showing results in the widespread ignorance among the recently-qualified of the true essence of professionalism and its code of practice. If this tendency continues much of the value of professionalism as now understood may die out.

## Examinations

The examination system is in no way peculiar to the consultant professions and we are only concerned with it on two points. One, which will be dealt with below, is whether, and how far, the public requires protection by the law's insisting on an examination qualification. The other concerns the need to remember that the essence of professionalism cannot be tested, even today, by written examinations based on theoretical training. It depends on experience, and experience of the right kind. It depends also on prolonged and close contact with the right kind of professional person during the formative years. Indeed a close alliance of high academic and theoretical disciplines with a sufficiency of the right kind of practical training should produce professionalism of a better standard than in the past. The old idea that it was not necessary to make any strict enquiry into a young man's knowledge of the technicalities of his profession before he took up its practice is gone for good. The assumption that one who had received a liberal education could easily master the details of the profession as he went along, if it ever had any validity, lost it when the subject matter of the professions became as technically complex as it has now been for several generations. Reader gives a picture of the views held in the legal profession on the need for examinations a century or so ago. The Treasurer of the Middle Temple summed it up by saying: "I do not think that examination is really of any use. I think the advantage of dining in the Hall is associating together. The question of men associating together, I think, is of very great importance . . . if he (the new barrister) is not qualified, he will get no business, and if he is qualified, he will get business." (14)

It is to be hoped that the reaction from this point of view will not go too far the other way. There was after all some basis for the belief that what mattered was for the tyro to mix with his future colleagues on terms of intimacy rather than to shut himself up with dusty books. That the latter was done, and often done with more depth of true learning than is found today, we know well. Even Dickens, with no love for lawyers and drawing Mr Pickwick's tormentors in the most unflattering light, granted Mr Serjeant Snubbins, along with his lantern face and sallow complexion, "that dull-looking boiled eye which is often to be seen in the heads of people who have applied themselves during many years to a weary and laborious course of study".

There are by and large two sorts of learning to be tested by examination: the academic and the technical. In some professions it is not uncommon for the academic side of the work to be studied at university as a matter quite apart from vocational training. For many years future barristers have passed their time at Oxford or Cambridge in studying theoretical jurisprudence, with a concentration on judge-made law and a contempt for statutes which by no means gives them a thorough grounding in the field of learning of a fully-fledged barrister. It does however lodge in their heads a respect for legal theory and abstract reasoning of more value than a premature concentration on the minutiae of statutory provisions. Their brethren may have gained the same discipline by a study of classics or history before tackling the vocational exercises needed for the Bar examinations.

There is a danger that some of the newer professions, intoxicated by the thought of drawing their entrants exclusively from the universities, will abandon the role of examining bodies. To be sure there is considerable pressure in that direction from the universities themselves, and from their graduates. Impatience to begin earning a living, coupled with the absence of any compulsion to become a member of a professional body before practising the profession, may well lead to growing numbers of graduates by-passing the professional bodies and their qualification altogether. If a diploma in architecture or a B.Sc. (Estate Management) comes to be regarded as equivalent to, or better than, a qualification bestowed by a professional body a serious blow will have been struck at the viability of professional institutions. Already control of syllabuses is passing out of the hands of professional bodies, who are being compelled to grant exemptions from their own examinations to holders of university degrees. While the universities are still obliged to bear in mind the requirements of the professional body in framing their syllabuses, they often feel reasonably certain that if the Institutes hold out against syllabuses desired by the universities, and threaten to withhold exemptions, the upshot will be that the university student will save himself the cost of an annual subscription and opt for reliance on his university qualification. Somehow this must be avoided and the idea preserved that a person is not fit to practise a profession the moment he or she comes down from the university with an academic degree. Indeed if it is a genuinely academic degree the graduate will scarcely have begun to embark on the vocational side of his education. It is not a matter merely of applied practical training; the difference between say the papers in the examinations for the final school of jurisprudence at Oxford and those for the solicitors' final is great indeed, and rightly so.

This leads us to a central problem of today. Should a university course be framed on vocational lines, so that little except practical instruction is needed before embarking on the profession? Or should the universities concentrate on training the mental faculties by rigorous intellectual discipline, leaving the details of the expertise of the profession to be picked up later? With university courses being almost entirely financed out of public funds there is a strong tendency for the former of these alternatives to be adopted. This negatives the idea of a university, and equates it to a technical school. It denies the present generation of undergraduates the richness of true learning, and such a denial will in time seriously impoverish the professions and indeed the whole national life. It is not merely a matter of cultural poverty; progress in the improvement of techniques is closely bound up with the pursuit of pure science and abstract learning.

If this reasoning is accepted it follows that such moves as the recent transfer of the College of Estate Management to form part of the University of Reading may not be altogether desirable. For half a century the College has formed the main training ground for recruits to the land professions. A typical pattern of training has been by correspondence courses taken by young men working under articles to an established practitioner. One danger is that the purely vocational training thus given will continue in the guise of university instruction. If this does not happen, and the courses resemble more the academic syllabus of the Department of Land Economy at Cambridge University, the position will be unsatisfactory in the opposite direction, since the main source of vocational training will have disappeared. It is true that postal courses are to continue, but students taking them will find it difficult to attend lectures, as they used to do while the College was at London. This at a time when the subject matter of the profession of the land is becoming more and more complex. If university courses are indeed to become the main training ground for future professionals, there is a great need for a reversal of the trend against practical and vocational training being given in practitioners' offices.

Carr-Saunders and Wilson favoured the giving of professional training in universities on the ground that the association of students studying different techniques widened understanding and created diversity of interests. They also felt that since research is a common feature of universities "the atmosphere is less likely to be heavy with instruction than in purely teaching institutions". (15) These are of course reasons why entrants to the professions should be university graduates; they are not reasons why detailed vocational training, rather than intellectual and academic disciplines, should be given at university.

While traditionally accepting the role of examining bodies, the professional institutions have been reluctant to take any responsibility for the quality of the instruction given in preparation for their examinations. There have been honourable exceptions: the land profession established the College of Estate Management, which was granted a charter in 1922; the Law Society has its School of Law and the Bar its Council of Legal Education. Private coaches have been ignored however; Carr-Saunders and Wilson found only one instance of a professional institute extending anything in the nature of recognition to private teaching institutions. Unwillingness to take responsibility for recommending an establishment whose standards were not officially supervised has led to a regrettable refusal to give needed advice. While this attitude still persists, its practical effect is growing less important with the increase in university courses and corresponding exemptions from professional examinations.

## Maintaining Competence

Having bestowed a hallmark of competence, a professional institute has some responsibility for ensuring that it remains valid. The man who has been examined and passed as competent at the age of 25 can, if he remains out of trouble, describe himself by his professional designation for the rest of his life. He may even do it after a long interval when he has not practised his profession at all. That this situation does not prejudice the public in fact can only be attributed to the rarity of the case. Most people who acquire a professional qualification either practise the profession for the rest of their working lives or, having once given up, do not return to it.

A more serious problem exists in the case of those who, while still practising, do not keep up to date with new techniques. Some do not even refresh their memories of knowledge acquired in student days. Lord Greene, a celebrated Master of the Rolls, remarked in 1936 that there were some chambers in the Temple where the library consisted of an out-of-date edition of the Annual Practice. He went on: "Such chambers will be found to house a hack in his most perfect development." (16) To keep up with changes is all the more necessary in the present era when the corpus of professional knowledge does not remain virtually static, but is revolutionised every generation. In some cases, such as medical science, it is revolutionised every five years.

Most professional bodies accept the need to assist their members to obtain knowledge of developments in their expertise. They provide information services, lectures and similar aids for this purpose. The R.I.B.A. has a library which is one of the two largest architectural libraries in the world, with a stock of over 70,000 books and 500 current periodicals. The Institute publishes a handbook of architectural practice and management in four volumes of some 800 pages. To enable members to organise the flood of technical information and manufacturers' trade literature, the Institute has promoted the use of an international classification system. Most other professions provide similar services. The R.I.C.S. has recently started an elaborate technical information service; the Law Society supplies its members with handbooks on office management, costing, etc. Only the Bar Council maintains the older tradition of doing very little for its members; but this enables it to keep membership subscriptions at a low level.

Even if his professional institution does not do all it might in the provision of information services, the active and conscientious practitioner can usually find the means to keep himself up to date. There is, however, rarely any compulsion on members to take advantage of the facilities available and certainly there is no examination into whether or not they have done so. The R.I.C.S. intends to establish post-qualification studies, advanced diplomas and other refresher-course activities, but there is no suggestion that these should be made compulsory.

The mature professional man has an invincible distaste for taking examinations. He usually feels that he has got them out of his system for good by the middle twenties, and would certainly oppose any attempt to make him sit them again later. Ten-year tests may be all right for motor-cars; they have little future for professional people.

Some may say that the government should step in and impose statutory obligations in this respect. The precedents for this kind of action, however, are not happy. Carr-Saunders and Wilson record that the Board of Trade have been reluctant to use such statutory powers in the case of patent agents; "Not being a professional body the Board have shown great hesitation in using their powers except where offences of a very grave nature are concerned." (17) A recent attempt by the Ministry of Health to induce doctors to undergo postgraduate training by making this a condition of the receipt of seniority payments aroused the ire of the British Medical Association. The scheme, introduced in 1968, requires doctors to attend eight postgraduate training sessions in a two-year period if they are to qualify for payments ranging from £200 to £650 a year. The B.M.A. asserted that this went beyond the bounds of the Minister's functions by setting standards for doctors following their profession and trying to coerce them to accept these standards by financial sanctions. The Minister's justification was that attendances at the training sessions were inadequate, and that at least one-third of general practitioners had no postgraduate education. (18) Which was right? It seems that the British Medical Journal went too far in asserting that "in following his profession the doctor's allegiance is to the standards of knowledge . . . laid down by the profession's governing bodies." if the implication is that he has no business to aim for any higher standard. The professional bodies themselves should aim for the highest practicable standards. If they shrink from enforcing them on backward practitioners they are in a weak position to object when the State, which in this case happens to hold the purse strings, insists on adding economic inducements.

### Is Incompetence Misconduct?

While many may agree that it should be left to the professions to ensure that the standard of competence of their members is maintained, it cannot be denied that they have been singularly reluctant to do so. The institution man tends to say that the matter can be safely left to the civil law of negligence, or that the forces of the market will drive out the incompetent, since he will be unable to survive in competition with his abler fellows. While this may be the case in flagrant instances, a great deal of harm can be done by lack of competence before economic forces or the rage of his partners drives the offender into outer darkness.

Nor are legal remedies altogether adequate. While the law enables damages to be claimed for loss arising through the failure of a professional man to exercise a reasonable standard of care, this standard will vary with the standing of the practitioner and the location of his practice. As has been said, "that might be negligence in a doctor of repute in the West of London which would yet come up to the highest warrantable expectations of the patient of a village doctor in remotest Kerry or Westmoreland". (19) Furthermore the aggrieved client is often reluctant to go to law, and a deaf ear coupled with an incapacity for answering letters has seen many an erring professional man out of trouble without loss to himself.

Even where the client does bring legal proceedings, and meets with success, the practitioner often effectively opts out by handing the claim over to his insurance company. Admittedly an insurance company will raise the premiums or withdraw altogether if it finds too many claims are being made on the policy. By the time that stage is reached, however, the incompetent practitioner can do a lot of harm.

Another defect in the protection given by the law of negligence arises from the fact that it is very easy for a practitioner to relieve himself from liability by inserting a suitable term in the contract with the client. This defect may be remedied in the near future, since the Law Commission is examining the possibility of altering the law to make it impossible to contract out of negligence where this would be contrary to the public interest. In the case of barristers the law of negligence gives no protection to clients, as the law exempts barristers from liability. In a few cases the law specifically provides for practitioners to be deprived of the right to practise where incompetence is proved. Thus a pharmacist may be struck off the register for selling poison in a bottle not properly labelled.

The extreme reluctance of professional institutes to penalise incompetence among their members is due to the fact that institutes are, after all, made up of professional people themselves who, while showing no mercy to dishonesty, always shrink from castigating examples of inefficiency which carry little or no moral blame. Two striking examples may be given, one from the last century and the other from very recent times.

The Tay Bridge disaster has passed into folklore. In 1877 the first railway bridge over the river Tay in Scotland was opened. It was the widest span over water yet attempted in any country, and the civil engineer responsible for designing it, Thomas Bouch, was knighted by Queen Victoria in recognition of his feat. Two years later, in a great storm the bridge was brought down, together with a passenger train which was crossing it at the time. 75 people lost their lives and the official court of enquiry concluded "that this bridge was badly designed, badly constructed and badly maintained, and that its downfall was due to inherent defects in the structure which must sooner or later have brought it down. Sir Thomas Bouch is, in our opinion, mainly to blame". (20) Sir Thomas did not long survive this condemnation and the public odium it incurred. Yet he remained a member of the Institution of Civil Engineers to his death, and there was no attempt by the Institution Council to deprive him of his membership or penalise him in any other way for his incompetence. It is not without significance that the report cited above was in fact a minority report, since it was made by the one of the three members of the court of enquiry who was not himself a civil engineer. The other two members (who were engineers), while not dissenting from the attribution of the chief blame to Bouch, felt that it was not for the court of enquiry to say so.

E

John Prebble, in his book *The High Girders*, attributes this attitude to "professional sympathy, or loyalty, or caution". (21)

The more recent case concerned a two million-pound county hall at Bedford. The building was designed in the early 1960s by the County Architect's department. At an early stage in the construction serious weaknesses in the design were discovered and work was stopped. The design of the reinforced concrete structure had been entrusted to a structural engineer who was a member of the staff of the County Architect's department. A firm of consulting engineers who were called in to investigate reported that this engineer was diligent and industrious and that "where he was in any doubt he sought answers". The structural faults arose entirely "from the fact that he adopted a number of his own ideas and unusual design principles". The consultants went on to say that the case was quite unique in their experience, adding: "We cannot logically explain how an engineer, who was so diligent and industrious and who has displayed professional integrity, could possibly have so distorted his appreciation of accepted rudimentary engineering principles, which must have been the very foundation of his professional training." (22)

The matter was thoroughly reviewed by the engineer's professional body, the Institution of Structural Engineers, who concluded that no action should be taken against him by the Institution. The reason given is highly significant: "The erroneous design criteria adopted, which led to such disastrous results both for the County Council and for the member personally, were used in good faith and no charge of negligence could be sustained." (23) In commenting on the case, the journal *Building* said, "as the failure of the County Hall design proved, a university degree and membership of a professional society are not necessarily in themselves a guarantee that a structural engineer is competent to undertake important work". (24) That this comment was undoubtedly justified as a general pronouncement is a matter which should give the professions great concern.

The fraternal nature of professional institutions is an important element in the effectiveness of professionalism. Confidence in the professions requires, however, that loyalty to a comrade should not stand in the way of removal, from one who has shown himself inadequate, of the hallmark on which the public ought to feel it safe to rely. In the medical field, figures for incompetence in operating techniques are increasing, according to the Medical Defence Union. In 1967 there were 44 cases of retained swabs and instruments and 33 wrong operations reported to the Union, which paid out £127,000 in damages, costs and legal charges. These figures were the highest recorded, though the matter is put in perspective by the fact that the total of operations in British hospitals is about 1,500,000 a year. (25) This century has seen a change in the attitude of the courts towards professional negligence and the adoption of, in the words of Lord Devlin, "a much higher standard of skill and care than heretofore". (26)

The attitude of many professions towards incompetence is illustrated by the submissions made by the R.I.B.A. to the Monopolies Commission in 1967. After pointing out the legal remedies for negligence and stating the R.I.B.A.'s policy of strongly urging members to take out insurance against this risk, the statement goes on: "The R.I.B.A. itself, however, cannot usurp the function of the courts. It cannot award damages to a client who has suffered from a member's misfortune, error or worse; and damages are usually the main concern of an injured client. The R.I.B.A. must therefore confine itself to issues of professional misconduct". The R.I.B.A. is exploring the possibility of framing a "Code of Performance" which would indicate in detail the service a member should give his client. It is not yet certain whether such a code will be forthcoming, or whether breach of it would constitute a matter for disciplinary action.

Incompetence goes wider than lack of professional skill, and covers delay, neglect and even sheer disobedience to the client's instructions. Solicitors have been found guilty of misconduct for failing to pay over money advanced by a debtor to buy time from his creditors, for failing to complete a conveyance after being put in funds and thus losing the property, and for disobeying instructions to invest property in a particular way. (27)

Worthy of praise is the attitude of the Institute of Chartered Accountants, whose practice it is in serious cases of neglect by members of their clients' affairs, to bring disciplinary proceedings on the grounds that such neglect is a discreditable act. In the years 1962-66, disciplinary action of this kind was taken in 29 cases, in only two of which was the complaint found not to have been proved. Frequently, in less serious cases, the Institute, by means of advice or the exertion of its influence, manages to rectify the situation without disciplinary proceedings. In the case of solicitors, gross delay or gross neglect of a client's business is regarded as professional misconduct, whereas "simple" delay or negligence is not. (28) This view is shared by the courts: in *Felix* v. *General Dental Council* it was held that a dentist was not guilty of disgraceful conduct in not keeping proper National Health Service records and overcharging, since he was merely careless without dishonesty or recklessness. (29) Powers to punish this type of misconduct in the case of solicitors have been recently strengthened, and the Council of the Law

Society can now deal effectively with complaints of undue delay and failure to act. (30)

## Covering

There is one matter on which the professions are quick to act, and that is "covering" or the practice of allowing an unqualified person to act under the cover of a qualified person who in fact exercises no supervision or control. It is a breach of the first of the fundamental rules of the Chartered Accountants. The General Medical Council has laid down that any doctor who knowingly enables or assists a person, not duly qualified and registered as a medical practitioner, to practise medicine becomes liable to disciplinary proceedings. No doctor should enable any uncertified person to attend a woman in childbirth, save in urgent necessity. Similarly, the Solicitors Acts provide that if a solicitor knowingly acts as agent in any legal proceedings for an unqualified person, or permits his name to be made use of by an unqualified person, or does any other act to enable an unqualified person to practise as a solicitor, his name shall be struck off the roll.

The reason why the professions are not slow to act in these cases is that they smack of fraud, and encourage the doing of the work of the profession by persons beyond its pale. In the eyes of professional people these acts are far more blameworthy than mere incompetence, but the harm to the public may be no different. So heinous is covering by solicitors that it is the sole offence for which striking off the roll is mandatory. According to Sir Thomas Lund it was the cardinal offence for any solicitor to commit up to the beginning of the present century. (31)

## "Closed" Professions

We have seen that in the consultant professions competence is highly important. The subject-matter closely affects life, property or rights and it is in the public interest that adequate advice should be available. It can scarcely be denied that within this field, where individualism matters so much, the most satisfactory arrangement for securing competence is one where the profession itself accepts the responsibility for this and carries it out. To do so it must first be effectively organised, preferably with a single professional body coverin the whole field of the profession.

What this field should be is debatable in particular instances and may not be static. The question where one profession ends and another begins is often difficult. Sir Christopher Wren was styled Surveyor-General to Her Majesty, but would now be called an architect. Many surveyors also practise as architects, however, and the line is not easy to draw. Architects' work also overlaps with engineers'. Solicitors overlap with accountants in giving tax advice and (particularly in Scotland) with estate agency. Surveyors are forbidden by their charter to do work which is properly that of a solicitor, but there is no corresponding restriction the other way round. The distinction between solicitors and barristers is not found in most other countries, and the Prices and Incomes Board grumbled recently at the fact that it had never been independently looked at. Accountants claim to do the work of actuaries, while medical science has many confused and overlapping branches.

As expertise grows more complex there may be a case for reducing the area of the field covered by a single representative body. This is exemplified by the rise of town planning as a separate discipline during the period since the First World War, which led to the growth of a separate body, the Town Planning Institute, occupying part of the field held by architects and surveyors. Another example is the Institute of Landscape Architects.

The profession being organised in a unified way, it then falls to the professional body to place the hallmark of competence only upon those qualified for it, with due regard to matters such as regional variations in the expertise and the desirability or otherwise of indicating seniority by variations in the hallmark.

A further necessary step is to educate the potential users of the professional service so that they are aware of the significance of the hallmark. Ideally there should be no question of legal compulsion either on the public to go to particular practitioners or on practitioners to have obtained a particular qualification. If the public are generally aware that a guarantee of competence is only given where recourse is had to a practitioner who bears the hallmark, there should be no need to legislate upon the matter.

This is not to say that legislation has no place. It may well be necessary to legislate in order to assist in the development of the ideal situation outlined above. Once the legislation has had its effect, however, it should be possible to repeal it. This may be the case, for example, with the Architects Registration Acts. While they were needed in a formative period in the development of the profession of architecture, little harm is likely to result from their repeal. The public generally is well aware that almost all qualified architects belong to the R.I.B.A. and, even if the Acts were repealed, bringing freedom to anyone to use the appellation "architect", the public would be very unlikely to consult self-styled architects who could not display an R.I.B.A. qualification, though the smaller bodies giving architectural qualifications should not be overlooked.

The position is quite different in the field of estate agency. Here there are innumerable qualifications, of very different value. The public is confused and scarcely aware of the qualifications possessed by the estate agent they consult. The position has been improved by the setting up of the Estate Agents Council and its uniform register, but the effectiveness of this will be slow to be realised unless it is supported by legislation preventing unregistered estate agents from practising. After a generation the public should become so familiar with the Estate Agents Council qualification that it will no longer need to be supported by law.

If free professions are to flourish in a free democracy, there ought to be as little interference from the law as possible. This wholesome principle has led to all attempts at imposing a "closed shop" in the field of medicine being firmly resisted. This is striking, since matters of life and death are involved. Yet Parliament was only prepared to go so far, by statutory regulation, as to provide a means whereby, in the words of the Medical Act of 1858, "persons requiring medical aid should be enabled to distinguish qualified from unqualified practitioners". This was done by setting up a statutory register, but there is no prohibition of the practice of medicine by unregistered practitioners. The Medical Acts do provide however that no person who is unregistered is a "legally qualified" or "duly qualified" medical practitioner; and only a registered practitioner may, for example, hold appointments in most hospitals or in the public services, or practise in the National Health Service, or prescribe dangerous drugs, or give death certificates.

It is only in the legal field that, until recently, anything like a "closed shop" has been imposed by law. Barristers and solicitors have an exclusive right of audience in the courts. In the case of the superior courts the right is limited to barristers. It derives in some cases from statute, in others from decisions of the courts themselves. The Bar Council defend this position on the ground that the more important litigation is conducted by a small body of specialists, numbering just over 2,000 and this, coupled with the fact that the judges themselves have all been practising barristers, contributes largely to the expedition and efficiency with which cases are conducted and to the high reputation which English justice has throughout the world.

Statutory provisions prevent anyone other than a solicitor from doing some forms of legal work. Only a solicitor may charge a fee for taking, on behalf of another person, certain necessary steps in conveyancing and probate. The Prices and Incomes Board recently examined these restrictions in its report on remuneration of solicitors (32) and concluded that the restrictions provided protection for clients — "in fact, a safeguard against those not subject to the discipline of a professional body". They felt that the possible legal difficulties which might have a considerable effect on the enjoyment of his title by a buyer of property formed a justification for denying the outsider the right to carry out conveyancing.

In 1921 the dental profession secured a statutory "closed shop", and it is now in general unlawful for an individual who is not registered in the dentists register or under the Medical Acts to carry on practice as a dentist. (33)

The professional man always tends to feel that the public should be protected from the ministrations of those not enjoying his qualifications. To provide this protection in the form of a legal bar on the provision of services by outsiders needs to be justified. In general the profession ought to rely upon impressing the public with the quality of its services, so that it becomes unthinkable to go elsewhere. This situation may be ideal but it is not always easy to bring about. The health and safety of the public must be protected, and ultimately this is the responsibility of society itself. In the field of property and rights the danger is less pressing but still real. Cut-price services can be provided profitably if desirable safeguards are omitted or the outsider picks on services that are lucrative and leaves professional people to provide the rest. We shall see later how it is a feature of professional practice to adopt a "swings and roundabouts" approach, under which high-cost transactions are subsidised by others where the service can be provided cheaply in relation to the value of property involved. This particularly applies to conveyancing by solicitors, and an outsider who could pick and choose the conveyances he was prepared to undertake (and left other legal business alone) would comfortably outbid the solicitors. The same feature is common in other services where a social element is involved.

## CHAPTER 4

# HUMANITY: A PERSONAL RELATIONSHIP

The basic proposition advanced in Chapter 1 of this book (page 15), at least so far as it deals with services provided to individuals, obviously calls for a close personal relationship between the practitioner and his client. This is self-evident in the case of medicine and other services concerned with bodily health. It is also pretty obvious in fields closely concerning the property and rights of individuals, such as that of the family solicitor. In matters like this the citizen needs to be able to go to an adviser whom he knows personally and who knows him, particularly if he is one of those out of the ordinary clients whom Reginald Hine, a country solicitor, described as "the fantastical, hysterical, unreasonable, half-certifiable sons and daughters of iniquity or obliquity who climbed the stairs and asked for one's advice". (1)

Any client will prefer to consult one whose outlook is sympathetic to his own and with whom he gets on as a person. The ideal consultant is a man or woman with a liking for people and a desire to understand them. Imagination, tact and sympathy are important characteristics, and the ability to create confidence is very necessary. With a client in trouble of some sort, the practitioner should be a person who actually or apparently enters into his client's problems and gives his client the feeling that here is a champion who will represent him fully and faithfully in any adversity. The value attached to the quality of sympathy is illustrated by the old Punch joke of the enquirer who asked what sort of doctor the new man was and received the reply, "Oh well, I don't know much about his ability; but he's got a very good bedside manner!" Much fun has been poked at the bedside manner, but it remains an attribute greatly appreciated when found and sadly missed when absent. All the efficiency and competence in the world will not suffice to meet human distress if humanity and sympathy are lacking, and as Hine says the ideal relationship with clients is "not a mere bowing acquaintance, but a pleasant and jocular friendship". (2)

This does not involve treating serious matters with flippancy or departing from that "kind of solemnity" which Dr Johnson required in the manners of a professional man. It was Lord Hewart who said that a

judge should try to look as wise as he is paid to look, and the same goes
for other professional men – and women too. The human touch must
not be lacking however. A well-known chartered surveyor recorded
that he often brought home a point by vivid metaphor: "For example,
if advising a client not to sell at present land likely to be valuable for
development in the future . . . one might say to him 'I think you will
agree that it is always a mistake to pick an apple before it is ripe'.
Again, if advising a client, who bought as a speculation, to sell (on a
rising market), it may be well to say to him that 'a tree never grows
up to the sky'." (3) A recent survey has shown the value of a humane
approach in dentistry. Many people, it seems, are deterred from regular
visits to the dentist by fear; and gentleness is the quality in a dentist
most esteemed. (3a)

The intensely personal relationship between the professional consultant and his client has led professional institutes to take note of factors
which might otherwise be regarded as the concern only of the
individual practitioner. The Hippocratic oath, formulated in the fifth
century B.C., included the sentence: "With purity and with holiness I
will pass my life and practise my art." (4) The Hippocratic corpus went
into considerable detail about the appearance and character of the
physician. He should have a worthy appearance, and look healthy and
well-nourished. He must look to the cleanliness of his person; he must
wear decent clothes and use perfumes with harmless smells, since it was
held that physicians who are not tidy in their own persons cannot look
after others well. As to his character: "Let his character be that of a
noble man; as such let him restrain himself in the face of everything
that is high-principled and philanthropic; for a hasty and busy life avails
one nothing except when it can be used usefully." (5)

The Hippocratic corpus did not neglect the bedside manner: "The
physician must have a certain degree of sociability, for a morose dis-
position is inaccessible both to those who are well and those who are
sick. He must respect himself as much as possible; he must neither allow
much of the body to be exposed to view, nor must he have much conversation with the uninitiated, but only what is necessary." (6)

Professional institutions today show the same concern for this aspect
of their members' attributes. In their submissions to the Monopolies
Commission in 1968, the Royal Institution of Chartered Surveyors and
kindred societies said:

"We believe that all professions involve a vocation, a sense of dedica-
tion and a willingness to accept a measure of self-discipline as well as the
ability to reflect deeply and sympathetically on the problems referred
to them by clients. These qualities of mind and spirit are not called for

in the same degree in commerce or industry, where forcefulness, ambition and enterprise (and sometimes even ruthlessness) may be valuable assets from the point of view of the national economy as well as the individual. It follows that it is the function, and indeed the duty, of a professional body to seek to establish in the profession it represents conditions which will attract to the ranks of that profession the right type of recruit." (7) Elsewhere in this submission, the point is made that professional rules of conduct are designed to raise and maintain a number of qualities, including personal service "and last, but not least, good manners". (8) A reference to good manners is also made in a well-known attempt to define professional attributes made by a former President of the Institution of Electrical Engineers. This mentions a standard of conduct "based on courtesy, honour and ethics, which guides the practitioner in his relations with clients, colleagues and the public". (9)

The idea that a client will not repose confidence in a practitioner whom he does not respect as a person has led to the adoption of rules to preserve the "dignity" of the professions. It is fashionable to sneer at these, but the need for them is felt very strongly by most professional people. One of the reasons used to justify restrictions on the carrying on of trades or businesses by practising barristers is that there are a number of these which it would not be in conformity with the dignity of the Bar for a practising barrister to carry on. (10) It is the express duty of a barrister "at all times to uphold the dignity and high standing of his profession, and his own dignity and high standing as a member of it". (11) A solicitor must not engage in a business unless it is "an honourable one that does not detract from his status as a solicitor". This is construed widely and has been held to permit business as a building contractor, a theatre manager or even a coal merchant, but not a bookmaker. It is permissible to hold elocution classes for articled clerks "provided they are not held at the Law Society's Hall"! (12) The Institute of Chartered Accountants regards it as undesirable for a member to engage in any activity which is disreputable, undignified or likely to lower the standing of the profession in public esteem. An example of such an activity, given by the Institute, is for a practising member to hold a moneylender's licence. (13) Also incompatible with the dignity of the profession is carrying on a retail shop from the address from which a member practises. "A member whose wife ran a shop would not be allowed to practise in a room behind the shop particularly if the entrance to the office were through the shop. Nor regrettably would you be allowed to put up your plate outside a public house." (14) The Declaration of Geneva binds the doctor to practise his profession "with conscience and dignity". (15)

That this reasonable and proper desire to engage the confidence of the client may shade into a less laudable wish to increase the social status of the professional man's work, and therefore of himself, cannot be denied. Many criticisms have been levelled at this tendency. Reader quotes a nineteenth century opinion that it would be better if the idea of gentility could be divorced from professional occupations. (16) Carr-Saunders and Wilson point out that throughout the eighteenth century the professions were regarded first and foremost as gentlemen's occupations. "Though they might not offer large material rewards, they do provide a safe niche in the social hierarchy." (17) This attitude has persisted and many members of professions or near-professions have openly sought to raise their status, first by forming professional associations and later by seeking Royal Charters for them. It is undoubtedly a criticism of the professions today that their less enlightened members form one of the last strongholds of the old disdain of "trade". There are chartered surveyors, for instance, who look down on those of their number who practice estate agency or, far worse, mere house agency. Such activities are commonly regarded as not really professional — even when carried on by persons who have had the same long and arduous training as purely consultant surveyors. This attitude is indeed difficult to justify since all the skills acquired in such training may well be brought into play in the proper carrying out of the functions of an estate agent. It is the touch of the market that offends, however, and it is difficult to acquit those holding this attitude of the taint of hypocrisy. Indeed there are professional surveyors who, while also practising as estate agents and indeed making most of their income in that way, do so through separate firms acquired for the purpose and prefer that the fact shall not be known, or at least remarked upon, by their professional brethen.

## The Ideal of Service

Without countenancing false dignity and unworthy striving for position, it is necessary to defend any practice which promotes the confidence of the client. One old-fashioned virtue which is perhaps on the wane is the "tradition of service". In a presidential address celebrated among chartered surveyors, this was expressed in the following words: "The finest tradition of any calling is a readiness to serve. The spirit of a great profession is the spirit of service . . . It is a spirit which derives, I suggest, from an interest not in things but in people — which alone begets understanding." (18) It goes without saying that "readiness to serve" involves assiduous attention to the client's needs and prompt dispatch of his business. It calls for personal attendance wherever needed, as in court proceedings. It is the duty of a solicitor to attend throughout a court hearing, even though his client is represented by Counsel. If it is impracticable for him to attend personally he must send a capable deputy. (20)

The estate agents' ideal of service was expressed as follows by the R.I.C.S.:

"The services of a professional estate agent are devoted to the best interests of the public as represented from time to time by the client who retains him, and this involves him in a fiduciary relationship with that client. The best interests of that client must be served in preference to the interests of any members of the public (provided that the latter are treated openly and fairly) and always in preference to any private interest of the estate agent, such as a quick sale to make sure of commission when some patience would have achieved a better result for the client." (21) This concept is also seen in the B.M.A. statement that "it is the long-standing tradition in the medical profession that the rendering of professional services is not dependent upon payment of a fee". (22) In the days before the National Health Service many poor patients were grateful to the general practitioner who was ready with everything except his bill, and indeed lived up to the Declaration of Geneva's statements that "I solemnly pledge myself to consecrate my life to the service of humanity" and "The health of my patient will be my first consideration". (23)

The Bar Council submission to the Monopolies Commission mentions the professional man's duty often to give advice which is contrary to his own financial interests, and says that it is inherent in the profession of a barrister that he should hold himself out as ready to serve any client and to give equal attention to every client. (24) This is known as the "cab-rank" rule and, in the words of the submission, "serves to ensure that no client, however notorious or unpopular with government or public he may be and whatever may be the odium which will be suffered by the person who appears for him, will fail to find a spokesman". (25) The rule was established in 1792 when Erskine was deprived of his office as Attorney-General to the Prince of Wales for defending Tom Paine in the prosecution for publishing Paine's *Rights of Man.* Erskine said in a famous speech: "From the moment that any advocate can be permitted to say that he will or will not stand between the Crown and the subject arraigned in the Court where he daily sits to practise, from that moment the liberties of England are at an end." (26)

The Bar Council maintains that the "cab-rank" rule operates in no other profession, but it is to be hoped this is not so. The position probably is that, since we are fortunately still blessed with a plentiful supply of private consultants, it is always possible for a person rejected by one to find another who will take on his case. This means that instances of a person being refused professional assistance by every practitioner he goes to just do not arise. The nearest approach nowadays is perhaps where the patient of a National Health Service practitioner is asked to transfer to some other doctor's list and finds difficulty in doing so. The B.M.A. regards it as essential to safeguard the free choice of doctor by the patient. (27) While most professional institutions would probably frown on a member who declined to act for a person except for some weighty reason, it would probably be unreasonable to deny in the last resort the right to turn away a would-be client. Barristers are in a special position, since they have no direct dealings with those they represent — except in rare cases, such as the dock brief, where no solicitor intervenes between the barrister and his lay client.

A striking instance of willingness to serve beyond the call of duty, coupled with a humane approach, is afforded by Reginald Hine, when arguing the claims of the family solicitor to act as executor, rather than the bank or public trustee: " . . . what you need is not a cold, correct official, an impeccable machine, but a human being, even if he be a fallible mortal, someone who has been the repository of the family secrets, the trusted adviser and friend". Hine recounts how as executor he has done many things not strictly required by law — even on one occasion completing an unfinished manuscript in the style of the deceased author and then publishing it in the latter's name. (28) Another solicitor demonstrated his humanity by personally injecting a female client in the thigh to calm her before a divorce case. His zeal was rewarded by a three-year suspension. (29)

The tradition of service which leads the true professional consultant to place the interests of his client before his own, and to give of his utmost without regard to material reward, is a most precious concept. While difficult to create, and of slow growth, it is all too easy to dissipate. It needs to be taught to young entrants, if not explicitly at least by contact with practitioners imbued with its spirit. From the nature of things it flourishes more in private offices than in salaried employment, and is a telling reason why no one should be given the hallmark of a professional consultant unless his training has included a spell in private practice.

## The Consultant as *alter ego*

A further aspect of the need for services of the kind we are discussing to be rendered on a "person to person" basis lies in the fact that very often the practitioner is acting as the *alter ego* of his client. The most complete example of this is of course the solicitor acting under a general power of attorney, which gives him the power in law to do any act which his client could himself have done. Less complete examples arise in many fields. Litigants and accused persons are represented by counsel; a property owner threatened with compulsory acquisition is represented by a chartered surveyor; a taxpayer seeking to cut down his assessment is represented by an accountant; a developer wishing to persuade a planning committee is represented by an architect; and so on. In every case where an individual appears to argue or defend himself through the medium of another he is to a greater or lesser extent identified with his representative, and naturally desires that representative to be in no way inferior to himself. This identification is strikingly illustrated by the old mannerism of the barrister who, in explaining his case to the judge, would often say not "my client is an elderly lady and she has suffered much . . . " but "I am an elderly lady, my Lord, and I have suffered much . . . " It is perhaps symptomatic that this construction is seldom heard today.

## Partnerships

The stress we have laid upon the need for a personal relationship between the practitioner and his client might seem to indicate that ideally the practitioner should be entirely a freelance, acting alone. There are many practical considerations, however, which render it desirable in most cases for the practitioner to be associated with colleagues in the same profession, and the usual machinery for achieving this is the partnership. The Bar prohibits partnership, and the Royal College of Physicians prohibits it except where the College gives permission, which it occasionally does. (30) Other professional bodies place no obstacles in the way of partnership.

Partnership is recognised by law as a distinct type of business organisation with certain characteristic qualities. These include the following: every partner is entitled and bound to take part in the conduct of the practice, unless otherwise agreed; every partner is liable for the debts of the partnership to the whole extent of his private property; as between the partners, each partner is bound to contribute to the debts of the partnership in proportion to his share of the profits; as regards third persons, the act of every partner, within the ordinary scope of the business, binds his co-partners, whether they had sanctioned it or not; the relation between the partners being personal, no one of them can put a stranger in his place without the consent of the others. (31)

Sometimes a "partner" takes a salary instead of a share of the profits. He may then in law be no more than an employee, though if his name appears on the firm's writing paper he will be taken to be held out as a full partner and liable as such. (32) It is possible to create a limited partnership in which, although there must be one or more partners responsible for all the liabilities, there may be other partners whose liability is restricted to a fixed sum. (33) In theory a partnership comes to an end whenever there is a change in the partners, though in practice a partnership firm can be continued indefinitely. In this it resembles a body corporate, though differing from it in confining the "equity" or ownership of the partnership assets (including goodwill) to the partners themselves, rather than to shareholders who may have no concern in the management of the enterprise.

The reasons which justify the carrying on of a practice in partnership rather than individually are numerous. They have to be weighed against the intensity of the personal relationship with the client, which of course varies according to the nature of the services in question. The following are among the more important reasons for setting up a partnership; and are equally reasons against sole practice:

1. If a practitioner is absent through illness or other cause, the client's affairs can be dealt with by one of the partners who, because of the continuous exchange of information which goes on within a partnership, may well already know something of the affairs of the client. The Law Society point out that great difficulties arise where a solicitor practising on his own has made no arrangements for another solicitor to look after his affairs in an emergency — to maintain office records, to conduct client's affairs and to see that Law Society regulations are complied with. The *locum tenens* is of course well known in other fields as well, notably medicine. He is usually inferior to a partner in the estimation of clients because he is unfamiliar and inevitably lacks the authority, because the responsibility, of a full partner. That these difficulties can be at least partially overcome is demonstrated by the Bar, which prohibits partnerships. The arrangement under which half a dozen or so barristers share office accommodation in one set of chambers, with common clerking and secretarial facilities, gives some of the advantages of a partnership. If one member of the chambers is unable to take a case, as frequently happens because of the unpredictability of court proceedings, it is the normal practice for another member of the chambers to act instead. So firmly entrenched is this system that it is a positive rule that a barrister must not practise unless he is a member of professional chambers or the pupil of such a member. (34)

2. It is difficult for a single practitioner to make full economic use

of the clerical and secretarial services he needs. A solicitor who spends a day in the County Court, for example, may well leave his secretary under-employed. The more principals there are in a firm the easier it is to rationalise the working time of ancillary staff. Here again we find that professions where partnership is not allowed get round this difficulty. The Harley Street consultant operates from premises where there is one receptionist dealing with perhaps half a dozen separate practices.

3. A firm with several partners can provide a more specialised service. N.A.H. Stacey has noted the increasing specialisation in accountancy from the beginning of this century, individual partners specialising in bankruptcies, liquidations, formation of companies, or accounting for certain trades. (35) This factor tends to be more important in the "general practice" type of firm. The medical profession is of course organised on the basis that the patient first takes his case to a general practitioner who, through his knowledge of consultancy services, is able to direct the patient to the appropriate specialist consultant either via a hospital or straight to the consulting rooms.

4. A professional man with very great skill or experience can spread his talents more widely by operating with the aid of junior partners or assistants. This particularly happens in the field of architecture, where a leading architect may see a client once only, sketch a few rough drawings showing his basic solution to the client's problem, and leave the rest to junior members of the firm. This illustrates an important principle of the organisation of work, namely that those with rare talent should not waste any of their time doing work which less gifted or experienced persons can undertake.

5. A lone practitioner cannot accumulate savings in the form of goodwill, and the practice lacks continuity in record-keeping, the accumulation of experience among ancillary staff, and the increased authority that comes with a long-familiar firm name. The problem of capital formation and transfer is by no means satisfactorily solved by the partnership formula, as appears below, but it is considerably better than with the sole practitioner. The continuity of the firm following the death of a partner is indicated by Hine: "The lawyer is dead; long live the law. But in a sense the lawyer does not die. Clients will come flocking into his office as of old, feeling somehow that his friendly spirit is still there. His room may be taken by another, but his mantle will have been taken too. The partner will bear the same impressed stamp of office personality. The advice given will be the advice he would have given." (36) Continuity, and emphasis on personal service, are illustrated by the family nature of many firms. F.M.L. Thompson,

the historian of the chartered surveyors' profession, comments: "The hereditary, or dynastic, principle is as readily ascertainable in surveying as it is in other professions such as medicine or the law. The atmosphere of being brought up in a professional family is a strong inducement to some at least of the sons to follow in father's footsteps; the profession being in the main run as small, family, practices, there is family loyalty and pride on hand to see that a son takes over the business." Thompson adds that the dependence of firms on clients' goodwill gives a son taking over the firm a flying start. (37)

6. Finally, there is the position of new entrants to the profession. It is difficult for the sole practitioner to give adequate tuition to pupils while at the same time carrying on a practice single-handed. To be sure this is done at the Bar, but only with the aid of the "chambers" system. Furthermore newcomers find it very much more difficult to become established if they have to stand entirely on their own feet from the beginning rather than entering a firm as junior partners. In the latter case they can take their share of the work brought to the firm by the connection of the more senior partners, and clients are usually quite satisfied with this arrangement. It is different where the youngster has no connection with the practitioner whom he is assisting. The tendency then is for his work to be passed to the client as the work of the senior practitioner, after the latter has put the finishing touches to it. This is the old system of "devilling" at the Bar, which has often led to a struggling newcomer losing the help he would have gained from a well-written opinion if the professional client had known its real origin.

The strict rule of the Bar that no practice in the least degree resembling partnership is permissible has often been criticised. It was investigated by a special committee of the Bar Council in 1959–61 and by another such committee in 1968–69. The committees concluded that there should be no change in the rule. They felt that the institution of partnerships at the Bar would be wholly incompatible with the traditional conception of barristers as individual practitioners enjoying an independent and individual status. They found there was no real demand for partnerships and no case in their favour had been made out. The present system, they felt, had been shown by experience to foster the strength and independence of the Bar while affording a satisfactory service to the public. In justifying this rule to the Monopolies Commission, the Bar Council contended that a partnership was a restriction on competition, "since a man cannot compete with his partners". Whereas under the present system members in the same chambers could appear on opposite sides in a case, this would

F

obviously be impracticable if they belonged to one partnership. In some specialist fields, and at local Bars in provincial towns, there are a very small number of practitioners and partnerships might cause difficulty. The Bar Council shared the view that partnership would tend to blur the individual responsibility of the barrister, and make it more difficult for him to exercise an independent judgement. "Barristers are in fact individual performers, and the legal basis on which they work should correspond with this fact." (38) With the confidence that could only be shown by an economist, Professor D.S. Lees says that there is no case for the Bar's rule against partnerships, and that its relaxation "could not but lead to the growth of more efficient legal units". (39) Evidence for this assertion is not provided.

One problem of professional partnerships is likely to become increasingly pressing, especially as the removal of the limitation of twenty on the number of partners in 1967, and the economic considerations which brought this about, are likely to lead to very large firms in future. This is the difficulty arising from the inability of most young entrants to partnerships to provide capital, coupled with the need of retiring partners, or the families of deceased partners, to withdraw their capital. While the working capital needed by a professional partnership is not large, it is nevertheless an appreciable amount. It is tending to grow with the increase in data-processing equipment and the sophistication of office machinery. With some professions, e.g. aerial surveys, the capital equipment required may be very large indeed. One solution is the creation of a service company as a separate entity from, but controlled by, the partnership. This can be financed as an ordinary trading company, with some of its capital provided by persons outside the profession, and looking for its profits to a rental return on equipment used by the partnership (see page 103). The service company does not of course meet the problem of capital such as goodwill, which may be a large element in the value of a firm. The main reason underlying these difficulties is the rule that no person other than a member of the profession may partake of the profits of the profession. While this rule, which is discussed in a later chapter, remains in force there seems little prospect of a solution to the problem of capital provision and withdrawal.

A profession not troubled by the problem of goodwill capital is the Bar. Since they can only practise as individuals barristers do not accumulate goodwill as transmissible capital. By a quirk of tax law they were until 1968 partly compensated for this in not being taxed on "post-cessation receipts," i.e. those paid to them after retirement. This concession was rather meanly abolished in the 1968 Finance Act.

## Incorporation

If it is accepted that professional services of the kind we are discussing are best rendered in a personal relationship between the practitioner and his client, it follows that the practitioner should operate as an individual (whether alone or in partnership) and not a body corporate. Although corporations act of course by means of individuals, the legal relationship is with an entity which is a legal fiction. While a corporation can be organised so that its relationship with outsiders is hardly different in practice from that of a partnership and, as the joint stock banks have shown, can still retain the human touch, the essence of incorporation is to substitute the impersonal for the personal. Diffusion of responsibility within a corporate body may make personal accountability for breaches of professional ethics difficult: "a corporation cannot blush". Nevertheless these are not the main reasons why incorporation has been frowned on by professional bodies; the reason usually given is connected with limitation of liability. Most corporations are companies incorporated under the Companies Act with limited liability. They are disapproved of ostensibly for this attribute, rather than their corporate status. It is convenient, therefore, to deal with the whole question of incorporation as part of a discussion of limitation of liability, which will be found in Chapter 7.

CHAPTER 5

# DISCRETION: THE SECURE CONFIDANT

George Farquhar remarked that, "there are secrets in all families", (1) and it is often necessary that these should be shared with a professional adviser. Carr-Saunders and Wilson said of the client:

> "He places his health and his fortune in the hands of his professional advisers, and he entrusts them with confidences of an intimate and personal kind. He is interested therefore not only in the technical, but also in what may be called the moral, quality of the service." (2)

## Why Confidences are Imparted

The need for entrusting confidences is fairly obvious. If the professional adviser is to act as the *alter ego* of his client (see page 63) he needs to know as much about the client's affairs as the client himself. If he is to give competent advice in a more limited field he must be supplied with all the facts of the case. Sometimes sound advice on a particular matter depends upon thorough familiarity with the client's history and temperament. This particularly applies to advice by a medical adviser or family lawyer. Carr-Saunders and Wilson point out that the doctor can be much helped in making his diagnosis if he knows the whole man – habits, foibles, past and present surroundings, and so on. (3) Another commentator has observed: "No one save the priest in the confessional is so near a witness as the physician of the failings, weaknesses, degradations and nobility of human beings. No one comes so close to another in suffering, or is thus so privileged, at times, to witness the heights to which human dignity can reach." (4)

## Types of Confidential Information

The sort of confidential information that comes a doctor's way is infinitely various. The patient may be suffering from a grave disease, such as cancer, which he or his family are anxious should not become known. He may have a complaint with overtones of moral turpitude, such as venereal disease or the effects of drug taking. Patients may have suffered injury in circumstances they do not want talked about, such as the wife beaten up by the husband or the thief injured in the course of his criminal activities. There may be mental trouble or personality defects such as homosexuality. Apart from the endless possibilities in the realm of medicine itself, the physician very often acquires non-medical information about his patients. The psychiatrist in the course of analysis, the anaesthetist listening to the murmurs of a patient returning to consciousness, and others similarly placed may acquire information far removed from the purely medical.

Other types of professional practitioner may well acquire information which it would be a grave embarrassment to the patient to have widely known. The cosmetic dentist who equips the television "personality" with a flashing artificial smile may hold a career in the palm of his hand. The family solicitor builds up a host of facts about his client which would cause inconvenience or worse if revealed. The fact that his house is mortgaged, or that his will makes rather smaller provision for his wife than she might expect, or that he was born out of wedlock or has been in trouble with the police are things the client would prefer to see securely locked away behind the facade of Lincoln's Inn Fields or Bedford Row. The estate agent who could tell you what your neighbour paid for his house, the literary agent who could reveal the plot of the best-selling author's next two or three novels, the surveyor who knows just how many structural flaws there are in your apparently desirable residence — all these could cause great embarrassment if they did not respect their clients' confidences.

More than mere embarrassment is involved, however. Professional people acquire information that, if revealed, could cause great economic loss to their clients. The accountant knows more about the financial position of the company whose accounts he audits than many of the shareholders. Although certain information is required by law to be made public, its premature disclosure, or the disclosure of other facts not covered by these legal rules, could often cause serious damage. An architect called in to design a new factory may learn trade secrets that his client's competitors would gladly pay to acquire. The patent agent has many opportunities of enriching himself and others by disclosing details of inventions. It is needless to multiply examples: the propensity of professional consultants to acquire confidential information is plain. This is not of course limited to the professions: bank managers and inspectors of taxes, to name but two obvious examples, acquire as much confidential information as many professional consultants. It is however a dominant feature of professional practice.

## The Need for Security

A client needs to feel completely secure that information acquired by his professional consultant will be kept confidential. If he does not have this feeling of security he is likely to withhold information, and thus receive advice which is less complete or effective than it might otherwise be or may even be completely wrong. If the client feels there is a risk of disclosure he may worry and, in medical cases, may even worsen his complaint. With this in mind, the law has created a special privilege in legal matters, the object being "to ensure that a client can confide completely and without any reservation whatever in his own solicitor". (5)

## Professional Rules

Realising the importance of secrecy, the professions, particularly those of medicine and law, have devised appropriate rules for preserving it. The Hippocratic oath says: "Whatever, in connection with my professional practice, or not in connection with it, I see or hear, in the life of men, which ought not to be spoken of abroad, I will not divulge, as reckoning that all such should be kept secret." (6) The Declaration of Geneva, produced by the World Medical Association, requires a newly-admitted doctor to swear that "I will respect the secrets which are confided in me" and the international code of medical ethics, which is based on this declaration, includes the requirement that "a doctor shall preserve absolute secrecy on all he knows about his patient because of the confidence entrusted in him".(7) In commenting on these rules the British Medical Association point out that the basis of the relationship between a doctor and his patient is one of absolute confidence and mutual respect. The doctor's awareness of the patient's reliance in his trustworthiness "serves to invoke the observation of ethical standards and the need to act always in the best interest of the patient". The effect of this is somewhat weakened by the statement that "the complications of modern life sometimes create difficulties for the doctor in the application of the principle, and on certain occasions it may be necessary to acquiesce is some modification". (8) The wording of this qualification is disquieting. The circumstances in which it is justifiable to break confidence, if they exist, should surely be set out with precision and not left to be inferred from language as vague as this. Such a relaxation of the proper strict standards may be used by some doctors as a justification for revelations which may seem to them harmless, but could in fact cause embarrassment to the patient. It should be possible to go to the doctor with a simple cold and feel certain that its existence will not be disclosed

without one's consent. A reputation for absolute fitness may be important to the patient in his work. Even if it is not, the medical man has no
business to gossip about his patient's ailments.

Similar rules are explicitly laid down for the Bar (9) and solicitors. (10)
The strictness of the rule in the case of solicitors is illustrated by its
application to wills:

> "Where a testator is alive, a solicitor having the custody of
> his will is not free to disclose the contents of that will to
> anyone, even to the testator's wife and even if the testator
> is in a lunatic asylum. If the testator is dead, the solicitor
> who has the custody of the will must not disclose any inform-
> ation before probate is granted, except to the executors,
> without the consent of the executors." (11)

Chartered accountants regard it as fundamental to their professional
status that they should treat the information contained in accountancy
records as being available to them for the purpose only of carrying out
their professional duties. "All members are well aware that to divulge
information about a client's affairs would be a breach of professional
confidence having the most serious consequences." (12) Other professions have not made express rules for this purpose, but would no
doubt treat breaches of confidence as professional misconduct. An
example from the surveyor's profession is furnished by Norman J.
Hodgkinson in his book *Debit Experience Account* (p. 43): "In the
case of a sale or purchase by private treaty, the sale price must not be
divulged, although a reporter will often press for this information."
He goes on to sanction disclosure to the press of the reserve price or
last bid in an auction of property withdrawn without sale, presumably
because this information will have been made public in the auction
room. A professional rule partly designed to ensure that clients' confidences are preserved is that precluding the sharing of professional
offices with persons outside the profession (see page 66).

## Employed Practitioners

While professional people in private practice would find no difficulty in observing these rules of confidence, the same is not always
true of employed practitioners, who may come under pressure from
their employers. The B.M.A. has made rules to deal with this situation.
For example, it has laid down that medical records should be sent to
medical officers employed by government departments only when
written consent has been obtained from the patient. (13) Again, personal medical records of workers treated by doctors employed by

industrial firms are to be kept in the custody of the doctor, who, on termination of his appointment, is required to hand them over only to his successor. If there should be no successor, he must retain the custody of the records himself. (14) While the practitioner will no doubt strive to observe these rules, they are not of course binding on his employers. Cases not infrequently arise where doctors get into the news by resisting demands from the employer to be shown medical records. An example in 1968 was the case of the University College of Aberystwyth, where the authorities applied pressure on the director of the student health service, Dr. John Hughes, to supply details of pregnancies among women students. When Dr. Hughes refused to do this, he was dismissed but later reinstated under pressure from the B.M.A. (15) In another 1968 case the coroner at an inquest on a university student who had committed suicide criticised the medical officer for not telling the university authorities and the parents when he observed a propensity to suicide. The doctor replied that if he did that sort of thing students would not come to him at all, and a medical spokesman described the coroner's remarks as "quite ludicrous". (15A)

### Duration of Duty

The duty to maintain confidences does not of course end with the practitioner-client relationship. As Sir Thomas Lund puts it, "The duration of the privilege is for ever". (16) Barristers who formerly practised in another profession are specifically precluded from accepting instructions in any matter in which they have been previously instructed in their former professional capacity (17).

### Exceptions

While the principle of secrecy is clear, the detailed working out of the rule can give rise to difficulties. It cannot be an absolute rule, and must be applied with common sense. Sir Thomas Lund gives six categories of information not covered by the  rule. These are:

1. Information derived from collateral sources and not through professional confidence.
2. Facts patent to the senses, that is facts which are obvious to anyone, as for instance that the client is of unsound mind.
3. Information which the client intends or authorises to be disclosed.
4. Records of public proceedings.
5 Information disclosed by one client to an adviser acting in the same matter for several clients.

6. Communications made in furtherance of a fraud or crime. (18)
Another possible exception occurs in the case of an accountant who is
being replaced as auditor of a company. The rules of the Institute of
Chartered Accountants require that no accountant shall become the
successor to an auditor without first obtaining from him full information
about the reasons for the change.

## Knowledge of Client's Guilt

Laymen often ask how an advocate can conscientiously defend a
client who has confided his guilt. This is an old conundrum and reveals
a misunderstanding of the advocate's function, which has harmed his
reputation throughout the ages. English law is proud of the tradition
which enables the biggest villian unhung to find without difficulty
someone who will speak for him, and make the best case possible without deliberately misleading the court. The full statement of the position
is as follows:

> "As regards confessions of guilt, different considerations
> apply to cases in which the confession has been made before
> the advocate has undertaken the defence and to those in
> which the confession is made subsequently during the course
> of the proceedings.
> If the confession has been made before the proceedings
> have been commenced, it is most undesirable that an ad-
> vocate to whom the confession has been made should
> undertake the defence, as he would most certainly be
> seriously embarrassed in the conduct of the case, and no
> harm can be done to the accused by requesting him to
> retain another advocate.
> Other considerations apply in cases in which the confession
> has been made during the proceedings, or in such circum-
> stances that the advocate retained for the defence cannot
> retire from the case without seriously compromising the
> position of the accused.
> In considering the duty of an advocate retained to defend
> a person charged with an offence who, in the circumstances
> mentioned in the last preceding paragraph, confesses to
> counsel himself that he did commit the offence charged,
> it is essential to bear the following points clearly in mind:-
> (1) That every punishable crime is a breach of the common
> or statute law committed by a person of sound mind and
> understanding; (2) that the issue in a criminal trial is always

whether the accused is guilty of the offence charged, never whether he is innocent; (3) that the burden of proof rests on the prosecution. Upon the clear appreciation of these points depends broadly the true conception of the duty of the advocate for the accused.

His duty is to protect his client as far as possible from being convicted except by a competent tribunal and upon legal evidence sufficient to support a conviction for the offence with which he is charged.

The ways in which this duty can be successfully performed with regard to the facts of a case are (a) by showing that the accused was irresponsible at the time of the commission of the offence charged by reason of insanity or want of criminal capacity, or (b) by satisfying the tribunal that the evidence for the prosecution is unworthy of credence, or, even if believed, is insufficient to justify a conviction for the offence charged, or (c) by setting up in answer an affirmative case.

If the duty of the advocate is correctly stated above, it follows that the mere fact that a person charged with a crime has in the circumstances above mentioned made such a confession to his counsel, is no bar to that advocate appearing or continuing to appear in his defence, nor indeed does such a confession release the advocate from his imperative duty to do all he honourably can do for his client.

But such a confession imposes very strict limitations on the conduct of the defence. An advocate "may not assert that which he knows to be a lie. He may not connive at, much less attempt to substantiate, a fraud".

While, therefore, it would be right to take any objection to the competency of the Court, to the form of the indictment, to the admissibility of any evidence, or to the sufficiency of the evidence admitted, it would be absolutely wrong to suggest that some other person had committed the offence charged, or to call any evidence, which he must know to be false having regard to the confession, such, for instance, as evidence in support of an alibi, which is intended to show that the accused could not have done or in fact had not done the act; that is to say, an advocate must not (whether by calling the accused or otherwise) set up an affirmative case inconsistent with the confession made to him.

A more difficult question is within what limits, in the case supposed, may an advocate attack the evidence for the prosecution either by cross-examination or in his speech to the tribunal charged with the decision of the facts. No clearer rule can be laid down than this, that he is entitled to test the evidence given by each individual witness, and to argue that the evidence taken as a whole is insufficient to amount to proof that the accused is guilty of the offence charged. Further than this he ought not to go." (20)

Except in cases, mentioned below, where the law imposes a duty to reveal facts of a criminal nature, the general position of a professional man who learns of such facts (otherwise than as defending advocate) is that he should advise his client to disclose them, or otherwise deal with them in a way which avoids impropriety, and if the client refuses should decline to act further in the matter. Thus where a solicitor learns that documents handed to him by his client have been forged he should advise the client to disclose the forgery and if this is refused should decline to act further. In that event the solicitor would be under a duty to disclose the forgery to any solicitors subsequently instructed by the client to carry through the same transaction. Where a client is engaged in an illegal transaction (e.g. in breach of building regulations) his solicitors should discourage him from continuing and should themselves decline to act for him. (21)

## Knowledge Derived from Other Clients

Many problems arise through information relating to one client proving material in the affairs of another client of the same practitioner. Although normally a barrister must accept any brief offered to him, he is justified in refusing to accept a brief if thereby he would be embarrassed through his possession of confidential information acquired in a previous case. Where counsel advises a client how to change a design to avoid infringement of a patent he ought to regard his advice on the changed design as confidential and not repeat it to another client with the same problem. (22)

It is considered to be the duty of a patent agent, where two inventors come to him independently with the same invention, to proceed with both applications without informing either client of the existence of the other (23). Solicitors who acted for one client and obtained confidential information are not at liberty to disclose it to new clients, even though it might be of the greatest possible assistance to them. Where a solicitor is concerned in non-contentious business for several clients, but it becomes clear that litigation is probable and that the solicitor would be embarrassed in acting for any of the clients by reason of knowledge acquired by him of the other's case, he should ensure that both clients are represented by other solicitors (24).

## Non-Clients

A practitioner may have a duty to preserve confidences even in the case of persons who are not his clients. Sir Thomas Lund gives the example of solicitors acting for a creditor and receiving a visit from the debtor, who was unrepresented. The debtor asked if he could talk to the solicitors in confidence, and they agreed, whereupon the debtor gave them highly confidential information. The Law Society advised the solicitors that they had acted quite wrongly in putting themselves into the position of giving the debtor a chance to speak to them in confidence, but that having done so they ought not to disclose the information and their only fair course was to tell their client that they had been supplied in confidence with information by the debtor which they were not at liberty to pass on, and therefore they could no longer continue to act. (25) In another case where solicitors received instructions to institute divorce proceedings purporting to come from the husband but in fact coming from the wife, the Law Society advised that there was no objection to their disclosing the information to the husband and his solicitors (26). A solicitor collecting a debt for a client is not allowed to communicate with the debtor's employer or anyone else whose knowledge of the unpaid debt might prejudice the debtor. (27)

## Rules Imposed by Law

Having discussed the professional rules relating to the keeping of confidences, we turn briefly to the legal position. The law has found it necessary for the furtherance of justice between parties to invest communications between a party and his solicitor, or between the solicitor and counsel, made during and with reference to judicial proceedings or in anticipation or for the purposes of such proceedings, with a legal privilege which protects them from being ordered to be disclosed. The privilege is that of the client and not the legal adviser. If the client elects to waive the privilege it therefore ceases to operate. The law has not extended this protection to other types of professional communication, e.g., those between doctor and patient. It is clearly however the professional duty of a practitioner to resist disclosure as far as he possibly can without himself incurring legal penalties. If he does hold out to the extent of incurring such penalties they are unlikely to be regarded as a ground for disciplinary proceedings by his professional body. This is indicated by the B.M.A.'s statement of the position:

> "The doctor's usual course when asked in a court of law
> for medical information concerning a patient in the absence
> of that patient's consent is to demur on the ground of
> professional secrecy. The presiding judge however may over-
> rule this contention and direct the medical witness to supply
> the required information. The doctor has no alternative to
> obey unless he is willing to accept imprisonment for con-
> tempt of court." (28)

The B.M.A. have acknowledged that there may be circumstances in
which a medical witness would be acting in accordance with the highest
principles of medical ethics by refusing to obey the judge and taking the
consequences, but they recommend that "this serious step should only be
taken after consultation with those who are competent to advise". (29)
C. Croxton-Smith takes the view that an accountant should not answer
questions about his client's affairs unless under subpoena. "Even in
this event" he goes on "I think it should be made clear to the court
that the only information the member has was obtained by him in the
course of carrying out his professional duties and that he, therefore,
has a strict duty of confidence to his client which he cannot break
unless ordered by the court to do so. If the court does so order then
the member must of course comply." (30)

While a professional man may thus be compelled by law to disclose
confidential information, there are few occasions when he is required
by law to *volunteer* such information. One example is the statutory
requirement to notify cases of infectious disease. The Law Society have
advised that solicitors should volunteer information to the authorities
in certain cases where the national interest requires it. This probably
arises only in time of war or serious national emergency, in relation to
enemy aliens. Sir Thomas Lund does however mention a case where
a solicitor was advised that he should disclose to the Home Office certain
details of an anarchist client. (31)

A duty of disclosure formerly existed (in theory at least) where a
criminal offence amounting to felony was known to have been committed, since failure to disclose itself mounted to the crime of misprision
of felony. This crime has now been abolished however.

## Privacy

The above discussion has been mainly concerned with the preservation of confidences. A word may be added however on the subject
of privacy in consultations. A client may feel confident that his secrets
will not be disclosed to the outside world, and yet be hampered and

embarrassed if he is required to speak of intimate matters, or undergo physical examination, in surroundings where his privacy is not respected. If this happens the consultation is likely to be less effective than it should be. Dr. Willoughby of Derby recorded in his *Observations* (1863) that on one occasion when an important lady patient was in labour and he was called in by the midwife he paused at the door of the lady's chamber, crouched down and crept into the room on hands and knees so as to examine the patient unperceived. His examination over he crept out again in the same way. (32) For centuries obstetricians were forced to examine their patients in darkness, or without drawing back the bedclothes. This kind of prudery is not unknown today. Peter Fryer records that a reader of *Woman's Own* wrote in 1962: "I have always attended a male doctor but now I have to undergo a rather intimate operation and my husband says it is a job for a woman doctor . . . This argument is causing trouble between us." (33)

One may smile at such absurdities, but the fact remains that acute discomfort and distress can be caused by lack of privacy. A notorious case is of course that of the teaching hospitals, where many patients undergo the most appalling indignities in full view of the interested gaze of perhaps twenty or thirty youths acquiring medical knowledge. This may be difficult to help, since professional knowledge must be acquired by practical demonstrations. It should however be done discreetly and sympathetically, and avoided so far as possible. Official policy is to allow patients the right to refuse to be examined or treated in the presence of students.

The qualities of tact, forbearance and sympathy which a professional practitioner ought to display towards his clients will ensure that proper privacy is observed in consultations. It is a subtle characteristic of the relationship between a private consultant and his client that these conditions should prevail. With a service provided by a large organisation such as a government department or big company the relationship will be more impersonal, the client may come "as of right", and the practitioner may not feel disposed to accord him more than his bare legal entitlement.

## CHAPTER 6

# IMPARTIALITY: NO AXE TO GRIND

It is axiomatic that professional advice must be untainted by any private interest of the practitioner. It is a prime justification of the basic proposition laid down in chapter 1 (page 15) that advice should ideally be given by an individual who is beholden to no one, free from personal concern or involvement, and subject to no pressures or influences restricting his independence. The professional bodies have rightly regarded the securing of this state of independence, both for their members and for themselves, as one of the principal objects of their existence. W.J. Reader begins his book *Professional Men* with a nineteenth-century quotation which bears repeating: "The importance of the professions and the professional classes can hardly be overrated, they form the head of the great English middle class, maintain its tone of independence, keep up to the mark its standard of morality, and direct its intelligence." (1)

It is obviously of the greatest public concern that anyone who consults a professional practitioner should feel completely confident that the advice he receives will be impartial, and it is a paramount duty of the practitioner to decline to act if he has any commitments or connections whatever which might prevent, or appear to prevent, this being so. The last qualification is important, for he must not only be impartial, he must manifestly appear to be impartial. Any factors which might arouse suspicion if discovered by the client should be treated as precluding the acceptance of instructions, even though the consultant feels confident he would be able to ignore them in practice. The cruder forms of partiality, e.g., that induced by a bribe, are of course punishable by the criminal law. The professions echo the criminal code, as instanced by the consulting engineers: 'a member shall not receive directly or indirectly any royalty, gratuity or commission' without the written authority of the client. (2) The professional code goes much further, however, and embraces a large number of possible situations.

## Personal Financial or Property Interests

Little difficulty arises where the practitioner has a direct pecuniary interest in the matter on which he is instructed: unless his interest is merely trifling he should decline the instructions. Thus members of the Bar are told that it is in general undesirable for a barrister to appear in a matter in which he is himself pecuniarily interested. (3) He should not, for example, act for a creditor in a bankruptcy petition when he himself is also a creditor of the same debtor. (4) Similarly, a barrister who is a member of a group of underwriters at Lloyds should not act professionally in any case relating to a policy on which his name appears. (5) Again, it would be improper for an accountant to hold the position of auditor of a company in which he held a substantial block of shares. (6) Strangely enough, although the Companies Act, 1948 disqualifies directors from acting as auditors it has nothing to say about shareholders, though a major shareholder would be likely to act as a director within the widened definition of that expression used in the Act.

Complete impartiality is safeguarded by the rule which discourages professional people from becoming personally involved in the actions of their client − especially where this could have financial consequences for the consultant. Thus the Council of the Law Society have expressed the opinion that it is in general undesirable for a solicitor to stand bail for a person for whom he or any of his partners is acting. (7) Some professions also feel that advice may be less than completely objective if the consultant's remuneration depends on the nature of the advice given. Thus the Institute of Chartered Accountants frowns on the calculation of fees as a percentage of the value of the subject matter of the work. It is felt, for example, that an accountant reporting on profits for prospectus purposes might be embarrassed if it were thought that his fee was related to the estimate of profits stated in his report. These considerations have not prevented the scale fees laid down by the R.I.C.S. for valuations of real and personal property from being calculated as a percentage of the value found by the consultant.

Particularly frowned on, as contrary to the whole spirit of professionalism, is the practice of "no win, no fee". By this the professional man, usually a lawyer, takes a stake in the success of his client's case by agreeing to share in the proceeds if victory is won but going unpaid if it is lost. Until 1967 such an arrangement was illegal for lawyers, amounting to the crime of champerty. It is outlawed by the professions as tending to produce inequality of effort, since a hopeless and therefore unproductive case is likely to be ill-prepared; and also as giving the consultant an unduly large stake in the success or failure of his efforts, thus imperilling proper professional disinterestedness.

In the field of estate agency, the Chartered Auctioneers' and

Estate Agents' Institute has a rule that "agency and dealing are two incompatible occupations, and any attempt to combine them in one person or firm must inevitably be fatal in any pretension to a professional reputation." This view is supported by a well-known chartered surveyor, Norman J. Hodgkinson:

"I suggest that a practising surveyor should not himself speculate in property. This may seem a surprising statement when so many individual surveyors and firms have made fortunes in this way. It may be asked why should not a surveyor speculate in the one thing about which he should have special knowledge. There is no reason why he should not speculate in property in respect of which he is not acting for a client, but in my experience once he speculates he is likely to be tempted to do so in cases where he is retained to advise a client, and even sell his own property to a client or buy from a client. It makes little difference whether or not he explains the position to his client, as when he once begins doing this sort of thing it becomes impossible for him to give a client sound and impartial advice." (8)

The same view was taken by the majority of the House of Commons committee considering the Estate Agents Bill in 1966. An amendment was moved by Mr Shepherd, the Conservative member for Cheadle, to require the code of conduct of the proposed Estate Agents Council to include regulations designed to prevent any registered agent from dealing in or developing property, or taking any equity share in such dealing or development, either directly or indirectly, except with the permission of the Council. Mr Shepherd complained that whereas the professional societies said that an agent should not be a dealer at the same time, they did not attempt to enforce this regulation. In discussing the advisory function of estate agents Mr Shepherd said: "I assure the Committee that very big sums of money are staked on the advice given by professional agents. The outlay of millions of pounds is often determined by their advice. It is therefore crucially important that an agent who gives advice should be free from the complication of being involved in dealing or development, either directly or indirectly."

Mr Shepherd's amendment gained general support and was added to the Bill. It raised in acute form the question whether a professional man should refrain altogether from financial or property transactions likely to lead to conflict with his professional duties, or whether the position is adequately met by imposing a duty of disclosure. In the case of solicitors full and frank disclosure is considered adequate, (9) and the same view is held by the R.I.C.S. Mr Shepherd and his supporters

G

thought otherwise however. Arguing that a client might be harmed in circumstances where no particular property was in question, and disclosure did not therefore arise, he went on: "If I say to Mr X, 'I am thinking of doing this or that. Would you advise me to do this or that?' and he is engaged in the activity, either directly, through a nominee or as an equity shareholder in a property company, there will be a clash between his personal interest and the advice which he tenders to me as an individual."

Architects observe a similar rule in a slightly different field. They are forbidden to carry on business as builders or manufacturers of building components, or be concerned in any business of dealing in land or buildings to an extent which might affect the independent exercise of professional judgment. (10) A consulting engineer may not, without disclosing the fact to his client *in writing*, have any substantial financial interest in, or be an agent for, any business operating within the field in which he practises. (11)

## Links with Commerce

The professions are usually wary about links between their members and commercial undertakings. In part this may spring from a snobbish disdain of "trade", but it is also founded in a genuine apprehension of the risks and temptations involved. The B.M.A. has laid it down as a general ethical principle that a doctor should not associate himself with commerce in such a way as to let it influence, or appear to influence, his attitude towards the treatment of his patients. He should not allow use to be made of his professional status in order to enhance a business; nor, conversely, should he allow a business to enhance his professional status. (12) These are rules which the other consultant professions would agree with, and enforce.

An obvious abuse arises where a professional man has entered into arrangements with commercial interests providing him with a commission or "rake-off" on goods sold through his recommendation. Clearly there is a serious risk that advice as to an appropriate remedy will not be impartial if the practitioner stands to gain financially by recommending one remedy rather than its competitors. The Royal Institution of Chartered Surveyors, and kindred societies adopting the same code of conduct, have laid down the explicit rule that "no member shall accept or give any illicit or secret trade or other discounts, commission, or allowance in connection with any professional business which may be entrusted to him, or any goods he may order on behalf of clients". (13) The wording of this rule absolves the practitioner if he discloses the fact that he is receiving a financial benefit to his client.

The medical profession goes further and lays down that it is undesirable for a doctor to have "a special direct and personal financial interest" in the sale of any pharmaceutical preparation he may have to recommend to a patient. The possibility is recognised that this may be unavoidable in certain cases, but he is then required to disclose his interest to the patient. This rule does not apply to the acquisition of shares in a public company marketing pharmaceutical products. (14) The B.M.A. state that collusion between doctors and chemists for financial gain is reprehensible. A doctor should not arrange with a chemist for the payment of a commission on business transacted, nor should he hold a financial interest in a chemist's shop in the area of his practice. To avoid even the suspicion of profiteering of this kind, doctors are advised not to recommend that a patient should go to a particular chemist unless they are specifically asked to do so by the patient. (15)

Where a doctor invents a new form of medical instrument or appliance, or develops a new drug, he is permitted to take a financial reward. Wherever possible however this should be in the form of an initial lump sum payment from the company which is to market the article; only where this cannot be arranged is it legitimate to receive royalties on sales. Remuneration in the form of royalties clearly offers an inducement to the doctor to encourage the greater use of his invention, and thus prescribe it unnecessarily. (16)

Another possibility of abuse relates to testimonials given by professional people. There is always the suspicion, even if it turns out to be unfounded, that a person giving such a testimonial has been paid for doing so and that it does not represent his own sincerely-held conviction. The Architects Registration Council has laid down a specific rule that an architect must not allow his name to be used as recommending specific building materials in advertisements in the press or otherwise. The B.M.A. say that testimonials written by doctors on the value of proprietary products have often been abused by the manufacturers. Doctors are advised to refrain from writing a testimonial on a commercial product unless they receive a legally-enforceable guarantee that the testimonial will not be published without their consent. (17)

Most professions discourage their members from taking up private practice while they are in the employment of a commercial firm if the interests of the employer might influence the advice they would give in private practice. The Bar goes further and discourages a practising barrister from holding salaried employment in any business concern. (18) Even more extreme has been the attitude of the R.I.C.S. and the R.I.B.A. towards employment with building contractors. The R.I.C.S. has a rule that no member shall in any way be connected with any occupation or business if such connection is, in the opinion of the Council of the Institution, inconsistent with membership. (19) This was introduced in 1902. It was soon taken to mean that a chartered quantity surveyor could not remain a member of the Institution if he entered the employment of a building contracting company, or became a director of such a company. The Architects Registration Council has laid down a similar rule, though strangely it does not extend to employees of building companies. (20) The Association of Consulting Engineers forbids a member to be a director or salaried employee of any company, firm or person carrying on any commercial, contracting or manufacturing business which is or may be involved in the class of work to which his appointment relates. (21)

These rules were criticised by a committee set up by the Government in 1962 to report on the placing and management of contracts for building work. The committee, whose chairman was Sir Harold Banwell, felt that a new searching examination of the case for retaining the rules was required. (22) In consequence of this recommendation, the R.I.C.S. re-examined the rule and concluded that they were not justified in depriving quantity surveyors who entered the contracting field of their membership of the Institution. The rule was therefore modified in 1967, but its essential principle was preserved. The Institution felt that there continued to be a need, in the public interest, for chartered surveyors in private practice to be independent of the building industry. Accordingly it remains forbidden for a member to practise as a private consultant at a time when he is employed by a building company. Thus the public may continue to be aware that when they appoint a consultant chartered quantity surveyor for a particular project there is no risk of his being influenced in the advice he gives by a link with a particular contractor.

The Minister of Public Building and Works hailed the modification as "a historic decision", and the Architects' Journal commented that the architects might be obliged to follow suit, and stressed the view that "the built environment must be designed by independent professional people, for it is only in this way that we can ensure that the vital decision-making is free from commercial interest". (23) Another similar rule of the surveyors' profession, known as the Harrods rule, precludes a member from employment in the estate department of a multiple store. It is felt that a conflict of interest could arise between a surveyor's duties in advising clients on all matters relating to the sale or purchase of a house and a department store's interest in pushing the sale of furniture or the provision of removal services needed by the same clients.

Another aspect of connections between a professional practice and commercial interests is the possibility that business may be attracted to the professional firm because of the commercial connection. Apart from the risk, discussed above, that such a connection will give rise to partial advice, or may arouse suspicion of this, it is also frowned upon by the professions as tending to attract business unfairly.

## Links with Other Professions

The consultant professions have traditionally preferred to avoid forming connections with other professions. This has led to rules restricting a person carrying on one profession from at the same time carrying on any other profession, and restricting a member of one profession from being in partnership with members of other professions or sharing premises with them or indulging in "fee-splitting". A number of reasons combine to produce this result, not all of them concerned with preserving impartiality. The tradition of the exclusiveness of each profession involves that a specialty forming a distinct avocation is to be regarded as the preserve of one set of people, organised in a single professional society. The mysteries of the profession are jealously preserved, and so is its independence and freedom from outside interference. Claiming self-determination for one's own profession, one readily yields the same principle to members of other professions. The boundaries are clearly defined and movement across them is discouraged. The Pilkington Commission found that less than one per cent. of professional people practised in more than one profession. (25)

Apart from the tradition of exclusiveness, the factors operating to discourage intermixing of professions include the desire to maintain the qualities of impartiality, independence and responsibility, the belief that the client should not be influenced in his choice of a consultant, an occasional snobbish reluctance to be associated with activities regarded as lower in the professional scale, and detestation of the practice of attracting business unfairly. The last-mentioned is dealt with in Part III of this book, since it essentially concerns relations of professional people with each other. The other factors are dealt with in the course of the following discussion.

The most sweeping condemnation of attempting to carry on another profession along with one's own applies to the Bar. A Bar student is obliged to give an undertaking that he will not, while practising as a barrister in England or Wales, also act as a member of any of the other consultant professions. Nor must he do so anywhere else, unless the local rules of the Bar so permit. (26) The position of other professions is as follows:-

*Solicitors.* Apart from the usual ban on professions which might detract from status as a solicitor, the only test is whether business might be attracted unfairly or there might be encouragement of any other breach of practice rules. There is no objection to a solicitor in practice as such also acting as a stockbroker, land agent, insurance agent or patent agent. There is however a ban on practising solicitors also acting as barristers (since otherwise the separation of the two sides of the legal profession might be endangered), estate agents, auctioneers and mortgage brokers. (27)

*Architects.* A practising architect must not permit auctioneering or house agency to form part of his business; otherwise there is no restriction. (28)

*Chartered Accountants.* A practising chartered accountant is not allowed to carry on the practice of a barrister, solicitor, estate agent, auctioneer or stockbroker. Other professional activities are permissible, though accountants are advised that activities such as insurance broking, which have a close relationship to the accountancy profession, should preferably be carried on separately and from a different address. (29)

*Surveyors.* The only restriction in the case of chartered surveyors and members of kindred societies is that they may not engage in work recognised as being properly that of a solicitor. (30)

*Doctors.* Partnership of doctors with members of connected professions is discouraged, as is partnership between general practitioners and specialists. It is felt that such partnerships may lead to fee-splitting or undue direction of patients to the doctor, thereby interfering with the principle of free choice of doctor by the patient. (31)

How far can these restrictions be justified? The arguments for and against discouraging "unfair" attraction of business are examined in Chapters 10 and 14. Of the other underlying reasons, preservation of free choice by the client and securing impartiality and independence of the practitioner can hardly be faulted. It is doubtful however whether in themselves they ever justify prohibiting the carrying on of different professions by persons within the same partnership. In such a case the connection is overt, the firm is in effect a multi-purpose one, and the client's position is hardly different from that of a man who having hitherto gone to a firm of solicitors only for conveyancing transactions and having dealt with partner A, needs to make a will and is passed to partner B, or requires income tax advice and is passed to the firm's taxation specialist, partner C.

Preservation of the exclusiveness of the professions can be defended on two grounds: discipline and identity. It is axiomatic that a partner is responsible not only for his own misconduct but also for that of his partners and the staff employed by the firm. How, it is said, can this salutary principle be enforced when some of the partners belong to a different profession, with different practices and standards? The sense of identity of a profession, and its spirit and values, may be impaired by intermixing. This could strike at the roots of professionalism.

The advantages of multi-purpose partnerships within the same field are nevertheless coming to be recognised. The Banwell Committee noted that group practice of architects, engineers and quantity surveyors, in formal partnership or *ad hoc* consortia was already taking place in 1964. Since then it has grown considerably. The Prices and Incomes Board, reporting in 1968, saw no reason why a solicitor should not be free to enter into a partnership with, say, a foreign lawyer or an accountant. They quoted the Secretary General of the Law Society, Sir Thomas Lund, as saying that in 2000 A.D. "the larger firms will have in partnership accountants, surveyors and even doctors and other professional men, while smaller firms will work in the closest association with members of such other professions, in order to provide an efficient service for their clients". (32)

While overt links of this kind can be defended, the same is not always true of less formal or obvious connections. Two particular cases arise, the sharing of premises and "fee-splitting".

Many professional bodies frown on the sharing of premises with members of other professions not embodied in the same partnership. Again, the reasons primarily concern undue direction of clients and "unfair" attraction of business. The medical rules state that there is no objection to a doctor and a member of a profession supplementary to medicine practising from the same building if the premises are separate, with separate entrances and addresses, but not otherwise. The same rule applies in the case of a doctor and a pharmacist. (33) The Law Society regard it as highly undesirable for a solicitor in practice as such to share office accommodation, staff or telephone arrangements with any person who is not a solicitor. (34) The Institute of Chartered Accountants has expressed a similar view. (35)

The agreement to divide a fee received from a client with a practitioner of another profession who is not a member of the same firm is condemned. The reason usually given, and advanced for example by Carr-Saunders and Wilson, (36) is that "there results something very like a fraud if a general practitioner recommends his client to see a certain consultant, and the recommendation is based on any other ground than the ability and reputation of the consultant". If this were indeed the reason underlying the prohibition it would be met by imposing on the practitioner a duty of disclosure to the client. This is not considered sufficient however. Furthermore the rule is usually expressed the other way round, i.e. as a duty not to share the fees one receives rather than as a duty not to recommend another practitioner from whom one is to receive a share of *his* fee. Thus Rule 3 of the Solicitors' Practice Rules 1936 states: "A solicitor shall not agree to share with any person not being a solicitor or other duly qualified legal agent . . . his profit costs". The rule does not apply to receipts not falling within the phrase "profit costs". He is therefore allowed to share remuneration not being profit costs, such as brokerage or insurance commissions. (37) Again in their submission to the Monopolies Commission the B.M.A. condemned partnerships between general practitioners and specialists "as leading to fee-splitting or dichotomy". (38) This could hardly be objectionable on the grounds given by Carr-Saunders and Wilson, since it is common knowledge that the receipts of a partnership are pooled and no question of secret commissions can arise. It is true that the B.M.A.'s handbook "Medical Ethics" defines dichotomy as "the secret division by two or more doctors of fees on a basis of commission or other defined method", adding that any undisclosed division of professional fees "save in a medical partnership publicly known to exist" is highly improper.(39)This only shows what muddled thinking exists on the question.

The chartered accountants' formulation of the rule limits it to cases where the consent of the client is not obtained (40) but the chartered surveyors' rule is expressed in absolute terms, and separate from the rule prohibiting secret commissions: "No member shall directly or indirectly allow or agree to allow any person, other than a member of his own profession, to participate in his remuneration." (41) The Institute of Chartered Accountants explains its rule by stating that it is directed against the introduction of professional work to a member by a third party for some consideration and thus prevents corruption in removing the temptation for a member to bribe persons who would not otherwise introduce work. (42) The petition for the charter of the Institute, which was granted in 1880, stated that the charter was required to "put an end to the practice which has been much objected to of the division of profits with persons in other professions or callings in the form of commission or the like".

It is difficult to resist the conclusion that the real reason for the professions' almost pathological dislike of fee-splitting is not the desire to protect the public, but the belief that it is a means of attracting business unfairly. The Law Society indeed admit this, in saying that the rule was primarily designed to prevent unqualified staff 'using unethical means of obtaining professional business for their principals'. (43) In practice the rule does protect the public however, since it is obviously difficult to explain to a client that in advising him to consult X you are totally unmoved by the fact that X will give you 10% of the resulting proceeds. Such advice should be completely impartial, and the rule against fee-splitting helps to make it so.

## Combining Employment with Private Practice

The professions tend to dislike seeing a person who is in the salaried service of an employer engaging in private practice in his spare time. Ideally the private practitioner should be totally free from commitments which bind him to the service of one person or company, even though this service is apparently unconnected with his activities as a private practitioner. Employers are always in a position to exert pressure on their employees, or at any rate are commonly supposed to be, and therefore the client cannot be assured of impartiality. The same is true of any dominating relationship, such as that subsisting in the eighteenth century when solicitors and architects, for example, often had patrons to whom they were subservient. It is an aspect of the truth that impartiality presupposes independence. The Joint Consultants' Committee giving evidence to the Royal Commission on Doctors' and Dentists' Remuneration 1957-1960, recorded that "the great disadvantage of the whole-time consultant physician is that he lacks the sense of professional independence that is felt by a consultant not wholly dependent on his salaried appointment". (44)

The Bar Council take the view that the receipt of a salary leads to a relationship between a practising barrister and his client which "would be inconsistent with the independence which is necessary to the proper performance of a barrister's functions". (45) This has led to the imposition of a rule precluding a barrister employed as a company legal adviser from representing his company as an advocate before a court. This might be justified on the ground that the court expects an advocate to be committed to his client's cause only so far as is involved by the acceptance of a brief in the ordinary way. It is however a source of friction between the Bar Council and the Bar Association for Commerce, Finance and Industry. Similar reasoning leads to denial of a barrister's right to appear in any case involving a person or body with whom he is connected in any capacity such as that of a member of a local authority or company director.

The duty to give impartial advice cuts both ways. The client is entitled to expect that the consultant will not prejudice him by serving any indirect interest of the consultant's own. Equally he is not entitled to undue favour at the expense of, for example, the consultant's employer.

Thus the architects have a rule that an architect employed as a salaried and official architect by a public authority, who is by reason of his office in a position to grant or influence the granting of any form of statutory or other approval, must not undertake private work (even with the consent of his employer) "unless his position and action in the matter can be shown to be free from any suspicion or suggestion of abuse". (46)

## Previous Knowledge of Facts or Parties

It may be or appear difficult for impartial advice to be given by one who has prior knowledge of the situation gained through extrinsic means. There is of course no objection where other persons are not involved, so that previous friendship with a person would not prevent a solicitor, say, accepting him as a client — indeed familiarity with the new client's circumstances might well be a positive advantage. If however a solicitor has acquired knowledge of a potential client's circumstances through having held some office or appointment, or might otherwise be embarrassed in acting for him, he should not accept instructions. (47) Similarly it would be improper for a barrister who, in acting as a marriage guidance counsellor, had interviewed a married couple to accept a brief in divorce proceedings between them. (48)

Similar considerations arise where, although confidential information is not involved, the personal situation of the parties could cause embarrassment. Thus a barrister is justified in refusing to accept a brief where a witness whom it would have been necessary for him to attack is a personal friend of his. (49) Again, the Council of the Law Society has ruled that a solicitor should not appear as an advocate in a court in which his father is sitting as the judge, nor should any partner of his do so. (50) A similar rule applies to barristers, though there has been held to be no objection to a barrister practising in a court where his father is one of several judges, since in such a case it is impossible to know beforehand which judge will try a case. (51) It is illegal for a solicitor who is a magistrate for an area to act in any case before his fellow-magistrates. (52)

## Rules Against Direct Instructions

Some professional people, notably barristers and medical specialists, act as consultants in a narrower sense. They do not advise the lay client or patient direct, but only through the medium of a general practitioner. Often they are in effect advising the general practitioner on matters too difficult or specialised to be within his competence, and thus place him in a position in which comprehensive guidance can be given to the client. The rule is most strongly developed in the barristers' profession: as a general practice they do not see or advise clients or accept briefs or appear as advocates on behalf of clients without the intervention of a solicitor. (53) In certain limited fields instructions may be received from other types of practitioner, such as patent agents, parliamentary agents, local government officials and the Chief Land Registrar. The only case where the ordinary layman may be represented direct is in criminal defences where the accused has insufficient funds to emply a solicitor. (54)

What is the reason for these rules against direct instructions? Partly it is a question of function. If it is the function of a professional man to give specialised advice to other professional people in a form which, since it is couched in expert professional language, may be incomprehensible to the layman, the business can be conducted in no other way. The specialist will be organised to operate in a certain fashion and cannot be expected to carry out functions for which he is neither trained, experienced nor equipped. This particularly applies to the preparation of cases to be brought before the courts; barristers are not equipped for the assembly of evidence through factual enquiries. This is recognised as the function of the solicitor, and is invariably left to him.

A more fundamental reason for the rule, which does not merely depend on demarcation of functions, is stated by the Bar Council: "One of the great values of the services of the Bar as at present rendered is that barristers are less closely involved with the client and his affairs and are thereby enabled to bring a fresh and more objective mind to bear on the case. This is of great value both to the client, and to the administration of justice. Without it the barrister would be less able to do his duty to the court, which involves sometimes taking a course which is unwelcome to the client and may be against his interests." The Bar Council feel that if barristers were not kept at one remove from the general public in this way, they would soon find themselves expected to do the work which solicitors now do. This would involve a total reorganisation of the profession, for which the buildings and staff employed by barristers would be quite unsuitable. (55)

In the medical field the B.M.A. rule is that except in emergencies, and certain very restricted cases, a practitioner in any form of specialist practice should not accept a patient for examination and advice except on a reference from a general practitioner. The report of the specialist, and his advice, should be given not to the patient direct but to the general practitioner, who will pass it on to the patient in whatever form he thinks suitable. (56)

The "no direct access" rule of the Bar is carried to what some may

feel to be absurd lengths in prohibiting a barrister from accepting
instructions from another barrister who is employed as a legal adviser to
a company. If the company requires counsel's opinion it must obtain it
through the medium of a solicitor. Thus where the company's legal
adviser is a barrister he has to go through the formality of instructing a
firm of solicitors to act as an intermediary between himself and a
practising barrister. Alternatively he may brief counsel through the
medium of a solicitor employed in the same company, who may well be
junior in rank. In criticising the rule the Bar Association for Commerce,
Finance and Industry state:

> "The argument that is usually used today to support the
> rule . . . . . is that in accepting instructions from a solicitor,
> counsel can rely upon their being prepared by an indep-
> endent person who is himself personally uninvolved in the
> matter upon which instructions are given. This situation
> exists in the case of the solicitor in private practice, even
> when he is acting for a company. The same situation does
> not exist when the solicitor is an employee of the company
> concerned, for as an employee he is subject to just those
> pressures which the advocates of the rule find objectionable.
> His barrister counterpart is in exactly the same position and
> is penalised by the rule of his profession." (57)

The legal profession may well have lost work by insisting on the rule
against direct access where the client or would-be client is another professional man, such as an accountant. (57A)

## Acting for Two Competing Clients

It is difficult to give impartial advice to one client if another client
may be adversely affected. A professional man should therefore avoid
getting into a position of having two separate clients whose interests
conflict. If he finds himself in that position he should release himself
from it by parting with one of the clients.

An example of this kind of conflict is frequently met with by estate
agents. A prudent prospective purchaser of a house will have a structural survey made before binding himself to buy. For this he will usually
consult a local firm of surveyors, though not of course the one entrusted
by the owner with the sale of the house. Often the purchaser will need
a mortgage from a building society, and the building society will require
a valuation of the property before agreeing to lend. For this purpose
building societies instruct local firms of surveyors and thus the same
firm may well find itself instructed both by the prospective purchaser
and the prospective mortgagee. A conflict of interest can arise because

mortgagees are frequently unwilling to lend as much as the would-be purchaser needs if the purchase is to go through. The proper course is to decline the second instructions, though this is not in fact always done. (58) A ruling of the R.I.B.A. provides that an architect commissioned to prepare a plan for a planning authority must not concurrently accept an architectural commission from a private client to design a building within the area of the plan. (59)

Solicitors distinguish in this field between non-contentious business and contentious business, i.e. that involving litigation. Clearly, as soon as litigation is probable, the solicitor must see that one at least of the two clients concerned is separately represented, and if he would be embarrassed in representing even one by reason of the knowledge which he has acquired of the other one's case he should see that *both* are represented by other practitioners. In non-contentious business however the Law Society take the view that it is not necessary for clients with inconsistent interests to be separately represented, provided that they are aware that the same solicitor is acting for both. A solicitor acted for two women in forming a partnership, and when it was later desired to dissolve the partnership each partner wished the solicitor to act for her. He consulted the Law Society whose ruling was that he should advise both the partners in writing that they should be independently represented, but if they both persisted thereafter there was no professional objection to his acting for them, unless and until litigation ensued. (60)

The rule that the same solicitor may act for both vendor and purchaser of land has occasionally caused disquiet. This may be partly due to the Law Society's recommendation that full charges should be made notwithstanding that the amount of work involved is necessarily less. The Prices and Incomes Board feel that it may not be in the interest of clients that solicitors should act for both parties. By encouraging the practice, a reduced charge may therefore, in their view, be undesirable. The Board felt that if the practice were indeed undesirable it should be forbidden, otherwise a reduced charge not exceeding one and a half times the total charge if two solicitors had been involved should be permitted. (61)

### Independence of Government

We have stressed in this chapter that impartiality and independence are indissolubly linked; the one cannot subsist without the other. It is fitting therefore to conclude the discussion with a brief consideration of the question of state interference in the professions. This is a large subject, and we can only touch here on the professions' own attitude. The professions most affected by state intervention during recent years have been barristers, solicitors, doctors and dentists. They have been largely successful in retaining the essential attributes of private practice and in particular the independence of the individual practitioner. Dangers exist however, particularly from the State's command over the rates of remuneration of the practitioner. For this reason the Pilkington Commission recommended in 1960 that rates of pay of doctors and dentists in the National Health Service should be determined by an independent review body on the basis of external comparison with other professions. (62) Nevertheless the State uses its financial power to influence professional policy (see page 49).

The operation of the National Health Service and the Legal Aid and Advice scheme is a question of the operation of legal enactments which the practitioner is bound to obey. There is more flexibility in the case of government policies not for the time being translated into law. What should be the attitude of the professions to these? The subject was ventilated in 1966, at a time when the Labour Government were seeking to persuade the nation to adopt a voluntary standstill in prices and incomes. At a luncheon attended by Mr Enoch Powell, M.P., the President of the Institute of Chartered Accountants expressed the view that action by accountants which, though not illegal, was contrary to the spirit of the prices and incomes standstill was undesirable. He was immediately roundly attacked by Mr Powell for meddling in politics. Mr Powell felt that professional bodies had no business to advise their members one way or the other as to government policy which had not been made enforceable by law. The President of the Royal Institution of Chartered Surveyors sprang to the defence of his fellow-president, pointing out that it was a tradition of professional bodies that in matters affecting their members' practices "they give guidance which accords with settled government policy, whatever government may be in power". He went on:

"If members seek guidance from their own Society on matters of this kind, as they frequently do, that guidance must, in my submission, be consonant not only with the law of the land but also with general government policy. Otherwise professional bodies are setting themselves up in opposition to the government, and this would indeed be meddling in politics." (64)

It must be true that professional bodies have no business to sabotage operative government policies, even though not backed by legislation. Nevertheless they retain their freedom to differ where they feel compelled to do so, and whatever view his professional body takes the individual practitioner is of course free to act as he thinks fit. This freedom is vital. It could be undermined by a failure on the part of governments to ensure that the economic conditions necessary for the survival of private practice are maintained. If it is desperately difficult to make ends meet, that is when temptation becomes most acute — temptation to take secret commissions, even bribes; to play one client off against another; to spin out consultations unnecessarily; to advise action with the main purpose of inflating the consultant's bill and so on. To this extent responsibility for preserving the disinterestedness of the professions rests with the government, and through them with the public at large.

CHAPTER 7

# RESPONSIBILITY: ANSWERABLE IN FULL

One of the essential characteristics of the professional consultant is that he should accept full personal responsibility for the advice he gives. An explicit statement of this principle was published by the Council of the Institute of Chartered Accountants in 1961: "The Council emphasises the personal responsibility of every member of the Institute for his professional conduct; this applies regardless of the way in which the work of the member is organised and of the medium through which it is performed." (1) The code of the Architects' Registration Council forbids an architect to do any act which will have the effect of avoiding his responsibility to his client. (2) The Declaration of Geneva stigmatises as "unethical" collaboration in any form of medical service in which the doctor does not have professional independence, that is where ultimate responsibility lies with someone else. (3)

It is this undertaking of full responsibility which distinguishes the professional man from the auxiliary or technician operating in the same field. The complexity of most professional techniques requires that the fully qualified practitioner shall be assisted by subordinates who, while having some knowledge of the techniques involved, are without the full professional training. The technician of today is a valuable member of the team, very often trained for that purpose. He succeeds the untrained clerk, who nevertheless frequently made up in experience what he lacked in formal qualifications.

Many a solicitor's office has depended for its smooth functioning on the quality and experience of its managing clerks. These are now renamed legal executives, and in the case of newcomers undergo training as such. An Institute of Legal Executives was formed in 1963 and has a current membership of more than 13,000. Similarly in the architects' field there was formed in 1966 the Association of Architectural and Allied Technicians, embracing ancillary grades in the field not only of architecture but also engineering and surveying. It is significant that the tendency for technicians to develop organisational structures resembling those of the professions themselves is displaying a pattern under which they are grouped in separate entities rather than as junior grades within the professional bodies. This follows protracted debates in the professional bodies as to the relative advantages of having technicians under their own eye or organised in separate and independent groupings. The decisive factor has been the fear of the professional bodies that if they admitted technicians to membership in any shape or form the public would inevitably confuse fully qualified members of the profession with the technician grades, thus blurring an essential distinction. Professional bodies have nevertheless taken a leading part in founding the technicians' representative bodies and in helping them to devise syllabuses for training.

If responsibility is one of the essential characteristics of the full professional, to whom is it owed? The primary duty is to the client, but there is also a responsibility owed to the profession, and in some instances to a member of another profession. Finally a professional man may be looked on as owing a responsibility to society at large.

The responsibility to the client is primarily a legal one, usually though not always enforceable in the civil courts. This means that its exact nature and scope may be affected by the terms of any contract entered into between client and practitioner. In the absence of an express contract the law will imply a contract. This will not place an unlimited obligation on the practitioner. It will render him liable for fraud, bad faith or negligence, but will not go to the extent of treating him as a guarantor of the accuracy of his advice or its effectiveness in dealing with the circumstances to which it is directed.

Where, as sometimes happens, there is in law no contract governing the circumstances in which advice is given, the consultant's duty to take care is derived from the legal rules governing the tort of negligence. The practical difference between a duty arising under an implied contract or in tort is slight; in either case the law expects a person engaged in a transaction where he holds himself out as having professional skill to show the average amount of competence associated with the proper discharge of the duties of his profession. Whether or not legal liability exists to the client, the professional body may treat failure to display proper professional skill as amounting to misconduct. This is particularly important in the case of barristers, who cannot be sued in negligence. Thus the professional sanctions reinforce, or supply the lack of, legal sanctions. They would also in effect enforce a duty to a member of another profession. Thus if a solicitor failed to prepare a case properly, and his neglect caused the barrister handling the case in court to fail in his duty, disciplinary proceedings might be taken against the solicitor on the complaint of the barrister. The latter is specifically told that he should be able to rely on the responsibility of a solicitor as to the

H

statement of facts put before him. (4)

It is unrealistic to expect anyone to shoulder responsibility unless he is accorded a degree of authority sufficient to enable him to see that the responsibility is effectively discharged. Thus barristers are told that it is not becoming for Counsel to accept a brief limiting his ordinary authority or to take a position subordinate to a non-barrister in the conduct of a case. (5) An example of an improper limitation on Counsel's authority would be imposing a condition that his discretion as to offering no evidence is fettered.

Why is such a rule imposed? In many cases it is required in the public interest; thus a barrister who has had his authority limited may be unable adequately to perform his duty to the court. Apart from this sort of consideration however the client himself is likely to suffer if he attempts to deny his professional consultant the authority requisite. An example of this is given by Norman J. Hodgkinson in discussing the duties of an auctioneer. He tells how, before holding an auction of a large agricultural estate, he called on the owner to discuss what reserve prices should be fixed for the various lots. The client cut him short by saying that when he engaged Gordon Richards to ride one of his horses he did not tell him how to ride the race. Given unlimited discretion by his client, the auctioneer realised a very good total. Hodgkinson comments: "Such clients are exceptional, but it is usually possible to persuade a client to give certain limited discretion to the auctioneer conducting the sale. As I have said, it is always in his interest to do so, and great though the auctioneer's responsibility may be in consequence, such discretion should always be asked for and welcomed when given." (6) In another place Hodgkinson points out that it is never the slightest use trying to shelve responsibility by leaving the decision to the client. "If the decision turns out to be a wrong one, your client will blame you for it just the same, and will only be irritated if it is pointed out to him that it was, in fact, his decision." (7) Nor should the consultant take refuge in ambiguities. Lord Westbury in advising on a case was always clear and direct, saying he was 'paid for his opinion, not for his doubts'. (8)

The need for a professional consultant to be in a position of full authority is recognised internationally. Thus the European Code laying down the professional obligations of the accountant states that it is incompatible with professional practice to accept any public function or commission placing the accountant in a position of subordination. (9)

## Vicarious Liability

In professional practice, as in law, the responsibility of the consultant covers not merely his own acts and omissions but also those of his partners and the staff of the firm. Thus we find the byelaws of the R.I.C.S. stating specifically that "members who are principals will be held responsible for the acts of their partners and staffs so far as they relate to matters coming within the scope of their practice". (10) To discourage evasion of this responsibility by allowing an employee to act on behalf of the firm under his own name, the Institute of Chartered Accountants have expressly prohibited this practice in one of its five fundamental rules.

In the rare cases where professional activities are allowed to be carried on through the medium of an incorporated body the professional man who is a member of the company is vicariously liable for its acts. Thus a chartered accountant who is a member of a company carrying out accountancy services is responsible for the conduct of the company and its directors and officers as if the company were a firm and he were a partner. (11)

Although vicarious liability clearly exists, punishment for its breach is likely to be less severe. A solicitor's managing clerk took advantage of the ignorance of a client who wished to be represented under the poor persons rules by suggesting that if the client paid the usual fee his case would be dealt with more quickly. Only a nominal penalty was imposed on the employing solicitor in view of his absence on war service at the time in question. (12)

### Responsibility as an Employee

Where a person carries out the duties of his profession as an employee he remains responsible in the eyes of the profession, though in law the responsibility may be his employer's. Where he is employed by private practitioners in the same profession no problems are likely to arise. Where however the employer is a lay person, unfamiliar with the rules and practices of the profession, there may be conflict between the wishes of the employer and the professional duty of the employee. The professional institution will hold an employee in such circumstances responsible for ensuring that no act of his employer leads to a breach of any professional rule. Nor may the employee "cover" the employer by enabling him in effect to carry on the profession with the use of the employee's qualifications and name (see page 54). He must not permit the employer to receive, whether directly or indirectly, fees earned by him from clients other than the employer, even if the employer has assumed responsibility for payment of those fees (as when the other clients are lay persons in the same employment).

The Law Society have laid down rules designed to ensure that, so far as concerns solicitors' work, the legal department of a company is run as nearly as possible on the same lines as a private firm. The department must be controlled by a solicitor with a practising certificate and solicitors' functions must be performed by the solicitor in his own name. (13)

Architects are free to take salaried employment with companies which provide architectural services. This means that a firm of building contractors offering an architectural service in competition with architects in private practice is free to employ its own architects to enable it to do so. Such companies may in certain circumstances describe themselves as architects. (14)

### Practice Through Limited Liability Companies

Most professions regard it as a cardinal rule that members should not practise the profession through the medium of limited liability companies. The rule partly arises through a desire to maintain the personal relationship between practitioner and client (see page 68). In the main however it is directed to preserving in its full rigour the responsibility of the practitioner for the advice he gives. Another reason is that, while a member may be restricted in assigning his shares in the company during his lifetime, there is nothing to prevent them going on his death to an unqualified person who would thus in effect come to be carrying on a professional practice. As Carr-Saunders and Wilson point out, this is bound to undermine the responsibility of practitioner to client. (15)

Principle V of the Architects Registration Council Code forbids an architect to carry on his practice in the form of a limited liability company. The R.I.B.A. code does not include this provision, but the Institute say there is no special reason for the omission, and the R.I.B.A. has always accepted that all its members in private practice are bound to accept full personal responsibility for their professional conduct. (16) The chartered accountants have a similar rule, which is one of their five fundamental principles. It is justified on the ground that public accountancy is essentially a personal service calling for long training and experience and the assumption of heavy legal responsibilities and personal responsibility to the client for the standard and consequences of the work done. (17) The Association of Consulting Engineers prohibits practice in respect of work on sites in the United Kingdom under the protection of limited liability. (18)

Some professions only adopted the rule against limited liability comparatively recently. This was so in the case of the chartered surveyors, whose rule states that in order that members shall accept full personal liability for advice given to clients, they will not be permitted to convert their firms into limited liability companies, or otherwise to carry on practice under the protection of limited liability, unless special circumstances approved by the Council of the Institution exist. (19) This rule was only adopted however as late as 1932.

Professional people have at times felt that the rule imposed hardship on them in restricting their ability to withdraw capital and minimise taxation. The rule has also been criticised for its effect in keeping down the size of professional organisations and hampering the raising of capital needed for investing in expensive equipment. The chartered surveyors and kindred societies have avoided extreme hardship by sparing use of the escape clause allowing permission for limited liability to be given in special cases. Such dispensations have however been virtually limited to firms already practising when the rule was introduced, firms carrying on livestock auctioneering (which requires the provision of markets), photogrammetry companies engaged in aerial surveying, and firms practising overseas.

## Service Companies

The prohibition on limited liability only applies to activities carried on by way of the practice of the profession. Some of the disadvantages mentioned above have therefore been avoided by the creation of service companies. The function of these is to provide a service for a professional firm by acquiring, holding and maintaining the office premises, providing furniture, stationery and equipment and employing the unqualified members of the staff, such as clerks, typists, book-keepers and the like.* The service company makes a profit by charging the firm on a cost-plus basis for the services it provides. The fee paid by the firm is an allowable deduction for tax purposes, and the "profit" made by the service company represents an asset in the hands of the partners which, if kept to a modest proportion, avoids surtax. It should be noted that the shares in the service company are normally required to be held by the partners of the professional firm and not by outsiders. If they were held by outsiders there would be a risk of the firm's remuneration being shared with non-members of the profession (see page 89). The advent of corporation tax and capital gains tax has lessened the attraction of service companies, and it remains to be seen how far they will continue to be a useful device.

* The Pilkington Commission found in 1956-7 that the average capital outlay for each principal in firms of accountants, actuaries, solicitors, architects, surveyors and engineers returned in an enquiry carried out in 1958 varied from £1,995 (architects) up to £7,336 (engineers) — Pilkington Report, p.48. By 1968 the figure for solicitors had risen from £3,844 to £7,060 (Cmnd. 3529. p.10). The state-financed General Practice Finance Corporation lends capital for medical practices.

## Unlimited Liability Companies

The professions do not generally bar the carrying on of practice by companies if liability is unlimited, though the Solicitors Acts are so worded that it is legally essential to carry on a solicitor's practice in person and not through a body corporate. (20) The Companies Acts provide for incorporation with unlimited liability, and it may have advantages in assisting in the raising and withdrawal of capital. Although few have made express rules to this effect, the professions would presumably object to any arrangement under which the shares in an unlimited company were held by persons other than members of the profession. There are believed to be few unlimited-liability companies practising any profession, but the Institute of Chartered Accountants has considered it worth laying down fairly detailed rules about how they are to operate. They must conform to all the rules which apply to a member in practice, and must not have a name which indicates the activities of the company or use the designation "chartered accountants". They must not be used as a means of sharing profits or remuneration with a non-member of the profession. (21)

## Other Forms of Limitation on Liability

While attaching great importance to preventing limitation of liability through the formation of limited companies, the professions have done little to restrain another type of limitation. This is the entering into a contract including terms absolving the professional consultant from the whole or any part of his obligation to the client. There is nothing in law to prevent this being done, provided the client is made fully aware of it. That it is not done frequently is probably due to the fact that clients would speedily abandon any practitioner who seriously attempted to strike at the roots of professional service by taking away their legal protection.

While there is every objection in principle to contracts being so framed as to save a professional man from the consequences of his ineptitude, there is no such objection to a contract which relieves from liability by indicating what the professional man is purporting to do for his client and what he is not. A good example is structural surveys of buildings. A householder will often ask a surveyor to report on the state of the house at a time when it is fully equipped with furniture, carpeting and other furnishings. In such circumstances it is impossible for the surveyor to scrutinise every part of the fabric. A similar difficulty arises even in the case of an empty house where the client is not prepared to pay a fee adequately reflecting the amount of time necessary to examine every detail. In such cases the surveyor is justified in stating that his report covers only those parts of the building that he has been able to examine. This is not a limitation of liability but a clear indication of how far the professional service extends.

More controversial is the rule of law which exempts barristers from liability for negligence. As stated above, this rule will not absolve a barrister from disciplinary proceedings, but these will not afford any financial recompense to an aggrieved client. The immunity of a barrister from actions for negligence in respect of his handling of court proceedings was confirmed by the House of Lords in the recent case of *Rondel* v. *Worsley*. (22) A man convicted of causing bodily harm had been defended on a dock brief by a barrister who was alleged by the convict to have acted negligently. The convict sued, but it was held that no such action could be entertained. The administration of justice requires that a barrister should be able to carry out his duty to the court fearlessly and independently, without worrying about the possibility of actions against himself. He is obliged to accept any client — even the most awkward and litigious — and might be plagued with suits if the law were otherwise. Finally, such actions would virtually involve a retrial of the original case; this would be against the public interest, which requires finality in litigation. The same protection is given to a solicitor in relation to matters which might have been conducted by counsel.

## Compensating the Client

The rule against limited liability is based on the proposition that a professional man should back his advice with his whole personal fortune. While this has a splendid ring, and may once have been some protection to the public, it is hardly a valid safeguard today. Most professional people have little in the way of personal fortune, while frequently called upon to advise on matters involving very large sums. It is the clear duty of the professions therefore to insist that their members enter into suitable arrangements, by means of insurance or otherwise, to make certain that claims can be met. Strangely enough, however, although one or two professions have set up compensation funds, very few insist on indemnity insurance being taken out by members. The fact that for their own protection most professional people do insure against claims through negligence does not absolve the professions from making such insurance compulsory where no alternative safeguards are provided.

Most elaborate of such alternative arrangements is the Solicitors' Compensation Fund. The Fund was established by Act of Parliament in 1941, and is fed by contributions from solicitors themselves. Grants are made out of the Fund where loss is caused in consequence of dishonesty by a solicitor or his clerk or servant. It is not available to meet claims arising out of negligence or other misconduct short of dishonesty. The fund was set up under the initiative of the Law Society, and is administered by it on a discretionary basis. To date all admitted claims have been paid in full. (23)

Another form of protection, recently established in the case of estate agents, is the "honesty bond" system. As operated by the Estate Agents Council this involves the taking out of an overall insurance policy by the Council, to which each registered agent may become a party. It is a condition of registration that the agent should either become a party to the bond or make other adequate arrangements. The cover thus given enables persons who have suffered loss through dishonesty to be recompensed where the Council thinks fit.

The wide range of possible liabilities arising in the case of professional firms makes it desirable to have a correspondingly wide-ranging professional indemnity insurance policy. This would cover not only negligent advice to clients, but liability for negligent statements to others arising under a doctrine laid down by the Courts in 1963 in the case of *Hedley Byrne* v. *Heller*; liability for libel or slander; liability for damage to goods, including documents deposited with the firm; and, in the case of auctioneers, liabiliity for the torts of conversion and detinue. (24)

A further safeguard for clients is the rule that a separate bank account must be opened for clients' money, so that it is not mixed with money belonging to the firm. While this does not provide a complete safeguard, since the principals of the firm cannot be prevented from drawing on the clients' account, it does have certain advantages. The bank is put on enquiry if cheques for items obviously not relating to clients are drawn on the clients' account. Partners have no excuse for not being aware that their clients' account is overdrawn when such is the case.

The professions have again been strangely reluctant to impose the keeping of separate clients' accounts as a positive rule of conduct. The Chartered Surveyors, for example, did not adopt the rule until as late as 1966. The solicitors have the most developed rules, but even these only date back to 1933 and have been very greatly strengthened since the last war. Apart from separation of clients' bank accounts, they require the keeping of proper books of account which will show clients' moneys distinguished from those of the firm and the moneys of each client distinct from those of all the others. The money of one client must not be used for financing another, and there must always be in the clients' bank account a sufficient sum to meet the solicitor's total liabilities to his clients.

It is difficult to resist the conclusion that safeguards of the kind mentioned here would, if made universal, provide adequate protection without the need for a rule against the formation of limited liability companies. Preservation of such a rule suggests a more deep-rooted objection, which is probably really an objection to incorporation itself. This compares with the situation in other countries such as Canada, where the suffix "Limited" is regarded as a sign of status, welcomed by the public and therefore used by practitioners. In this of course the public deceive themselves; a far better safeguard would be knowledge that a particular firm bears the professional hallmark and that this involves compulsory safeguards such as indemnity insurance and proper accounting rules.

## CHAPTER 8

# INTEGRITY: 'SANS PEUR ET SANS REPROCHE'

Integrity, probity or uprightness is a prized quality in almost every sphere of life, and nowhere more so than in the professions. The best assurance the client can have that he will meet with the qualities discussed in the previous chapters is the basic integrity of the professional consultant. The professional bodies therefore attach great importance to its presence and preservation in their members; and do not hesitate to say so. Thus the code of the Association of Consulting Engineers states flatly: 'a member shall discharge his duties with complete fidelity'. (1)

The professions exact a higher standard of integrity than is found in many other walks of life. W.J. Reader comments: "It is this sense of being obliged to observe exceptionally high standards which, more than anything else, gives some sense of unity to the professional classes as a whole, diverse though the occupations of their members may be." (2) Standards in this respect are probably higher than they have ever been and mark a considerable advance from the days when Sir Walter Scott thought the only qualities needed in his nephew if he were to become an accountant were to be "steady, cautious, fond of sedentary life and quiet pursuits, and at the same time proficient in arithmetic". (3) Today the slightest falling off in probity is looked at askance by fellow-members of the profession. They believe, with St. Luke, that he that is faithful in that which is least is faithful also in much, and he that is unjust in the least is unjust also in much. (4) Like the nobleman of the parable they would say "because thou hast been faithful in a very little, have thou authority over ten cities". The true professional man asks nothing better for his epitaph than that of the eighteenth-century clock-maker: "Integrity was the mainspring and prudence the regulator of all the actions of his life."

## Unblemished Reputation

Since inward character can only be deduced from outward signs, a spotless reputation, "the purest treasure mortal times afford", is essential to a professional man. In words of advice to a young solicitor,

Sir Thomas Lund says that only the very highest conduct is consistent with membership of the profession and that his reputation is the greatest asset a solicitor can have. "When you damage your reputation you damage the reputation of the whole body of this very ancient and honourable profession of ours." (5) W.J. Reader, writing about the rise of the professional classes in the nineteenth century, points out that the new professional man brought one scale of values — the gentleman's — to bear upon another — the tradesman's — and produced "a specialised variety of business morality which came to be known as professional ethics". He adds that any professional man must cultivate and deserve a reputation for probity. "He must cultivate it even more zealously than the ordinary businessman, who deals with other businessmen who know what to expect." (6)

These sentiments may appear high-flown, and are often expressed in grandiose language. Notions of honour, even of self-respect, are becoming unfashionable. For those who follow fashion the importance of a good reputation does not depend on these things — it is grounded in self-interest, since a professional practice will not long endure if clients learn that the practitioner cannot be trusted.

A reputation for integrity is an indivisible whole; it can therefore be lost by actions having little or nothing to do with the profession. This was the case with one Dunch, the first man to be suspended from membership of the Surveyors' Institution (now the R.I.C.S.). The incident arose in connection with the purchase by the Metropolitan Board of Works of property needed for the site of what is now Shaftesbury Avenue. This was begun in 1878 and the Board official concerned was the notorious F.W. Goddard, around whom many tales of corruption circulated. The property included the Pavilion Music Hall which, until the site was needed, was let to one Villiers on stringent conditions which it was Goddard's duty to enforce. Dunch, who was a mutual friend, persuaded Villiers that he ought to accede to a demand from Goddard to be paid £50 a quarter for himself in order to smooth the way over compliance with the conditions. Dunch acted as bearer of this quarterly payment and was censured by the Royal Commission set up to examine the Goddard scandal. They commented that if he had, as it was his duty to do, communicated to the Board Goddard's request for payment, the confidence which the Board reposed in that official would have been at an end, and it would no longer have been possible for him to betray the interests of his employers for his own advantage. (6A)

The insistence by a profession that its members shall be without reproach raises difficult questions where a member commits some misdemeanor or indiscretion outside the professional field. Conviction of serious crime will usually lead to expulsion from the profession, but where should the line be drawn? If the offence demonstrates unfitness to carry out a necessary function of the profession the position is clear. A land agent, used to holding rents from his clients' estates, can hardly be trusted again in his profession after detection in the embezzlement of funds held in some other capacity, such as church treasurer or slate club secretary. A doctor, in duty bound to succour the injured, casts doubt on his seriousness of purpose if found guilty of some vicious and unwarranted assault. A solicitor, whose duties often include the production of documentary evidence to the court, can hardly survive a conviction of forging a motor-car log book to his own advantage. But suppose the conviction establishes moral turpitude of a kind not likely to arise in the course of professional practice? A recent illustration was the case of Dr John Petro, convicted of stealing a gold cigarette lighter left by a woman on a counter at Selfridges. The judge called it a "singularly mean theft" and a dirty trick, "especially for a professional man". The General Medical Council were not called on to decide the professional consequences, however, since a short time previously Petro had been struck off the register for failing to keep a drugs list. (7)

A conviction for dishonesty of any kind will usually be fatal — even if it is for travelling without a ticket on the Underground. "He that is faithful in that which is least . . . " Difficult problems arise however where a conviction relates to something further removed from the professional sphere. In a celebrated libel case Mr Justice Macnaghten remarked: "It cannot be said that chastity is a necessary qualification for the management or ownership of a garage". (8) The same might be said of the practice of a solicitor or accountant, though probably not that of a doctor. The test is whether knowledge of the offence is likely to impair the clients' trust in the offender as a professional consultant. Many so-called crimes today involve no moral turpitude, at least in the eyes of the ordinary citizen.

Difficulty can also be felt in determining whether a fall from grace should be considered permanent or of limited duration only. Again this must depend on the seriousness of the offence and its closeness to the sphere of professional activity. A solicitor who embezzles trust funds will never be given another chance to do so; if he has cheated the railway his offence may be deemed to be purged in time.

One test laid down by a famous judge asked to decide whether a conviction should result in professional disqualification was "ought any respectable solicitor to be called upon to enter into that intimate intercourse with such a solicitor (i.e., one who has been convicted) which is necessary between two solicitors even though they are acting for opposite parties? In my opinion if the offence is personally disgraceful he ought not to remain on the Roll." (9) Thus conviction for indecent assault, acts of gross indecency or persistent importuning for an immoral purpose will normally involve a finding of professional misconduct, at least in the case of solicitors. (10) Dentists have been struck off the register for such offences as drunkenness, indecency, bigamy, incest, embezzlement, fraud and receiving stolen property. (11)

If an applicant to enter a profession has already forfeited his reputation by incurring a conviction of a criminal offence, or in some other way, it follows that his application should be rejected. The converse is equally true, and Lund refers to the "oft-quoted proposition" that any conduct by a solicitor which would, if committed before he was a solicitor, have been sufficient to prevent him from being admitted, will be sufficient to warrant his being struck off the Roll or suspended. (12) Membership of a leading professional body is generally treated as an indication of good character in itself, and it therefore follows that investigations as to character ought to be, and usually are, made before admission is granted. Thus a person enrolling as a student with the Law Society has to provide three references as to his character, which are invariably taken up. The referee is asked, among other things, whether the candidate has at all times shown himself to be honest and trustworthy. The Inns of Court require two character references before admission of students. The medical profession relies on the teaching bodies not to grant qualifications to students who are not of good character. Strangely, the architects make no enquiry as to character from their students. Professions based on the system of articles, such as the chartered accountants and chartered surveyors, rely mainly on the articled clerk's principal to satisfy himself as to character. Offences committed during the period of articles are dealt with as they would be if committed by a full member. In serious cases articles may be cancelled.

In the case of solicitors the professional body not only considers the character of principals and articled clerks, but of ordinary staff as well. The Law Society has statutory power to prohibit the employment of any person who has been guilty of dishonesty or any other relevant offence. (13)

Integrity has many aspects and may be displayed (or not) in a wide variety of situations. We have examined some of these in earlier chapters; the preservation of confidences, the display of impartiality, the taking of full responsibility are all aspects of integrity. So is the question of competence. Few can hope to be fully proficient in all branches of their profession. Integrity demands that advice be given only where competence exists, and that competence be maintained within the chosen field of practice. Integrity is the fundamental quality, whose absence vitiates all others. In what follows we deal with other important attributes of integrity.

## Fairness

It is obvious that the professional man must treat his client fairly, and little needs to be said about this. The true professional takes pride in doing a good job without unnecessary delay; in other words he gives value for money. He does not mislead his client about the progress of the case or any other aspect of it; it has been held to be misconduct for a solicitor to tell his client that he was carrying out his instructions when in fact this was not so. The rule applies whether or not accompanied by circumstances of fraud, such as seeking to obtain from the client payment on account of costs of proceedings which have not in fact commenced. (14)

The consultant should always make full disclosure of the facts to his client, except where they are unimportant. It is indefensible to conceal vital information, even on the well-meaning ground that the client might be worried by it. This is a rule often broken by the medical profession — with of course the best motives. Every individual has the right to be told basic facts about his own health — particularly where disease threatens his life. As the senior surgical registrar of a London hospital pointed out, most members of the medical profession would wish for the truth when their own time came. "Why therefore should our patients be denied the same right?" He added that in hospital practice "too many are not told who ought to be . . . the deception this involves, though perhaps well-meaning, is not in the true interests of our patients as human beings". (14A)

There is a story of a hospital patient — called let us say John Smith — who could get little information about his case from the hospital staff. He asked for the bedside telephone provided by Friends of Hospitals and, after dialling the hospital number, asked to be put through to the ward he was in. He then asked the ward sister: "How is Mr John Smith today? How did his operation go, and are there any complications?" He was given full information, and then the sister asked: "Are you a relative?" "No," came the answer, "I am Mr John Smith." Whether true or not, this illustrates a grievance felt by many patients — the disinclination of the medical profession to tell them the full facts about their case. The practice rebounds upon itself, because many worry lest the truth of some dire (but non-existent) disease is being kept from them. Playing fair with the client always involves resisting the temptation to give him advice which he wants to hear, rather than sound but unpalatable guidance.

A professional man must not take improper advantage of the youth, inexperience, want of education, lack of knowledge or unbusinesslike habits of a client. Thus a solicitor who exploited the inexperience of a client by inducing him to pay a sum in advance of costs which was far larger than the costs were likely to amount to was disciplined. (15)

If presents are accepted from clients they should not be allowed to influence the quality of services bestowed. Reginald Hine, in his *Confessions of an Uncommon Attorney,* describes a picture hanging in his firm's office called "A Lawyer's Office in 1515" by Peter Breughel. "It portrays a group of country clients rewarding their family solicitor with the fattest of capons, the ripest of grapes, and score upon score of eggs, whereas the client who ventured in empty-handed is left standing, and likely to stand, by the door." (16) We think differently today.

Fairness does not stop with the client. While the interests of the client should be served, this must not be done at the price of unfairness to others. This is only another way of saying that the interests of the client must not be pursued beyond a legitimate stage. Nothing must be done which would harm the reputation of the profession or transgress the moral code. Thus the Declaration of Geneva requires medical practitioners to promise: "I will maintain the utmost respect for human life from the time of conception; even under threat, I will not use my medical knowledge contrary to the laws of humanity." (17) The public interest must be served, and this involves that barristers and solicitors, who are officers of the court, must not deceive the court. An advocate may not assert that which he knows to be a lie, or forward a fraud. On matters of law he is under a duty to draw the attention of the court to points of law which might otherwise be overlooked, even if they are to the disadvantage of his client.

A duty to the public is in danger of being broken whenever a professional man extols his client's case in extravagant terms. An obvious example is the estate agent who describes a property for sale in terms which even the owner himself might find excessive. This may lead members of the public to undertake fruitless journeys to inspect properties which, if they knew the truth, they would not trouble to visit. The danger of over-enthusiasm at the expense of the public is lessened by the system of private practice, where no one client's interests are of predominating importance to the practitioner. A professional person who is in the service of one employer only may be under greater pressure to advance his employer's interests beyond what is legitimate. A planning officer in the employ of a local authority has been known to justify decisions of his planning committee on grounds other than the right ones.

For example, where the councillors refused permission for redevelop-ment of the site of an old building because one of their number was sentimentally attached to it, the planning officer explained the decision as having been taken on "general planning grounds".

Other parties to a transaction or dispute have a right to fair treatment. A small minority of solicitors offend in this respect, through excess of zeal for their client's cause or an unworthy desire to prolong a litigious dispute. Reginald Hine refers to "the niggling, cantankerous, litigious, lesser breed of solicitors who gain a catchpenny or catch-six-and-eight-penny reputation for smartness but do our profession no good". He goes on: "Alas, from time immemorial, we have been plagued with these rabbling and tumultuous lawyers who specialise in the chicane or wrangling or captious part of the law. With such men it is impossible to pursue gentle arts of compromise. Their breast-pockets are stuffed with writs. Their dictated letters are dictatorial, each sentence barbed with a threat." (18)

A striking instance of a duty of fairness owed to parties to a transac-tion other than the client applies in the case of architects and quantity surveyors. Although retained and paid by the site owner they are en-joined to preserve impartiality and fairness towards the building con-tractor. Principle IV of the Architects Registration Council code states: "An architect must at all times apply the conditions of a contract with entire fairness between employer and contractor. In all questions arising between the employer and contractor and in all cases in which an architect is acting between parties, he must act in an impartial manner." The fact that the architect is being paid by his client must not be allowed to influence his responsibility for the proper fulfilment of the contract between the parties. (19) Thus although in many respects the agent of the building owner he must assume a quasi-judicial role in interpreting the building contract, and this is reflected in the terms of the R.I.B.A. forms of building contract. Similar rules are applied to quantity surv-eyors by the R.I.C.S.

Since he owes these duties to other persons, to his profession and to the public at large, it is clear that the professional man should not con-sent to act for a client whose ends are dishonest or otherwise improper. Lord Esher, when Master of the Rolls, once said that if a solicitor were instructed to take proceedings which could legally be taken but which he knew would injure the other party unnecessarily, and were only sought by his client in order to gratify his own anger or his malice, it would be "unfair and wrong" if the solicitor took the proceedings. (20) Even less should a client be assisted in illegal activities. A professional man ought not to give a reference for a client whom he knows to be dishonest. As

Sir Thomas Lund says, "you should never do, or agree to do, anything dishonest or dishonourable, even in a client's interests or even under pressure from your best and most valuable client; you had better lose him." (21)

While these principles are tolerably clear, their application in practice may cause difficulty. Some arts legitimately practised by professional people necessarily involve concealment of facts, and the laying of red herrings. Of nothing is this more true than of a central feature of several professions: the art of negotiation. This is a difficult practice, and distasteful to many laymen. It is therefore frequently left to professional representatives, be they solicitors, accountants, valuers, architects or estate agents. An element of bluff is inseparable from negotiation, and therefore cannot be condemned. How far is it legitimate to go? Norman J. Hodgkinson, an experienced chartered surveyor, gives as examples of legitimate prevarication in negotiation the following: to say "I feel sure my client would not be willing to sell at that price" when the price is one you actually feel sure your client would accept, and to say "I could not possibly advise my client to sell at that figure" when you have, in fact, already done so. (22) In another place Hodgkinson gives his approval to what many might feel is a less excusable deception. In describing the technique of the auctioneer he discusses fictitious bids. These are actual bids put in on behalf of the vendor "although the auctioneer may try to give the impression that the bids he puts in are actually made by other bidders". He goes on:

> "Every auctioneer has his own ways of taking fictitious bids. For example, he may pretend to take the bid from someone behind the actual bidder, or if the genuine bidder is at the back of the room the fictitious bid may appear to be taken from the front seat. Again, an auctioneer who has no bidder at all may start the bidding by saying: 'That is my bid to start proceedings', and then, having looked round for a bid and failed to get one, he may take a fictitious bid, saying: 'Thank you', and ostentatiously write the bid down on the particulars of sale, thus hoping to emphasise the impression that here at last is a genuine bidder. Again, the auctioneer may start a sentence, break off to take a fictitious bid, and then complete the sentence. This is a good plan if not used too often." (23)

Perhaps the last word should rest with Lord Esher, who said that how far a solicitor might go on behalf of his client was a question far too difficult to be capable of abstract definition, but when concrete cases arose, everyone could see for himself whether what had been done

I

was fair or not. (24)

### Fearlessness

A professional man may know what he ought to do, and wish to do it. This is useless if he lacks courage in the face of opposition and allows himself to be browbeaten into yielding his client's position. According to the best traditions of the Bar, a barrister should, while acting with all due courtesy to the tribunal before which he is appearing, fearlessly uphold the interests of his client without regard to any unpleasant consequences either to himself or to any other person. (25) There are many stories illustrating the fearlessness of advocates in defence of their clients.

The American defender, William Henry Seward, became very unpopular locally when he undertook the defence of the negro Freeman on a murder charge. Feeling ran high against Freeman, and he had been narrowly rescued from lynching. Seward stuck to his task, and maintained that no state was civilised which did not guarantee a fair trial and an adequate defence to every accused person. He expressed the hope that after his own death someone might put on his grave the words "He was faithful". This was in fact done. (26)

In lighter vein, two stories concerning F.E. Smith (later Lord Birkenhead) also illustrate the courage of the advocate. In his early days at the Bar "F.E." was appearing in a county court on behalf of an insurance company fighting a workman's compensation claim. The plaintiff was a little boy who was alleged to have lost his sight as a result of an accident. The judge was visibly affected by the sight of the child and, greatly to the annoyance of "F.E.", kept murmuring "Poor boy! Poor boy!", finally saying to the usher "Put the poor boy over there. Put him where the jury can see him."

"Perhaps", said "F.E." suavely, "your Honour would like to have him passed round the jury box?"

"That is a most improper observation, Mr Smith", said the judge angrily.

"It was prompted by most improper observations from the bench", replied counsel.

The other case also concerned a county court judge, who was a worthy but somewhat dull and ineffective personality. He tried a number of times to restrain the exuberance of "F.E." but the advocate took no notice of his rebukes. Finally the judge asked irritably "Mr Smith, why am I here?" The future Lord Chancellor replied politely: "It is not for me, your honour, to attempt to fathom the inscrutable ways of Providence".

The Judge: "Mr Smith, you are very offensive."

Mr Smith: "As a matter of fact we both are. The only difference between us is that I am trying to be and you can't help it. I have been listened to with respect by the highest tribunals in the land and I have not come down here to be browbeaten."

While courage needs to be displayed in defence of a client's interests, it may occasionally be needed to stand up to the client himself. The Bar Council point out that "the customer is not always right" and that the professional man has a duty on occasions to deny to the client what he wants, or thinks he wants. (27)

A professional man called on to certify that the client has behaved correctly – for example has kept a proper set of accounts – may well be under pressure from the client. He should of course resist such pressure, if he believes it to be improper, and where necessary should accept the loss of his appointment rather than yield. It is an important professional principle that where an appointment is lost in such circumstances a professional successor should not take up the appointment without careful investigation. The Institute of Chartered Accountants lays down detailed rules for this. An incoming auditor must communicate with his predecessor and find out the full reasons for the change. The appointment ought not to be accepted if this investigation discloses that the predecessor is being displaced "because he has stood his ground and carried out his duties as auditor in the teeth of opposition or evasion on an occasion on which important differences of principle or practice have risen between him and the directors". (28)

A similar situation may arise where an actuary is appointed to make a statutory valuation. In such a case the actuary must take an impartial standpoint between the directors of the insurance company and its policy holders, and must be free to criticise the conduct and procedure of the directors.

Acute problems may well arise in any profession where a member of the profession is in employment and there is a conflict between the employer's wishes and the rule of the profession. Here it is important, but often very difficult, for the professional man to resist the employer's demands and maintain the standards of the profession. In all cases of conflict, at least where public bodies are concerned, the professional institutions can play an important role in supporting their members against improper demands. They are usually very ready to do so. Thus the President of the Institute of Actuaries has said that "in any difficulties which might face actuaries in the conduct of their business . . . in resisting any undue pressure which might be brought to bear upon them, they would be assured of the support of the Institute". (29)

## Nest-Feathering

It is repugnant to the professional code for a practitioner to profit from dealings with a client otherwise than by the receipt of the normal professional fee. The consultant must not, in the guise of an impartial adviser, feather his own nest. Abuse of the professional relationship can take many forms, not all relating to material advantage; and standards are continually rising. As Sir Thomas Lund points out, what is entirely proper for one generation may be slightly irregular for the succeeding generation and highly improper for the next. A generation ago there was nothing improper in keeping clients' money in one's own bank account and making free use of it — even drawing interest. Nowadays many professions would regard this as improper. (30)

The most serious ways, apart from downright fraud, of making a financial profit from a client or his affairs are: taking bribes or "sweeteners", dealing in clients' property, borrowing from clients, persuading clients to make gifts or legacies, and exploiting trade secrets and similar information.

Hodgkinson gives the correct attitude to bribery in recounting how, as auctioneer of a landed estate, he was approached by a prospective bidder, a speculator, who asked: "What would you want out of it if I buy? Would £500 meet the case?" When the auctioneer explained to him that he was acting for the vendor, and could not possibly take anything from the purchaser, the speculator expressed surprise, saying: "I thought all you people were prepared to accept a sweetener in order to get a sale through." (31) Unless it is common practice for them to do so, professional practitioners should not receive payments from third parties; in this way suspicion of abuse is avoided. Thus the architects' code prohibits the insertion of any clause in tenders, bills of quantities or other documents which provides for payments to be made to the architect by the contractor unless with the full knowledge and approval of the employer. (32) The engineers have a similar rule. (33) (See also page 93).

A clear abuse arises where a professional person is entrusted with the sale of his client's property and, unknown to the client, sells it at an undervalue to another person with whom the consultant is connected. A solicitor was found guilty of professional misconduct when, in the course of administering an estate, he sold part of it to his own daughter at a price less than the full value without either disclosing the connection between the purchaser and himself or advising his client to be separately represented in that transaction. (34) In another case a solicitor was found guilty of professional misconduct even though there was no direct evidence that the price received was not a fair market price. Here the solicitor was concerned in a number of sales of real property on behalf of both vendor and purchaser. In each case the purchaser was an associate or nominee of the solicitor and in each case the property was speedily resold at a profit which the solicitor and his associate shared equally. (35) Estate agents are frequently placed in a position of temptation in this respect, and do not always resist the opportunity for private profit (see page 83).

While professional people are encouraged to maintain a friendly relationship with their clients they should not carry friendship to an extent which is excessive, even though it might be considered reasonable in other relationships. Thus solicitors are discouraged from borrowing money from their clients. If they do so they must ensure that there is sufficient security, and where there is even the slightest doubt of this they should insist on the client being separately represented in the transaction. Cases held to amount to professional misconduct include one where a solicitor who claimed to be a spiritualist advised a client to dispose of his life interest in certain settled property and place the proceeds in the solicitor's hands, contrary to the client's interest. (36) Many abuses have arisen where elderly and feeble clients have been induced by their solicitors to leave them substantial legacies. These have led the Council of the Law Society to lay down rules aimed to secure that where the legacy is more than trifling the testator should be independently advised.

A particularly reprehensible practice is for a professional consultant to use knowledge gained in the course of his relationship with his client to enter the client's own field of operations, perhaps even in rivalry with him. In one case a chartered accountant, in the course of his professional duties, acquired information about a specialist manufacturing process and subsequently used this information to set up a business which competed with the former client. Similarly objectionable is use of "inside information" to buy or sell shares of client companies for personal profit. (37) Some professions discourage any activity by their members which could cause them to be tempted to make use of information gained from clients. Thus patent agents are discouraged from taking out a patent on their own account. If the idea for the patent derived from a client the property in the idea should be regarded as belonging to the client. If on the other hand it occurs to the patent agent independently he is recommended to communicate it to a learned society or technical journal. (38) Similar considerations apply to land development and speculation by estate agents on their own account (see page 83).

Where the professional relationship involves bodily contact and examination, as in the case of doctors, sexual intimacies are held to constitute misconduct. The Judicial Committee of the Privy Council recently pointed out that a doctor gains entry to the home in the trust that he will take care of the physical and mental health of the family. He must not abuse his professional position so as, by act or word, to impair in the least the confidence and security which should subsist between husband and wife. His association with the wife becomes improper when by look, touch, or gesture he shows undue affection for her or does anything else to show that he thinks more of her than he should. The Judicial Committee dismissed the suggestion that a doctor might be in a different position when he became a family friend, in other words that his conduct on social occasions was to be regarded differently from his conduct on professional occasions: "This looks very like a suggestion that he might do in the drawing-room that which he might not do in the surgery. No such distinction can be permitted. A medical man who gains the entry into the family confidence by reason of his professional position must maintain the same high standard when he becomes a family friend." (39) The rule ceases to apply once the professional relationship has ended.

These rules all reflect the need for trust. In the words of the great physician Galen, "he cures most in whom most have faith."

# PART III: BROTHERLY BEHAVIOUR

## CHAPTER 9

# PROFESSIONAL SOLIDARITY

We have seen above (page 20) how a profession regards itself as a brotherhood, and we turn now to examine in detail what this involves. The reasons for banding together are various; the degree to which solidarity is pursued is not always the same. Nevertheless the pattern is consistent: solidarity is maintained through the organisation of the professional institute, and by this also the autonomy of the profession is expressed and safeguarded.

The law is generous in according autonomous rights to the professions. It has decreed that it will normally be for a profession itself to decide its standards and its code of behaviour "and the mere fact that certain rules are laid down which are severely restrictive will not warrant attack upon them if in the interests of members and in the public interest such rules are reasonable". (1) These words were uttered in the 1968 case of *Dickson* v. *Pharmaceutical Society of Great Britain.* In this case Lord Wilberforce said of the charter of incorporation of the Pharmaceutical Society: "I have no doubt that this Charter, as other similar grants of corporate status and privileges to the members of a profession, ought to be construed so as to give to the members a wide degree of autonomy. Particularly is this so in relation to standards of professional conduct." (2)

In turn, the profession does its utmost to exact from its members conduct upholding its standards and tradition. "I will maintain", says the International Code of Medical Ethics, "by all the means in my power the honour and the noble traditions of the medical profession". (3) Each practitioner thus recognises his personal responsibility. Within the scope of his own practice he will be seen as the embodiment of his profession; in the eyes of the client his acts will be the profession's acts. We find, for example, dentists enjoined "to avoid, as far as possible, any word or action which might disturb the confidence of the patient in the dental profession". (4) Consulting engineers must order their conduct "so as to uphold the dignity, standing and reputation of the profession" (5). A chartered surveyor must not conduct himself in such a manner as would prejudice the reputation of his professional institution. (6)

121

Architects are required to uphold and apply the R.I.B.A. conditions of engagement, since the Institute regard professional solidarity in maintaining fees as necessary to aid small firms in dealing with powerful clients. (7)

Though professional people may believe that "the principal influence to be cultivated is that of good fellowship" (8); though they hold, with the Bar Council, that everyone should have available to him within the profession "a body of colleagues and friends to whom he can turn for advice and support" (9), this does not override the paramount concern for the wellbeing of the profession itself. It is therefore the duty of a professional man to report to his institute a colleague who has been guilty of professional misconduct. "In the view of the Council," say the Law Society, "that is a professional obligation, unpleasant though it may be, which, in the general interests of us all, it is your duty to discharge, subject only to the prior interests of your client". (10) Nor will the professional body tolerate lack of frankness to itself. It has been held on several occasions that to offer a false explanation to the Law Society on an allegation of misconduct itself amounts to a breach of the code. (11)

It is remarkable, in view of this desire to maintain solidarity, that few if any professional institutes are able to compel practitioners to become members. This applies even where, as in the case of solicitors, unqualified persons are prohibited by law from exercising certain functions of the profession. Although since 1941 there has been statutory power to make membership of the Law Society compulsory for solicitors, this has not yet been exercised. Nevertheless solicitors who are in practice are compelled to hold a practising certificate for which a separate fee is charged. This applies equally to non-members of the Law Society, which regards it as being in the public interest that a solicitor should be subject to such control through the Law Society, his professional body, and that he should thus contribute to the provision of machinery for regulating the profession. (12)

Almost all rules embodied in the professional code of conduct are relevant to the duty to maintain the standing of the profession. We select for mention in this chapter rules which have a particular bearing on professional solidarity, but lack a wider application.

Much importance is attached to preserving the confidence of the public in the advice given by practitioners. This has its difficulties where, as in so many fields today, new discoveries and developments are constantly being made. The sound advice of today often becomes the culpably unsound, because superseded, advice of tomorrow. Even worse, there may be several opinions as to what is the sound advice of today. Not unnaturally, the professions prefer to see debates on such topics conducted out of earshot of the public. The doctors go so far as to lay down a specific rule: "Discussions in the lay press or in broadcasting on controversial points of medical science and treatment should be avoided by practitioners." (13) The doctors also dislike anything which tends to induce the public to treat themselves, rather than seeking medical advice. Medical practitioners are therefore told that they should not have a direct association with any commercial enterprise engaged in the manufacture or sale of substances claimed to be of value in the prevention or treatment of disease and recommended in a way calculated to encourage self-diagnosis or self-medication. (14) This reinforces the prohibition imposed by law on advertising to the public remedies for diseases such as cancer, diabetes and epilepsy. (15)

Professional solidarity is endangered where one practitioner does any act calculated to injure a colleague. Such practices are therefore discouraged. The consulting engineers, for example, lay down that a member "shall not act as to injure or attempt to injure, whether directly or indirectly, the professional reputation, prospects or business of another member." (16) This is not held to prevent the expression of technical opinion on behalf of a client before a tribunal or in a commission's report. Nor of course does it prevent the lodging of an allegation of misconduct by a colleague with the professional institute.

The complaint is often made of professional people that, in pursuance of the honourable maxim "dog doesn't eat dog", they are most reluctant to give evidence against one another. This, it is said, often makes claims difficult to pursue. Conscious of this feeling, the Law Society has ruled that while it is commendable for a solicitor instructed to act against a colleague to give a prior informal communication of this to the colleague concerned, nevertheless the Council consider "in view of the feeling among certain sections of the public that solicitors are averse from taking proceedings against other solicitors", that no unusual procedure should be adopted. (17)

A well known instance of a profession acting to rid itself of one who attacked his fellow-practitioners unmercifully was *Allinson* v. *General Council of Medical Education and Registration* in 1894. Allinson was a homeopathic practitioner, and advertised widely that patients should avoid the doctors, "who poisoned with their drugs", and come to him instead. The court upheld the view that to defame brother practitioners and deter their patients was infamous conduct in a professional respect, especially when done "to discredit and defame the medical professional generally".

Sometimes professional solidarity is disturbed by the setting up of breakaway institutes, where the members of the parent body feel it is not catering adequately for their needs. Two examples within the legal field are the British Legal Association and the Bar Association for Commerce, Finance and Industry. The former was established by solicitors who felt that the statutory functions of the Law Society hindered it from adequately representing all the interests of solicitors, while the latter arose from the refusal of the Bar Council to concern itself with the interests of barristers not actually in practice before the courts.

## Professional Courtesy

The earliest known propounder of professional ethics was Hippocrates, whose precepts were laid down around 400 B.C. He forbade physicians to quarrel jealously, competing among themselves. Those who did so were acting less like reputable practitioners than like "people connected with the business of the market place". (18) Medical practitioners have continued ever since to be concerned with standards of courtesy within the profession. A modern doctor "ought to behave to his colleagues as he would have them behave to him". (19) He must display goodwill and recognise the other fellow's point of view. (20) Solicitors are similarly enjoined, and are asked to display in relations with other members of the profession the maximum of frankness and good faith consistent with the overriding duty to the client. (21)

Examples of the courtesy expected are legion in the professional codes. An architect must not copy the design of another architect without his consent. (22) A dentist must not take advantage of information obtained during unsuccessful negotiations for a partnership. (23) There is a convention, but no rule, that a barrister must notify his opponent whose pleading he intends to strike out. (24) A solicitor should not communicate with the client of another solicitor without the latter's consent, though an exception is permitted where the other solicitor has consistently failed to reply to letters. (25) A solicitor should not use a tape-recorder to record a conversation in which another solicitor is taking part without first warning him. (26) An estate agent should not publicly criticise a competitor. (27) A dentist should do nothing to entice an employee from a fellow-practitioner's employment. (28)

As we shall see in more detail later, it is regarded as particularly heinous to seek to supplant a fellow-practitioner. Wherever a professional man is invited to act in a case where he has reason to believe a colleague was previously engaged it is his duty to notify the colleague. In some cases this goes beyond mere courtesy and serves to protect the public. Thus an accountant or auditor may be supplanted because he is unwilling to aid directors in pulling the wool over shareholders' eyes. An enquiry by his successor will bring this fact to light. The dentists' rule indicates the general approach:

> "When a dentist is consulted by a patient who normally attends another dentist, the reason for the consultation may be either to seek advice or treatment for some special condition, or to obtain advice or treatment owing to the usual practitioner, for some reason, being unable to give it. In the first case the patient's regular practitioner should be consulted, and in the second case only such work as is immediately necessary should be undertaken, unless with the consent of the patient's usual dentist. In either case no attempt should be made by the dentist consulted to secure for himself the permanent care of the patient, nor should a dental practitioner take the place of another during a course of treatment." (29)

Doctors have always been sensitive on the subject of second opinions, and meticulous rules are laid down. The doctors concerned "shall confer together with the utmost forbearance, and no one of them shall prescribe, or even suggest, in the presence of the patient, or the patient's attendants, any opinion as to what ought to be done, before the method of treatment has been determined by the consultation of himself and his colleague". Arguments must not take place in the patient's presence: "If any difference of opinion should arise, the greatest moderation and forbearance shall be observed, and the fact of such difference of opinion shall be communicated to the patient or the attendants by the physician who was first in attendance, in order that it may distress the patient and his friends as little as possible." (30) Thus the Royal College of Physicians. The B.M.A. go into more detail, and even lay down the order in which the doctor in charge of the case and the attending consultant should enter and leave the patient's room! (31) The doctor in charge "should carefully avoid any remark disparaging the skill or judgment" of the consultant. (32) Similar rules apply to dentists: "It should be appreciated that there is room for genuine differences of professional opinion on the scope and type of treatment needed in many cases and nothing should be said or done by either practitioner to disturb the patient's confidence in the other." (33)

Professional courtesy is to be observed even at the cost of financial loss. A solicitor who employs another as an agent should personally discharge the agent's costs whether or not he receives payment from his client to enable him to do so. In Sir Thomas Lund's words this is part of "the close and friendly relationship which ought to exist between us as members of one profession". (34) Similarly Sir Thomas feels that as between solicitors one's word should be one's bond. It should not be necessary for a solicitor to have committed himself to writing: "Even if it may cost you personally something to live up to what you have said you will do or refrain from doing, you should live up to it." Thus if a colleague says on the telephone that a solicitor may have another seven days to deliver a defence it should be known with certainty that this can be relied on, "and that you will not have a judgment snapped against you". (35)

## The Helping Hand

The solidarity of a profession is demonstrated by the readiness with which professional people help one another, particularly those in distress. With Francis Bacon, the true professional man feels a deep sense of obligation to his profession and everyone in it: "I hold every man a debtor to his profession". (36) A duty is felt to help those entering it, as by training apprentices or articled clerks. To take proper pains with the training of a young entrant is time-consuming and unrewarding financially. Yet upon the loyal shouldering of this burden by the established practitioner depends the wellbeing of the profession and the handing on of its practices and traditions.

As between qualified practitioners, the tradition of mutual help is exemplified by a willingness to discuss problems and give advice on them. The Bar Council points out that to a practising barrister "the influence of the other members of chambers and of a circuit mess, and the advice which they can give, are invaluable . . ." (37). The chambers system has no counterpart in any other profession; the close ties it provides give great cohesiveness to the Bar. Willingness to help is not limited to professional matters, and senior members will not withhold the benefit of their worldly experience on any personal topic. A senior will not stand on his dignity with a junior: members of the Bar, from the newly-called to the loftiest Queen's Counsel, address one another by surname (or Christian name) alone. Use of 'Mr.' or other prefix is a breach of etiquette.

Within the professional field, services are usually provided to a colleague without charge. The B.M.A. desire that "every effort should be made to maintain the traditional practice of the medical profession whereby attendance by one doctor upon another or upon his dependants is without direct charge." (38) The Bar has a similar practice.

Most professions have accepted a duty to provide for members who through ill health or age have ceased to practise. Benevolent funds are established for this purpose and dependants also share in their benefits.

The feeling of being part of a sympathetic brotherhood undoubtedly sustains private practitioners in what can be a lonely and precarious existence. The sense of solidarity, fostered by frequent meetings of colleagues, helps maintain the tone and spirit of a profession. Nor are such meetings necessarily confined to strict matters of business. Professional people are usually gregarious and sociable. They form local branches and hold meetings and dinners. Such activities nourish the roots of the profession as well as the bodies and minds of its members. The professional man who takes no part in them is depriving himself and his colleagues of many benefits.

## Disputes Between Members

"Never", said Hippocrates, "must a distinguished physician envy the others, for that might appear despicable." (39) There have always been some professional people who, for one reason or another, have fallen out with their colleagues. It is a concern of the professions to minimise the effects of such internal disputes, and therefore to provide machinery for settling them. Few have express rules on the subject. The usual procedure, where the matter cannot be disposed of by completely informal discussions between the members concerned and the secretary of the institute, is for the president to appoint one or two senior members to hear both sides and give a ruling. Sometimes this is only done where the disputants have previously agreed to abide by the ruling and not take the matter to the courts if dissatisfied with it. To litigate is to invite publicity, and it can only weaken a profession if fraternal quarrels are conducted in the public gaze.

## Inter-Professional Solidarity

How far does fraternal feeling extend? It is strongest of course between members of a single society. Where, as in accountancy or surveying, there are several societies the feeling spreads, no doubt in somewhat weaker form, throughout the profession. There is usually a "pecking order" and members of a senior body may feel little kinship with what they regard as the lower reaches of the profession. Often there is obscurity about where the line is to be drawn. By a bye-law of the R.I.C.S. a chartered surveyor is forbidden to allow any person to participate in his remuneration "other than a member of his own profession". The bye-laws throw no light on the meaning of this expression, but it certainly extends beyond R.I.C.S. members to what is known as the profession of the land generally. The bounds of this are left unstated, and there would be much argument if anyone sought to define them.

When it comes to relationships between professions a sense of solidarity is often found, though jealousies and rivalries may exist also. The similarity in their methods and organisation gives members of the consultant professions a feeling of kinship, and this is even recognised in some of the codes. Thus the Dentists' Code refers to "the general cordial relationship which should exist between the members of all professions". (40) The position is affected by whether members of the different professions commonly work together. Barristers and solicitors do so very frequently, and are often collectively referred to as the legal profession. Close relations also exist between doctors and dentists, and again between architects, surveyors and engineers. Inter-professional consultations frequently take place between the governing bodies on matters of common concern, though as yet no formal structure exists (see page 234). There is as it were a comity between professions, which manifests itself for example in respect for each other's rules of conduct. Thus, while there is no professional objection to a solicitor accepting a commission from an estate agent or surveyor in respect of business introduced to the latter (provided the client consents), the Law Society deprecates the practice on the ground that it is contrary to the rules of conduct of the bodies representing the other professions. (41) Comity is aided by demarcation rules, such as that preventing a chartered surveyor engaging in work "recognised as being properly that of a solicitor." (42)

Comity between the professions does not prevent occasional sniping. Solicitors object to the statutory rule prohibiting a solicitor from acting as an advocate in the county court in a case where he is the agent of another solicitor. The rule operates to the advantage of barristers, and the Law Society have roundly declared it to be contrary to the public interest. (43) Similarly the surveyors object to the architects' and accountants' rules prohibiting connection with house agency. (44)

Where two professions are in the habit of working closely together rules are developed to govern their relations, and these illustrate the comity of the professions. Thus a solicitor who has briefed Counsel accepts responsibility for the payment of brief fees whether or not the lay client pays up. Disputes between barristers and solicitors are not unknown however, and a tribunal exists for the purpose of settling them. This consists of a member of the Bar Council nominated by the Chairman and a member of the Council of the Law Society nominated by the President. This method of settlement was adopted at the suggestion of the Law Society and has been successfully used on many occasions. (45)

## Poaching of Clients

The biggest threat to the solidarity of a profession is the attempt to attract business by unfair means at the expense of one's colleagues. The attraction of business is felt to be most unfair and improper when it takes the form of deliberately poaching a practitioner's existing clients. This is regarded as a grave offence by all the consultant professions, and most codes contain express prohibitions. The most picturesque formulation is in the code of the Royal College of Physicians, which states that no member "shall officiously, or under colour of a benevolent purpose, offer medical aid to, or prescribe for, any patient whom he knows to be under the care of another legally qualified medical practitioner". (46) The international code of medical ethics states more succinctly: "A doctor must not entice patients from his colleagues." (47) The duty of an architect is equally plain: "Whether in private practice or salaried employment, he must not attempt to supplant another architect." (48) The consulting engineers go further and ban any intervention in engineering work by an engineer who knows the work has already been entrusted to another. Nor must an engineer review or take over work of another acting for the same client until he has either obtained the consent of the other or been notified by the client in writing that the connection of the other with the work has already been terminated. (49)

Nevertheless in all cases the professions are at pains to safeguard the right of the client to terminate the engagement whenever he thinks fit. No professional man worth his salt would wish to go on acting for a dissatisfied client against that client's will, and any attempt to bind a client to continue to retain a practitioner who had forfeited his confidence would be frowned upon by the professional institute.

Generally, it is not regarded as a sufficient answer to a charge of poaching to say that one was not aware the complainant had been retained. The B.M.A. lay down that a practitioner, in whatever form of practice, should take positive steps to satisfy himself that a patient who applies for treatment or advice is not already under the active care of another practitioner, before he accepts him. (50) This even applies in the field of estate agency, where touting for business is otherwise allowed — at least in the form of a letter individually addressed. Thus the R.I.C.S. bye-law laying down rules of conduct states that in work concerned with sales and lettings no member "shall, either directly or indirectly, orally or in writing, seek instructions for business which he knows, or with ordinary care could have ascertained, is in the hands of another agent". Even where there is no such knowledge or imputed knowledge by the estate agent a letter seeking instructions must contain what is known as the saving clause. This is "a definite intimation that if another agent has already been retained, instructions can only be accepted from, and as sub-agent to, that agent". Even a body so impatient of old-established professional rules as the National Association of Estate Agents lays down that where it is indicated by the client or otherwise that an agent has been appointed a *sole* agent a member must refuse to accept direct instructions, and can only act as sub-agent.

There are some situations which, by putting a practitioner in contact with the client of another, make it easy to poach. Special rules are laid down to deal with this. We have considered above some of the rules relating to cases where one practitioner is called in to give a second opinion. This was from the general viewpoint of professional courtesy. We may now briefly glance at rules directly concerned with poaching.

The chartered accountants have been worried about the problem of poaching in connection with firms specialising in management consultancy. This is traditionally a part of the accountant's function, but in modern times relatively few firms have made it a specialised part of their service. In consequence ordinary firms of accountants may find themselves needing to take specialised advice from another firm of accountants accustomed to act as management consultants. Inevitably the latter are brought into contact with the client, and there is an obvious risk that the original firm will lose him to the newcomer. The Institute have therefore laid down a rule that a member who belongs to a firm which undertakes management consultancy work should not normally accept conventional accountancy work from any client introduced to him for management consultancy services by the client's own professional accountant. The rule is designed to encourage and facilitate access by clients to consultant services which their own accountant is not able to provide. Without the rule, say the Institute, there would be a natural hesitation on the part of the accountant to introduce a potential rival. (A prominent member of the Institute has however expressed the view that the fear is exaggerated.) (51) This is a special rule to meet a special case. Most professions have for general purposes a rule such as that applying to the dentists: "The dentist consulted should not attempt to secure for himself the care of the patient sent in consultation, nor should he treat the patient then or subsequently except with the consent of the dentist who referred the patient." (52)

Another situation where poaching might easily arise is when a practitioner who has been connected with a practice, whether as partner, employee or *locum tenens,* later sets up in practice on his own account. The partnership deed or other controlling document will often impose a legal obligation, subject to the laws governing restraint of trade. Apart from the legal aspect there is an ethical obligation on the practitioner not to damage the practice with which he was lately associated.

The B.M.A. requires the written consent of the partners running the former practice before a doctor associated with it sets up on his own account within the same area. (53) Dentists have similar rules. In the words of a homely proverb, a man who transfers his practice must not "sell the cow and sup the milk".

A question may occasionally arise as to whether a patient or client of one practitioner has transferred himself to another. An approach may be perfectly permissible if made to one who is to be regarded as an existing client, but improper if the client has moved to another practitioner. For example a notice indicating change of ownership of a practice, or change of address, may legitimately be sent to existing patients but not to anyone else. The dentists deal with the matter by saying that a notice should not be sent to any patient of the practice who has not attended for treatment during the preceding three years. (54) It is presumably supposed that no one can go without dental treatment for any longer period, and therefore such a person must have acquired another dentist.

We have discussed in this chapter some of the more obvious rules and practices designed to preserve solidarity and harmony within a profession and among the professions generally. In the remaining chapters of this Part we examine in detail further rules dealing with the central feature of brotherly relations — the attraction of business. While the poaching of a colleague's client is obviously disruptive and unfraternal, ill-feeling is inevitably caused by *any* breach of accepted rules by which one practitioner steals a march on another. We turn first to the question of how, in the view of the professions, business ought to come.

K

## CHAPTER 10

# ATTRACTION OF BUSINESS

Medicine, it has been said, is a science; acquiring a practice an art. The professions have always attached great importance to the ways in which a practice is built up. Numerous rules have been laid down, and most of the remainder of this Part will be concerned with them. It is worth pointing out by way of introduction that there are two aspects to the matter. One is the *content* of the rules governing the attraction of business. The other is the fact that, whether or not a professional man agrees with the rules, if he does not obey them he is gaining an unfair advantage over his colleagues who do. There is no objection to anyone seeking to persuade his colleagues that a rule needs altering; until he is successful in this, however, his colleagues will feel very strongly that he ought to abide by it.

### "Letting the Work Come to you"

The essence of the professional approach to acquiring business is that it should be allowed to come without being actively sought by the practitioner. As the Law Society put it, the proper method is "by his name becoming known to prospective clients in the neighbourhood without the solicitor himself actively participating in that process". (1) The professions warmly agree with the view expressed by Thomas Carlyle in his *Past and Present* in 1843:

> "Nature requires no man to make proclamation of his doings and hat-makings; Nature forbids all men to make such. There is not a man or hat-maker born into the world but feels, or has felt, that he is degrading himself if he speak of his excellences and prowesses, and supremacy in his craft; his inmost heart says to him, 'Leave thy friends to speak of these; if possible thy enemies to speak of these; but at all events, thy friends!' " (2)

Admittedly the professions do not altogether prohibit a man from plates. We shall come to these in Chapter 12. Some practitioners perform in public and can make their abilities obvious. As the Bar

Council point out, much of a barrister's work is done in this way: "He can be judged by his successes and failures, by the quality of his public performance." (3) Most professional people however are not in this position, perhaps to their relief.

The building up of a practice can be very difficult, and the way is often particularly hard for newcomers. A family connection still counts for something. W.J. Reader, writing of the nineteenth century, observes that the professional classes, having got rid of aristocratic patronage in the public service, had no intention of doing the same for their own affairs. Openings in family businesses or practices, like family livings, were family property, only to go to outsiders under the most unusual circumstances. (4) Today there are still many old-established firms, especially of solicitors or surveyors, where representatives of each family generation take their place among the partners almost as a matter of course. Naturally they have to satisfy the increasingly rigorous demands of the examiners, and a fool will not be tolerated long even if he has managed to acquire paper qualifications. The Bar Council point out that a young barrister may benefit at the start from family connections, "but this is of no advantage to him (indeed may be a disadvantage) if he cannot sustain it by his personal qualities and performance". (5)

Skill is of course needed in building up a practice. The words of H.B. Thomson, a nineteenth century writer on the professions, are still apposite: "The great struggle is for a connection, and every art is necessary to extend it, so far as it can be done without . . . compromising the integrity of the mind." (6) Certainly a professional firm whose partners spend their entire time wrestling with problems of law or accountancy will not prosper, though it may be highly respected. Lewis and Maude put the point in perhaps a slightly cynical way: "There are contented and prosperous partnerships in accountancy, architecture, and several other professions, in which the labour is shrewdly divided between the partner who plays golf, bridge and billiards, attends cocktail parties and dances, and the partner who just does the work." Professional advertising, they add, is a little art of its own – clothes, manner, politics, technical and popular journalism, all play their part in it. (7) Are these authors accusing the professions of hypocrisy? It seems not – they merely recognise that realism comes into the matter, and it is a question of drawing the line in the right place. Undoubtedly the view taken by the law itself is widely supported. Lord Upjohn in *Dickson* v. *Pharmaceutical Society,* remarked that the professional man must submit to such "elementary" restraints as prohibition against advertising and touting. He added parenthetically: "but of course there is no harm in letting the work come to you". (8)

### Reasons for the Rule

Professional men and women do not easily find words to justify a rule they regard as fundamental. As the R.I.C.S. said in their submission to the Monopolies Commission, it is not altogether surprising that when professional people are asked why they refrain from commercial methods of obtaining business their reply is apt to be on the lines of saying "We are professional people; it is against our professional creed to do these things; and therefore we do not do them." (9) Nevertheless reasons can be found, and perhaps the most significant is that it is wholly to the public advantage if success in a profession comes through merit rather than other causes. Advertising, say the Bar Council, cannot advance the public interest; and may be detrimental to it. "The corollary is that, in a profession, success should depend only on individual ability." (10) It is also felt to be important that the public should have a free choice, and should not be directed or persuaded to consult a particular practitioner. The B.M.A. regard it as essential to safeguard the free choice of doctor or dentist by the patient. (11) The Law Society feel that "it should always be left to the individual freely and without pressure or financial inducement to choose his own solicitor." (12)

The professions believe that it is undignified to solicit business, and harms the confidence of the client in his adviser. Provided the public find no difficulty in learning the whereabouts of suitable consultants (a point we shall return to later), the professions regard canvassing and advertising as wasteful in time, effort and money. Good wine, they say, needs no bush.*

At the bottom of it all is probably the fact that people choose to go into a profession because they are interested in its expertise, perhaps being of a thoughtful or academic turn of mind. They often have little taste for the hurly-burly of commerce – if it were otherwise they would have chosen a different occupation. The point is well put in the R.I.C.S. submission to the Monopolies Commission:

> "We believe that all professions involve a vocation, a sense of dedication and a willingness to accept a measure of self-discipline as well as the ability to reflect deeply and sympathetically on the problems referred to them by clients.

---

\* E.S. Turner observes that this proverb inspires in an advertising man the same reaction as "the Lord will provide" does in an insurance agent – *The Shocking History of Advertising*, p. 105.

These qualities of mind and spirit are not called for in the
same degree in commerce or industry, where forcefulness,
ambition and enterprise (and sometimes even ruthlessness)
may be valuable assets from the point of view of the
national economy as well as the individual. It follows that
it is the function, and indeed the duty of a professional body
to seek to establish in the profession it represents conditions
which will attract to the ranks of that profession the right
type of recruit . . .
Ideals tend to be suspect in a cynical society, but the professional approach involves idealism; the professions are the
servants of truth and a professional man needs to be able to
apply this approach to the problems presented to him if he
is to give of his best to his clients. He needs some peace of
mind for this and if he has constantly to be looking over
his shoulder to protect his livelihood from deliberate poaching, his approach to his work, for he is human, will become
coloured by the need to protect himself . . .
The professional man has to make his living. We firmly
believe, however, that it should not have to be a professional man's prime preoccupation. The proper ambition of
a professional man is not to obtain more work for himself
at any price and without regard for his colleagues, but
rather so to improve his skill and the quality of the service
he provides as to attract more clients by the reputation he
builds up." (13)

### Gaining Work through Recommendation

A person needing professional advice, and having no first-hand
knowledge of the profession, is well advised to seek guidance from someone who has this knowledge. Often he will know of another person who
has faced a similar problem and received satisfactory professional advice
or treatment. He will naturally enquire of that person the name of the
practitioner concerned. In this way he will participate in the classic
method of building up a practice. As the British Optical Association put
it, "the whole basis of professional practice-building is by recommendations from satisfied patients or colleagues". (14) The professions are
not of course alone in this. Even in the commercial field advertising can
be relatively unimportant compared with recommendation from satisfied users of the product. Harris and Seldon report that in the case of
brands advertised on television most users when questioned attribute
their purchase to personal recommendation. (15)

Disinterested advice need not be sought only from satisfied clients. Those whose job brings them into contact with professional people, and who are themselves of unquestioned integrity, are very often in a good position to advise. The local bank manager can be relied on to recommend a suitable accountant or solicitor. A solicitor will recommend an estate agent, and so on. Indeed this form of recommendation may be more reliable than that of the individual satisfied client. The latter may have no basis of comparison, and may unwittingly have received below-average service which nevertheless satisfied him. The person who is in constant touch with several practitioners in the same field will acquire an accurate impression of their relative standing.

Some professions, such as law and medicine, are organised on a two-tier basis under which the prospective client or patient first approaches a general practitioner, who from his knowledge of the specialist services available advises on an appropriate consultant. This is one of the great strengths of the so-called divided professions. A family solicitor whose client needs specialised advice on a point of taxation, or patent law, or town and country planning, has a wealth of skilled advice available to him among barristers practising in the field. If the law were a unified profession this range of advice would in practice be restricted, since the lawyer consulted by the lay client would naturally wish to confine the client to his own firm if possible. Under the present system there may be a little chain of recommendation. Where the client of a country solicitor needs specialist advice the solicitor may first go to a London firm of solicitors familiar with Counsel practising in the field concerned, who recommend a barrister. He in turn may advise that a particular leading counsel's opinion should be sought.

Another important source of recommendations is the professional institute. If a prospective client tells the institute the nature of his problem and where he is located they will usually suggest the names of members who could advise him. To enable them to provide this service, the R.I.B.A. for example invite private practitioners to submit details of their capability, such as qualifications of partners and staff, buildings executed, photographs, etc., to be used as a basis for advising on choice of an architect for a specific job. Almost invariably the institutes will decline to name a specific firm alone, but will give a choice of three or more without indicating any order of preference. This is necessary because members are quick to resent any indication that their professional body regards them as sub-standard. Nevertheless if the institute is satisfied that the enquirer will not make trouble in this way it can sometimes be induced to indicate a preference. This is very valuable, because few outsiders have as much knowledge of individual practitioners as their own society.

## Attracting Business Unfairly

Solicitors are forbidden to do anything which is calculated directly or indirectly to attract business unfairly. (16) Other professions, while not using the phrase, apply what is in substance the same rule. We have incidentally considered some practices which infringe this rule, such as the sharing of premises and poaching of existing clients. There are many other types of infringement which are considered in detail in the remainder of this Part. Most of the rules are of long standing, though one ancient injunction to the medical profession is regarded by the General Medical Council as "démodé ": "Do not adopt, in order to gain a patient, luxurious headgear and elaborate perfume." (17)

## Taking Advantage

It is regarded as attracting business unfairly if one takes advantage of opportunities afforded by holding a post or other position giving contact with potential clients. The professions deal with this either by regulating the way in which new clients may be accepted or by forbidding the taking up of such positions altogether.

Where a salaried employee is allowed by the rules of his profession to take private work in his spare time he must exercise care in attracting clients. It is for example stated to be unethical for a hospital dental officer to use his position to influence patients to consult him in his private capacity, whether for dentures or otherwise. (18) Employers of solicitors often wish to use them to provide welfare services for other employees, for example free conveyances under a house purchase scheme. In agreeing to this the solicitor must observe the rules regarding attracting business unfairly. He must ensure that the employer neither directly nor indirectly touts for him, as would be done if the employer sent a circular round the staff stating that the services of the employed solicitor were at their disposal. A fellow-employee who consults him must be told that he is free to instruct any outside solicitor of his choice on equally advantageous terms. While the service to the fellow-employee may be free, this must not be achieved by any reduction in the normal remuneration payable to the solicitor for the service in question. In other words a "free" service to the employee must be paid for on his behalf by the employer. If the employee chooses to avail himself of the opportunity to consult an outside solicitor instead, he must be given time off to do so. (19)

Another case which has given the Law Society some anxiety is that of the solicitor working as a volunteer at a free legal advice centre. While this is not discouraged in itself, it must not be used to attract business unfairly. Where a solicitor is found to be acting for reward for a client first introduced through a free legal advice centre, it is presumed that an offence has been committed. "The presumption is not irrebuttable, but it imposes on the solicitor the onus of showing that the initiative resulting from his employment was entirely on the client's side, and that he himself did nothing to suggest that he was prepared to act personally in such a capacity." (20) In its submission to the Monopolies Commission the Law Society goes further and states that in such circumstances the solicitor cannot act for reward unless a waiver has been granted to him by the Law Society itself. (21) A barrister is bound by similar rules. "He should be particularly careful not to act in such a way as to give rise even to a suspicion that he is giving his services in order to obtain introductions to solicitors or for financial gain." (22)

Solicitors are subject to detailed rules preventing them taking advantage of the relationship with a client in order to attract business from other persons connected with the client. A company which is the client of a solicitor in private practice may for example be moving its factory and wish the solicitor to execute the conveyances on behalf of employees forced to move house. The same rules apply as govern an employed solicitor. It would thus not be proper for the solicitor to accept the instruction where the employer had told his staff that he would only defray their expenses if they employed the firm's solicitor. (23) A solicitor retained by a trade union or other association which wishes to supply its members with legal advice may only provide such advice if it is conveyed through the staff of the association and the identity of the solicitor is not disclosed. (24)

A solicitor is often in a good position to pick up business through existing clients. A client with funds to invest may become the mortgagee of another client who is buying property. The solicitor must not use the provision of mortgage money as a lever to secure the work of executing the conveyance. Similarly a solicitor acting for a house builder who is selling his houses with offers of free conveyances must ensure that purchasers are put in as good a position as if they had been separately represented, and must indeed enable them to be separately represented without financial loss should they so wish. (25) The Chartered Accountants Institute has found it necessary to warn members holding the secretaryship or other office of a trade association or similar body not to misuse their position for the purpose of obtaining professional work. "In particular a serious view would be taken of a member who used his influence with a trade association to obtain liquidation work." (26)

The possibility of taking advantage of the position to gain clients has led to rules prohibiting members of one profession from entering into a partnership with members of others (see page 85). For the same reason sharing of business premises is discouraged (see page 89). Little need be added here to the earlier discussion, and we content ourselves with a simple statement by the Bar Council, who impose the sternest restrictions of all: "A barrister who engaged in a second profession, business or occupation would have an advantage over colleagues in the sense that he would obtain or be in a position to obtain professional work at the Bar arising directly or indirectly out of his other profession, business or occupation." (27)

A censorious view is sometimes taken of the possibilities afforded by a wife's business activities. A chartered accountant is told that if his wife runs a secretarial service or an employment agency he must not use this to attract clients, and the wife's business ought to be carried on at a separate address. If the wife of an accountant set up to give advice on tax or any other accountancy subject the Institute would make very searching enquiries to make sure she was qualified to do so. (28)

In some cases the retiring holder of an office is expected not to return to private practice, where he may profit from the contacts he has made. This applies to a stipendiary magistrate contemplating return to the Bar. (29)

## Hob-nobbing

Professional people are sensitive about being seen in company with possible clients; they feel they may be thought to be seeking business. Taken too far, this would involve a self-imposed purdah, since in some professions the whole world is a potential client. The feeling is illustrated by Reginald Hine, a country solicitor, who had been lecturing to a village audience on mediaeval England. Afterwards, "a fine old country couple came up to me and said: 'Muster 'Ine, we proper fancied what you said about them 'dieval wills, and if you dunt moind the missus and me 'ud loike to 'ave ouren dun arter ther same fashun.' For a moment I was taken aback. It rather looked as though I had been touting for business." (30) A solicitor must be careful about whom he entertains, and tax inspectors have been known to disallow as a deduction for income tax purposes expenditure incurred in entertaining clients on the ground that such entertainment is contrary to professional etiquette. Sir Thomas Lund comments: "That ground for disallowing them is bad. It is not so. It would, no doubt, be unprofessional to entertain persons who were not your clients with the object of attracting business to yourself unfairly ... " (31)

The fact that barristers obtain their work only through solicitors has led to stringent rules restricting contacts by barristers with the other branch of the profession. A barrister must not seek out the company of, or unduly associate with, solicitors and their clerks. He must not have a seat in a solicitor's office, or become a member of a livery company of solicitors. (32) Until recently a barrister could not entertain a solicitor to dinner at his Inn of Court, but the rule is now relaxed. The restrictions are not confined to solicitors: "It has long been recognised that it is contrary to professional etiquette, as being a form of indirect touting, for a barrister to seek out the company of, or associate unduly with, persons (other than his personal friends) who are in a position to influence the sending of professional work to the barrister. Such persons include accountants, tax consultants, land agents, surveyors, consulting engineers and insurance agents." (33)

It is becoming common for people of different professions to attend conferences or seminars on matters of common interest. The passing of a new planning act or tax law may affect barristers, solicitors, accountants, architects and surveyors, and participation in the conference may well lead to the attraction of business. This is not regarded as objectionable, provided undue steps are not taken to give prominence to a practitioner or his firm. Chartered accountants, for example, are told that a member who is invited to give a talk, or to be a member of a panel or brains trust, or to attend a conference is expected to take reasonable steps to ensure that there will not be for the practice or professional business in which he is engaged any undue publicity. (34)

### Paying Commissions

It is often a temptation to a professional man to pay a commission (it might be called a bribe) to someone who can put work his way. This has occasionally given rise to scandal. In the 1860s, for example, one Frederick Marrable retired from the post of superintending architect of the Metropolitan Board of Works and set up in private practice. Another official of the Board put a proposition to him: "We are about to buy land for the Thames (South) Embankment. I shall meet with a number of claimants who are without a surveyor. I could say to them, 'Mr Marrable is a surveyor who has great influence with the Board, by reason of his former connection with it. If you put your cases into his hands he will get you a large compensation.' If I send such people to you, will you give me one-third of your fees?" Marrable accepted, and was sent many clients. The two men quarrelled over the commission payments and asked the great rating surveyor Edward Ryde to arbitrate. In the words of F.M.L. Thompson: "Very properly Ryde declined to touch the case, and when Marrable protested that he did not see anything wrong in the affair, he was given a straight lecture on professional ethics."(35) This is a nineteenth century example, but similar cases arise today and the danger to the public is obvious and real.

Most professions state explicitly that commissions should not be paid, and this applies even where there is no fraud or impropriety on the part of the recipient. The matter has already been dealt with to some extent in the discussion on fee-splitting (page 89). The chartered accountants justify the rule by saying that it removes the temptation for a member to bribe persons, "who would not otherwise introduce work or clients to the member, thereby inducing them to act against the best interests of any person so introduced". (36) There is also the point that if the full fee charged to the client is a proper one for the work done it follows that by giving some of it away in the form of commission the practitioner is putting himself in the position of being inadequately paid, with the consequent temptation to skimp the work. The rule is not limited to fee-splitting. In the version observed by the Bar it prohibits the giving by a barrister to anyone introducing business to him of any commission or present. This "would constitute most unprofessional conduct, and, if detected, imperil his position as a barrister". (37) The architects apply the rule to the giving of discounts or commissions in recognition of introductions *previously* effected. The Bar extends it to the granting of *any* favour, such as the lending of money to a solicitor. (38)

Further rules govern the attraction of business by touting or canvassing, advertising and undercutting. Each set is of sufficient complexity and importance to warrant a separate chapter. The question of whether the rules restricting attraction of business can be justified in modern conditions is explored in Chapter 14 (pages 199-211).

## CHAPTER 11

# TOUTING AND CANVASSING

Seeking for business may be direct or indirect. In this chapter we are concerned with more or less direct forms, where it is pretty clear to the person approached that he is being asked for work. We should first explain how the terms touting, canvassing and advertising are used. By touting we mean a direct approach seeking business from persons individually, as by a letter addressed to them by name. Canvassing is regarded as the circularising of prospective clients generally. Advertising means the seeking of business without direct contact with the prospective client, as by the use of mass media such as newspapers and television. It follows that touting may be done by letter, telephone call or personal visit. Canvassing will normally be done by use of printed circulars. Advertising will embrace virtually any other means of gaining publicity. It is immaterial whether the act is done by the professional man himself or someone else on his behalf.

The professional creed, as we have seen, is diametrically opposite to that of the advertising man who believes that "the public like to be asked for their custom and they naturally go to the people who invite them". (1) The professional view is invariably set out plainly in the code of conduct. A consulting engineer "shall not, either himself or through any person or firm, canvass, advertise for or solicit professional employment". (2) An architect "must not advertise for nor solicit business nor allow any member of his staff so to do". (3) A solicitor "shall not directly or indirectly apply for or seek instructions for professional business or do or permit in the carrying on of his practice any act or thing which can reasonably be regarded as touting or advertising or as calculated to attract business unfairly". (4)

The rule is of long standing in most professions. Sir Thomas Lund points out that before the rule governing solicitors was formally embodied in a statutory rule in 1936 there had been many decisions of the courts that a solicitor who touted for business was unfit to remain on the Roll, some of these being long before 1936. (5) The newer professions adopted it in their turn. As the R.I.C.S. said to the Monopolies Commission, the rule "is believed to be a fundamental rule of all the professions, and the profession of the land inherited it from the accepted practice and tradition of the older professions". (6) As we shall see, the surveyors did not however apply the rule to all aspects of their practice.

The rule does not only prohibit deliberate touting. As formulated by the Bar, for example, it expressly includes any act "which is calculated to suggest" that it is done for the purpose of touting. (7) The chartered accountants insist that the rule is not to be interpreted in a merely legalistic way: "A member is expected to carry out this principle in the spirit as well as the letter." (8) Members are supposed to use their own judgment in applying the rule, but in case of doubt are encouraged to apply for advice to their professional institute. Many professional bodies employ staff whose duties are concerned with little else than advising members on whether or not a proposed course of action would infringe the rule.

The rule is regarded by the professions as being for the benefit of the public. Thus the General Dental Council say that it is "contrary to the public interest and discreditable to the profession of dentistry for any registered dentist to advertise or canvass, whether directly or indirectly, for the purpose of obtaining patients or promoting his own professional advantage". (9) This is lent support by the way courts of law invariably uphold the rule when it comes before them. The rule is also backed by government departments. For example the Treasury impose, as one of the conditions under which approved auditors hold appointments under the Friendly Societies Acts and the Industrial and Provident Societies Acts, the stipulation that an appointment will be terminated if the holder solicits audits by advertisement, circular or otherwise. (10) The Bar Council defend the practice whereby Counsel are briefed through negotiations carried on not by them personally but by their clerks, on the ground that this is a further assurance of the maintenance of the high standards on which the public depend. (11) As we shall see, it was by reference to the public interest that the surveyors declined to adopt in its full rigour the rule against touting.

The rule is by no means confined to the professions in Britain. An American writer on medical ethics, Dean Willard Sperry, cites the following statement issued by the American Medical Association:

> "Solicitation of patients by physicians as individuals, or collectively in groups by whatsoever names these be called, or by institutions or organisations, whether by circulars or advertisements, or by personal communications is unprofessional . . . It is equally unprofessional to procure patients

by indirection through solicitors* or agents of any kind, or by indirect advertisement, or by furnishing or inspiring newspaper or magazine comments in which the physician has been or is concerned. All other like self-laudations defy the traditions and lower the tone of any profession and so are intolerable." (12)

## Approaches to Prospective Clients

Touting and canvassing are mainly thought of in terms of approaches to strangers who, it is hoped, will thereby be induced to become clients. It is possible, however, to seek a new assignment from an old client, or to attempt to persuade professional colleagues to farm out some of their own work. We deal with these two cases below.

We have said enough to show that direct approaches to strangers, asking them for work, are universally regarded as unprofessional, and little more needs to be added. Illustration is hardly necessary, but it may be of interest to give two straightforward examples from the legal field. Sir Thomas Lund tells us that it used to be very frequent for a solicitor retained to execute a conveyance on behalf of a vendor of land to write to the purchaser explaining the position and adding: "If you have no solicitor to act for you, I shall be very glad to do so." (13) This is now regarded as objectionable not merely as being a direct solicitation of business but as seeking to become the adviser of both parties to a transaction. The other instance was also formerly not uncommon. A solicitor in need of work would have an understanding with an official at the local gaol through which he would be notified of prisoners in need of legal advice. He would then ask for an interview with the prisoner on the ground that he had been instructed by friends of the prisoner to advise him. This was not only touting for business from a helpless and probably ignorant victim but also involved the further misconduct of lying to the prison authorities. (14)

Renegade professional men have often exploited the hapless position of people in trouble. Unscrupulous estate agents keep an eye on the deaths column of the local paper. They know that when a householder dies his house is often sold, and are quickly on the widow's doorstep, seeking instructions. A similar pest is the "ambulance chaser". Rarer than formerly but still extant he operates as follows. Through contacts with the police, firemen or ambulance workers, the so-called "claims

---

* The general reader may derive some amusement from the fact that in England a profession strongly opposed to touting for business should be known as "solicitors".

assessor" speedily hears of an accident involving personal injury and obtains instructions to prosecute a claim for compensation. This involves badgering the shocked victim or his immediate family, and getting a signature to a printed form which gives the tout the right to a percentage of any sum claimed. Usually this is 10% or more — far in excess of professional scales. While not members of a recognised profession themselves, these touts need professional help in prosecuting the claim. Solicitors have since 1936 been forbidden by a special practice rule from lending their aid. (15)

Sir Thomas Lund recalls a case long before this rule was made. A man was knocked down by a motor-car and injured. The local police constable, who had an arrangement with a "claims assessor" under which he was paid 10s. for every name submitted, telephoned this tout before asking the hospital to send an ambulance. The first the injured man's wife knew of the accident was the arrival on the doorstep of the claims assessor, who succeeded in getting a retainer from the wife and still managed to arrive at the hospital before the victim himself. (16) The British Hospitals' Association, disquieted by such practices, were grateful for the new rule. (17)

It sometimes happens that a person needing professional advice issues a general invitation to firms who might be interested in acting for him. Many local authorities maintain a panel of private architects from which they select firms to carry out a specific project. The R.I.B.A. code expressly allows architects to respond to an advertisement inviting inclusion in the panel. (18)

The only other matter calling for comment at this point is the special rule under which the Royal Institute of Chartered Surveyors and kindred societies expressly permit touting in relation to sales and lettings (page 130). As we have seen, the rule is strictly limited. It does not permit touting by telephone call or personal visit, or canvassing. In effect therefore it only allows an approach to be made by individually-addressed letter to the prospective vendor or lessor of property, and such a letter must contain the "saving clause" stating that if another agent has already been retained instructions can only be received from, and as sub-agent to, that agent. (19)

This relaxation of the no-touting rule does not represent a falling away from previous practice but rather the inability of a relatively new profession to match in every respect the standards of the older professions. Although the R.I.C.S. was founded in 1868 it did not issue any general rules of conduct until sixty years had elapsed. By that time there was considerable pressure from members of the Institution for a code of conduct to be laid down, and a circular condemning the practice of touting was issued in 1908. Many members of the Institution however derived a large part of their income from estate agency, which was nevertheless a depressed market. Numbers of dwelling houses stood vacant, and competition between agents was intense. If the Institution had forbidden touting in this field it would undoubtedly have lost many if not all of its estate agency members. This was felt to be against the public interest, since it would have removed from the estate agency field the influence of the Institution and other bodies seeking to raise standards. (20)

### Approaches to Existing Clients

The rule against touting governs the approach to existing clients, in that it prohibits any outright request for work. Approaches to clients are however permitted where there is no suggestion that work is being sought. Clearly the relationship between a professional man and his clients requires that from time to time communications of a general nature should be sent to them. Here the chartered accountants' rule applies throughout the professions, and any communication "should be dignified in content, manner of presentation and form of production . . . flamboyance should be avoided as being inconsistent with the dignity and standing of the profession". (21)

Clients may be informed of changes in the name, address or other particulars of the firm. They may be sent leaflets or brochures describing the services of the profession in general or those of the firm in particular. Some nervousness is however betrayed lest they should fall into strangers' hands. With this in mind the chartered accountants require any brochure describing a firm's services to be printed without the firm's name and address. (22) A number of professional bodies have recently prepared leaflets suitable for distribution in this way and explaining the services available from members of the profession. A series published by the Law Society comprises various titles in the form of a question: Buying a House?, Paying your Tax?, Starting a Business?, Spending your Money? and so on. In each case the answer supplied is of course "See a solicitor". Rather more personal questions are asked in the titles of similar leaflets published by the R.I.C.S.: Are You Structurally Sound? Are You Overrated? Are You Underdeveloped? Is It Worth It? The Institute of Chartered Accountants modestly contents itself with a booklet entitled *See a Chartered Accountant*.

Another type of circular often sent to existing clients relates to changes in law or practice which might affect the client's interests. The accountant or solicitor who sends round printed summaries of the latest Finance Act does his client a good turn. If the client is thereby jogged into thinking he needs more specific advice he knows where to turn for it, and there is no harm in that. In an ideal world a professional man who had advised a client on some matter would, where a later event such as an Act of Parliament rendered the advice in need of revision, notify the client accordingly. This would benefit both parties, but is seldom practicable. Another type of approach is where one client has money to invest and others may well be anxious to borrow. Indeed in such cases circulars need not be limited to existing clients. The Law Society has held it to be unobjectionable for a solicitor, when asked by a specific client, to circularise estate agents informing them that the client has a sum for investment in real estate. (23)

Somewhat more delicate is the question of when it is proper to remind a client that it is time he had another consultation. Only the dentists seem to permit this, perhaps because regular prophylactic treatment is most practicable in this field. The General Dental Council however sound a note of caution, and require such notification to be sent only with the previous agreement of the patient. (24) Doubtless this may be tacit.

### Approaches to Colleagues

The professions do not explicitly disallow touting which is confined within the bounds of the profession. In other words one member of a profession will not be disciplined for asking for work from other members. Exception might be taken to such touting if carried out on a large scale, as by circularising hundreds of members, (25) and there is always the likelihood that such approaches will be unsympathetically received. If handled properly however they can be useful, particularly where a firm offer specialist services beyond the scope of most practitioners. An example would be the offering of management consultancy services to an ordinary firm of accountants. Similarly the Institute of Chartered Accountants see no reason why pamphlets descriptive of the firm's services should not be sent to other firms of accountants. (26)

### Letter Headings

We have been briefly considering in this chapter approaches for business which are explicit in their intention. One final aspect of this which needs mention is the form of printed headings on letters, whether sent to clients or others. The contents of the letter may be quite harmless, but the form of letter heading may constitute a more or less obvious inducement to send work to the firm. Accordingly rules have been laid down. Obviously a professional firm would not consider

L

using the blatant kind of exhortation frequently found printed on commercial stationery. "Try Bloggs's tax avoidance technique" or "Have your next house designed by Snooks" are unlikely to be used, rules or no rules. The rules are there to deal with more subtle approaches. Merely to announce the name of the profession is held by some to smack of touting. A practising barrister may not use stationery giving his name followed by the words "Barrister-at-law". (27)* While the solicitors do not have this stern regulation, several old-established firms disdain to put on their note-paper the profession they follow. It is however a rule that a solicitor must not show that he is a member of a legal advice panel. (29)

Most professions discourage the use of a multitude of designatory letters or descriptions. The chartered accountants hold that members should be satisfied with the description "Chartered Accountant" and not add other phrases indicative of particular specialties; any addition to it, they feel, is apt to depreciate its character and value, and to draw special attention to details of qualifications and experience may appear to take a form of advertising. Other rules relate more to integrity than touting, for example the rule that if a professional man is a Justice of the Peace he should not add the initials J.P. to his name, since this would appear to be using his office as a means of professional advancement. Again, mention should not be made of worthless degrees. Sir Thomas Lund gives an example: "If you have obtained, let us say, from a gentleman living at Chipping Norton in exchange for a £5 note a certificate that you are a Doctor of Philosophy of the University of Sidi Barrani, that degree is not suitable for inclusion." He adds that this may sound unlikely "but it has been done". (30) Another instance based on preserving integrity is that there should not be printed after the firm's address "and at Paris" or "Madrid", followed by an address in that city, unless there really is a genuine branch of the firm there and not merely a foreign correspondent or agent.

---

* Some of the rules are very odd; for instance that allowing one employee of a local authority (the Clerk) to put 'barrister-at-law' on his official stationery while forbidding another (the education officer) to do so. (28)

## CHAPTER 12

# ADVERTISING

"There are rules of conduct which all professional men must observe. Refraining from advertising would, I think, clearly be one." These words by Lord Chief Justice Goddard in the case of *Hughes* v. *Architects Registration Council* (1) state the law's view of advertising and the professions. There are many other cases in which the courts have held that prohibition of advertising is an essential characteristic of a profession. (2) We have given above a definition of advertising and examples of professional rules prohibiting it (see page 143). Other brief statements of prohibition are: "An architect must not advertise, either directly or by any form of organised publicity paid for by the architect" (3); a medical practitioner "should not sanction or acquiesce in anything which commends or directs attention to his professional skill, knowledge, services or qualifications . . . or be associated with those who procure or sanction such advertising or publicity" (4); "it is contrary to professional etiquette for a barrister to do, or cause or allow to be done, anything with the primary motive of personal advertisement, or anything calculated to suggest that it is so motivated" (5).

The British Medical Association say that in considering this prohibition the word "advertising" must be taken in its broadest sense, and their view is shared by the professions generally. Anonymity is the aim of professional people, who feel that it should be departed from only where this is necessary in the interests of the general public or the profession itself. (6)

## Reasons for the Rule

As will be apparent from the preceding chapters of this Part, the rule against advertising is an expression of the belief that the professional man should not seek work but let it come to him. Nevertheless the particular abhorrence of advertising calls for more detailed examination. Lord Justice Singleton, in an address to young barristers, once said that "advertisement is looked down upon by all right-thinking members of the Bar". (7) This is the general view, and is usually regarded as self-evident. How has it come to be so firmly held?

To answer this question we need to take a look at the disreputable history of the advertising industry. Throughout the nineteenth century, the formative period in the working out of professional codes, advertising was held in low esteem. The techniques of advertising were crude, and roguery was rampant. As Harris and Seldon remarked in *Advertising and the Public:* "At a time when many people could barely read or write and before modern techniques of typography and block-making had been developed, advertisements relied for their attraction on tricks and sensationalism." (8) There was no scientific technique of advertising: "Spending money on advertisements and judging the result depended on the crudest guesswork." (9) The advertisements produced were often "crude, meretricious, vulgar and dishonest". (10) E.S. Turner, in *The Shocking History of Advertising,* comments that an advertiser, unhampered by codes of ethics, scarcely restricted by legislation, unconfused by market research theorists, had little to guide him but his own judgment of human nature. "The leading showmen did very well at the game, but lesser men spent huge sums of money on badly-orientated advertising which produced no dividend except public exasperation. Rather was it 'the brazen age of advertising'." (11)

One of the main causes of the mistrust and disgust aroused by advertising was in a field connected with a major profession. This was the peddling of quack remedies, an abuse going back at least as far as the Great Plague of London in 1665. Daniel Defoe, in his *Journal of the Plague Year,* describes how there appeared in the streets of London a rash of posters proclaiming "INFALLIBLE preventive Pills against the Plague. NEVER-FAILING Preservatives against the Infection. SOVEREIGN Cordials against the Corruption of the Air . . . " (12) Patent remedies and sovereign specifics have been peddled ever since, and are even today by no means unknown. Much has however been done to bring them under control, notably by the British Medical Association itself with the publication of its pamphlet *Secret Remedies* in 1909, followed three years later by *More Secret Remedies.* These contained laboratory analyses of some widely-advertised patent medicines; "analyses which made it all too clear that the public were paying heavily for rubbish". (13) Turner comments that the first B.M.A. pamphlet had a similar effect on the medicine mongers to that produced by Samuel Plimsoll's *Our Seamen* on the shipowners. (14) A House of Commons Select Committee on patent medicines was appointed, and its report "is one of the most disillusioned documents of the century and contains enough criminal plots to last a novelist a lifetime". (15) A.J. Clark, in *Patent Medicines,* showed that the medical profession itself was not immune from the effects of patent medicine advertising,

and obligingly increased its prescriptions when invited to do so by
the advertisers. (16) The economist A.S.J. Baster, writing in 1935,
found that the "shameful scandals" of the patent medicine business
were still a public offence, even in the most advanced countries. (17)

Quack remedies were not of course the only source of complaint in
the advertising field. They were the most notorious abuse however, and
Harris and Seldon observed that it was reluctance to be allied with
"quacks" that deterred many manufacturers from making use of mass
advertising techniques. (18) Punch commented "Let us be a nation of
shopkeepers as much as we please, but there is no necessity that we
should become a nation of advertisers". (19)

It is scarcely surprising that with a general belief, even among traders
and manufacturers, that advertising was "ungentlemanly", professional
people should react against it. They were moreover acutely aware that
their predecessors among the consultant professions had taken part
freely and with gusto in the scramble for business through puffing
advertisements. In the medical field it was not only quack remedies,
but quack consultants as well, whose virtues were proclaimed. Defoe
quotes some of these advertisements:

> An eminent HIGH-DUTCH Physician, newly come over
> from HOLLAND, where he resided during all the Time of
> the great Plague, last year in AMSTERDAM; and cured
> Multitudes of People that actually had the Plague upon them.

> An antient Gentlewoman having practised with great Suc-
> cess, in the late plague in this city, ANNO 1636, gives her
> advice only to the Female Sex . . . (20)

There are even earlier records of posters advertising surveyors in
London. John Norden in *The Surveiors Dialogue* (1607) depicts a
farmer saying "As I have passed through London, I have seen many of
their bills fixed upon posts in the streets, to solicit men to afford them
some service: which argueth, that either the trade decayeth, or they are
not skilful, that beg employment so publicly". (21)

Another example, this time from the field of dentistry and dating
from the eighteenth century, is furnished by a Mr Gray, of the Royal
College of Surgeons, who announced an "unprecedented" development
in dentistry: he could fit artificial teeth constructed without springs,
wires or other anchoring devices. They could thus be taken out "with the
greatest facility", cleaned and replaced by the wearers themselves. (22)
Carr-Saunders and Wilson cite abuses in dentistry going on well into the
twentieth century. Dental companies began to flourish about 1906.

"Skilled in touting, advertising and canvassing, they employed men lacking any training and were able in most cases to avoid financial liability for injury." The departmental committee appointed to examine the working of the Dentists Act 1878 found in a report published in 1919 that there was nothing to stop any person, however ignorant, from practising dentistry and informing the public by advertisement and otherwise that he did so. The unregistered practitioner "is frequently a charlatan attracting business with blatant advertising or unscrupulous touting, who being subject to no control or professional code of ethics, brings discredit on the dental profession". (23) As a final example, take the following advertisement from the Economist of 1844:

> MANLY VIGOUR: a Popular Inquiry into the CAUSES of its PREMATURE DECLINE with instructions for its COMPLETE RESTORATION . . . Illustrated with cases, etc. By C.J. LUCAS & CO., Consulting Surgeons, London . . . Messrs Lucas & Co. are to be consulted from ten until two, and from five till eight in the evening, at their residence, No. 60 Newman Street, Oxford Street, London, and country patients may be successfully treated on minutely describing their case, and enclosing the usual fee of £1 for advice. (24)

It is scarcely surprising that uninhibited advertising of this kind, particularly in the field of human health, should induce practitioners to conclude that advertising needed to be brought under strict control. It was not felt to be enough however merely to require advertisements to be honest. The mere presence of advertisements could bring those responsible into disrepute. For example much public indignation was caused by defacement of towns and countryside through advertisement hoardings until the matter was brought under control by town and country planning legislation. Estate agents came in for their share of obloquy, through the proliferation of sale boards and other advertisements (see page 166).

While the unpopularity of advertising generally, and of medical advertising in particular, no doubt predisposed professional people against making use of it, this is not the whole story. Advertising has lost much of its former disrepute, and dignified professional institutions think it no shame to advertise the profession in the daily press and elsewhere. Yet we find the Law Society saying in 1968 that the prohibition is needed to preserve the dignity of the profession. (25) This is open to the objection that if it is undignified for an individual to advertise it must also be undignified for his professional body to do so, yet the Law Society engages in advertising. The medical profession is more consistent. The B.M.A. take the view that advertising on behalf of the profession "would certainly destroy those traditions of dignity and self-respect which have helped to give the British medical profession its high status". (26) They thus apply to the professional bodies themselves the same rule as restricts individual practitioners.

A reason often given for the no-advertising rule is the need to maintain the relationship of trust between client and practitioner. Dr Johnson once remarked that "promise, large promise, is the soul of an advertisement". The professions want the public to trust them, but dislike making promises express or implied. The Law Society argued before the Monopolies Commission that the need for trust renders certain common commercial practices incompatible with professional services. They cited Carr-Saunders and Wilson: "Professional men may only compete with one another in reputation for ability, which implies that advertisement, price cutting, and other methods familiar to the business world are ruled out." (27) The British Optical Association say that to achieve the necessary relationship of trust and confidence the client must have consulted the practitioner because of his accredited knowledge. "If his motive in consulting the practitioner is that he is cheaper or because he advertises better than someone else, he will not have this true confidence." (28) In their submission to the Monopolies Commission, the British Medical Association also argued that advertising would diminish the trust and confidence which a patient should repose in his doctor. They cite the recent case of the alleged cure for lukaemia made by M. Naessens as having caused disastrous effects through the publicity given. "Patients and their relatives had their hopes raised unjustifiably and the delicate relationship between seriously-ill patients and their doctors was gravely compromised as a result of this publicity." The B.M.A. go on to argue that if advertising were allowed, those aspects of medical practice which would attract the most interest as advertising material would inevitably be the most sensational and not those which characterised professional competence and expertise. (29)

A further argument used by the professions to support the no-advertising rule relates to the cost of advertising, and has several facets.

The purely economic argument runs as follows. Professional services differ from manufactured goods in that they are rendered individually and thus are not susceptible to the economics of standardisation and mass production. The argument that advertising increases demand and enables economies of large-scale production to be achieved therefore does not apply. This does not of course mean that the demand for services cannot be increased by advertising, but the increase will only be marginal in view of the restricting factor represented by the limited number of professional practitioners. Indeed an undue increase in demand would almost inevitably lead to a dilution of standards, since unqualified people would be drawn in to meet the demand and the existing practitioners would be tempted to skimp their service. The Law Society argue that it is not for a professional man to create a demand for his expertise — "indeed it is just because the demand is always there and the public have needed protection against the charlatan and the incompetent that his profession exists at all". (30) Is the demand always there however? Perhaps it is in the case of solicitors, though the Law Society still finds it necessary to publish its own advertising material (see page 146). Again, it could be argued that a practitioner would not spend money on advertising himself or his firm if he were already working full-time. If he thought it worth spending money on advertisement this would presumably be because he had some slack and could therefore absorb more work in his office. This has some plausibility, but the professions would argue that if advertising were accepted it would be necessary for *all* practitioners to spend money merely in order to prevent loss of existing business. This would be wasteful.

Another aspect of the cost factor in advertising relates to the maintenance of equality between practitioners. Professional firms usually have little capital — the rules we have considered in Part II of this book preclude the raising of capital by means open to commercial companies. Often professional people have nothing except their own acquired skills and native intelligence to keep them going. As the British Optical Association put it, in a profession all men, theoretically, have equal chances of success. "If one man can afford to advertise and does, while another cannot, this equality is disturbed." (31) Lewis and Maude make the same point: "The practitioner with large reserves of capital must not be allowed to use this (*sic*) to influence the public's judgment of his qualifications, prowess or suitability." (32) The last word may be given to the Bar Council:

> "If barristers were permitted to advertise, the advantages would go, not to the best qualified, but to the barrister with the longest purse and the least scruples. If the choice of barristers came to be made by the general public on the strength ·of advertisement, the choice would tend to be more ill-informed and the public not so well served as at present. If it became common for barristers to advertise, and all were compelled to fall in with the practicee, the costs of a bar rister's services would inevitably go up." (33)

In the nature of things there cannot effectively be a complete prohibition of all forms of publicity, and in the remainder of this chapter we consider in some detail the rules which have been devised to regulate essential advertising and draw the line between publicity which is allowable or at least venial and the rest. Before going on to these detailed rules we look briefly at one or two general points.

The rules are mainly designed to govern professional people in private practice. Since they are ultimately directed to means of attracting business they have little relevance where the person concerned is not in the market for business. Thus "publicity is rightly allowed to medical men not in actual practice of their profession". (34) This does not mean however that it is a defence to a charge of advertising to show that no pecuniary or other benefit was to be derived from it. "A doctor who attempts to justify unduly frequent publicity on the grounds that it cannot benefit him professionally is doing a disservice in that he makes it more difficult to condemn similar activities on the part of others who do stand to gain thereby." (35) In a recent instance the Bar Council went so far as to condemn a barrister who, in writing a preface to a legal textbook, was held to have "puffed" other practising members of the Bar specialising in the subject of the book. (36)

The extent of the no-advertising rule is not limited to Great Britain. Usually a member of a British professional body is expected to observe the rule so far as advertising in overseas countries is concerned. A dispensation may however be granted where the corresponding professional body in the country concerned permits advertising. The Bar Council state that advertising by a barrister that he is in practice, or intends to practise, is prohibited abroad as well as at home. (37) The ethical rules of the legal profession in Commonwealth and foreign countries are in the main similar to those prevailing in Britain. (38)

Finally we might mention that not all professional bodies carry the no-advertising rule to the same lengths. In particular some professions, such as the chartered surveyors (but not chartered quantity surveyors) and patent agents permit "card" advertisements — that is a simple advertisement giving the name of the firm and a brief indication of the type of practice (see page 161).

### Putting up the Plate

In a corner of Lincoln's Inn Fields, well back from the road, stands a large Wren building. To the casual passer-by its use appears obscure, since the exterior bears no indication whatever of who or what the occupants are. In fact it houses Farrer & Co., solicitors to royalty and the aristocracy, who prefer to practise in discreet anonymity. In this they resemble the firm of Frobisher & Haslitt in A.E.W. Mason's *The*

*House of the Arrow,* written about 1920. It was "the real thing as a firm of solicitors", and this was the reaction of the senior partner when a newcomer to the firm suggested that they ought to have a brass plate upon the door:

> "Mr Haslitt's eyebrows rose half the height of his forehead towards his thick white hair. He was really distressed by the Waberski incident, but this suggestion, and from a partner in the firm, shocked him like a sacrilege.
>
> 'My dear boy, what are you thinking of?' he expostulated. 'I hope I am not one of those obstinate old fogeys who refuse to march with the times. We have had, as you know, a telephone instrument recently installed in the junior clerks' office. I believe that I myself proposed it. But a brass plate upon the door! My dear Jim! Let us leave that to Harley Street and Southampton Row!' " (39)

Though Mr Haslitt's attitude is not unknown today, neither the solicitors nor any other profession go so far as to prohibit the placing of the name of the firm outside its premises. As the B.M.A. put it, "it is generally accepted by the profession that certain customs are so universally practised that it cannot be said that they are for the person's own advantage, as, for instance, a door plate with the simple announcement of the doctor's name and qualifications". The B.M.A. adds sternly that even this "may be abused by undue particularity or elaboration". (40) While no profession prohibits the display of the name of the practitioner or his firm, the Bar carries the concession no further. A barrister may not have the words "barrister-at-law" outside the place where he lives or has chambers. (41) Oddly enough, however, there is no objection to the letters "Q.C." being appended to the name. In this way, since most people know the significance of these initials, the senior member of the profession may enjoy an advantage over his juniors.

There is some lack of consistency about the reason why the brass plate or its equivalent is allowed. The most rigorous view is that taken by the dentists, namely, that the plate is purely to indicate to those who already know of the practice the location of, and entrance to, the premises at which the practice is carried on. (42) This also seems to be the attitude of the solicitors. (43) The doctors on the other hand say that the door plate on a doctor's house or branch surgery is the means by which he indicates to the passing public his availability as a medical practitioner. (44) The difference may be explained by the fact that doctors are often needed in emergencies involving life and death — though if this is really the reason it is surprising that doctors are directed that the plate should be unostentatious in size and form.

The professions go to some pains in telling members how far they may go in making their presence known. The size and positioning of the name plate, where it may be fixed, the type and size of lettering, the information to be displayed, and the degree of illumination are all laid down in detailed directions. A doctor's plate may bear his name and qualifications, and "in small letters" his surgery hours. Descriptive wording such as "Psychiatrist" or "Consulting Surgeon" is not permitted. (45) The solicitors have similar rules, though indications of actual offices held, such as Commissioner for Oaths or Notary Public, are permissible. An exception is membership of a legal advice panel. (46) Dentists regard it as unethical to exhibit the telephone number of the practice on professional plates. (47)

The British Dental Association go so far as to specify the maximum size of a name plate. For a partnership the aggregate area of the plate or plates shall not exceed 24 inches x 18 inches. For practitioners working on their own account the limit is 18 inches x 12 inches. (48) Several professions specify the maximum size of lettering; architects and dentists both favour a maximum height of two inches. Chartered accountants refrain from laying down the maximum size of lettering and say that "it should be able to be read without strain by the average person with the normal complement of eyes". (49) Solicitors are told that the size and design of the plate and lettering is really a matter of taste for them to decide, although it has been held to be "quite improper" to put the firm name and the description "Solicitors and Commissioners for Oaths" in gold letters about a foot high right across the width of the building. (50) Illuminated signs are frowned upon by the professions, although some have permitted these in exceptional circumstances. A solicitor whose office was in a dark arcade, the entrance to which was entirely surrounded by neon lighting, was allowed "modestly to illuminate his own name plate". Sir Thomas Lund, in giving this example, stresses that "I do not mean that a neon sign flashing on and off would commend itself even in Piccadilly Circus". (51) The chartered accountants have also firmly refused to allow flashing neon signs "or any of the other manifestations of modern advertising techniques". (52)

The question of where a name plate may be put has caused the Law Society difficulty. The general rule is that the plate must only be put on premises where the profession is actually carried on. This is not always straightforward however, particularly where the profession is carried on part-time, perhaps from a private residence. Accommodation addresses are frowned upon: "In no circumstances whatever may the plate be put outside the house of clients or friends even though it states that the solicitor will attend there on request, or that messages may be left for him there. That is highly objectionable." (53) The doctors stress that a trainee should not have a door plate, and a doctor should not put up a name plate on premises he proposes to occupy at some future date. (54)

## Posters and Hoardings

Advertisement of a firm by the use of posters, hoardings or other outside displays is in general forbidden, at least where no purpose of a client is thereby served. Only two exceptions need be noted.

Architects, engineers and quantity surveyors are allowed to put up boards indicating the names of their firms on building sites where the firms are currently engaged. The R.I.B.A. imposes limitations of size "as much for aesthetic reasons as to prevent ostentatious advertisement". (55) The Institute has produced boards of a standard size and design, and other professions have followed suit. These boards, in their standard colours of grey and white for architects, red and white for consulting engineers, and blue and white for chartered quantity surveyors, have become familiar features wherever buildings are constructed, altered or extended. While use of this board, rather than any other type, is not compulsory it is strongly recommended. Chartered surveyors are not allowed to use such boards where the work in progress is of an unimportant character.

The second exception arises in the case of chartered surveyors in general practice. The business of many of these consists wholly or mainly of house agency. In order to enable their members to compete with rival agents not subject to professional rules, the R.I.C.S. allows "restrained and dignified" name boards to be displayed. Unless these serve the purposes of the client, however, they are required to be located only within the precincts of a railway station, a coach station or an airport. Specific rulings have prohibited their use at, for instance, bus-stop shelters or within buses and trains. Other rulings have forbidden the use of sandwich men and town criers. (56)

It should finally be noted that rules against advertising do not prevent an architect from allowing his name to appear permanently on the outside of a building which he has designed, provided it is not done in an ostentatious way. Indeed the Architects Registration Council go so far as to say it is desirable that an architect should sign his buildings. (57)

## Directories

The professions are nervous about the use of directories. They recognise that there needs to be available for reference a comprehensive list of practitioners, giving addresses and other necessary information. They see a danger on the other hand that such lists will be used for the attraction of business. No one, they feel, should select a practitioner merely on the basis of an entry in a directory. Rules have been laid down to discourage this.

Most professions publish a list of members, and in the case of the registered professions copies of the register are published. The form of these lists is under the control of the professional bodies and many would prefer their members to refrain from inserting their names in any other directories. Such a restriction is not possible, however, since official works of reference such as telephone directories, and reputable compilations such as Who's Who, would be seriously incomplete, to the disadvantage of the professions, if their members were excluded. Nevertheless barristers are forbidden to include their names in the classified telephone directory. Doctors take the robust view that since their telephones are paid for at the business rate it is sensible to allow their names to be included among the businesses set out in the classified list. (58)

While the official roll of members is not always published directly by the professional body concerned, it is normally produced with the full co-operation and assent of the professional body and is therefore presumed not to infringe professional rules. Hitherto such directories have confined themselves to the barest details of members' names, addresses and telephone numbers. The R.I.B.A. however broke new ground in 1968 with the publication of its Directory of Practices. A fee is charged for the inclusion of a firm's name in this, and firms are permitted to go into considerable detail as to the nature of their practices and the type of work undertaken. They are even permitted to give a list of projects carried out by the firm. The publication of this list was challenged by a rival professional body, very much smaller than the R.I.B.A. This was the Incorporated Association of Architects and Surveyors, which went so far as to issue a writ attempting to restrain publication of the directory. The Association claimed that the directory was contrary to the spirit of professionalism and unfair to the small practice. Indeed it went further and claimed that the directory was a breach of the requirement laid down by the Architects Registration Council that an architect "must not advertise, either directly or by any form of organised publicity paid for by the architect". The I.A.A.S. considered that publication of the directory would cause dissension among architects and could well mislead members of the general public because the information included in it would refer solely to an architect's successes and exclude any of his failures. The writ was later withdrawn "owing to abstruse legal technicalities". (59) Such a directory is of course open to the precise objection mentioned above, namely that it is likely to be used by clients to select an architect, whereas they would be better advised to seek recommendations from persons with practical knowledge (see page 136). It is surprising therefore that the R.I.B.A. should commend the Directory on the ground that it would 'greatly assist potential clients, client organisations and members of the public in making appraisals of suitable firms prior to commissioning new work'. (60) At least a word of warning should have been added as to the dangers of relying on the Directory alone.

In relation to directories other than those produced by or under the auspices of the professions, certain rules have evolved. A fundamental rule is that the directory must be open to all members of the profession equally, or where it is confined to a particular area must be open to all practitioners in that area. The R.I.B.A. Directory of Practices infringes this rule, since it is only open to architects who are members of the R.I.B.A. Also objectionable would be a list of members of a body such as a local chamber of commerce, listed under particular trades or professions. Since this would exclude a firm in the area which did not choose to belong to the chamber of commerce, and would have the tendency of inviting those into whose hands the directory fell to confine their custom to firms listed in it, it would offend the notion of equality of treatment. (61)

Another rule commonly found is that precluding the use of leaded type or other devices to give special prominence to a practitioner's name. The chartered accountants make a special exception in allowing a telephone directory entry to be in small leaded type. This is a recent relaxation by the English Institute. The Scottish Institute had long allowed the use of leaded type in this way, and in a praiseworthy desire to secure uniformity the English Institute came into line. Croxton-Smith comments that "it is doubtful whether many members will bother to take advantage of this relaxation, but there seems to be no harm in it". (62)

The professions discourage the use of directories to give biographical details likely to attract business, or the names of clients or details of services offered by a firm. Sir Thomas Lund gives the example of a solicitor who took a whole page in the Irish Law List and filled it with the names of firms for whom he acted as professional agent. (63)

## Advertising in the General Press

The professions draw a distinction between advertisements in journals confined to members of the profession or those closely connected with it and advertisements in newspapers and periodicals circulating among the public generally. For obvious reasons, considerably more latitude is allowed in relation to the specialist press. With few exceptions, advertisements of a professional man or his firm inserted in the general press will offend against professional ethics.

The principle is that information which it is essential to convey to clients of the firm and others having dealings with it may be communicated by advertisement provided no unnecessary matter is included. Notice of a change of address or telephone number, or of the retirement of a partner or the dissolution of a partnership, or of the addition of a new partner may be advertised generally. Preferably there should be only one insertion. The solicitors refuse to allow advertisements of the opening of a new office, though the chartered quantity surveyors allow this. Also disallowed by the solicitors is an advertisement giving a change in office hours, though there was one occasion where, provided the description "solicitor" was omitted, one insertion in the local press was allowed where a firm reversed a century-old practice of closing on Wednesdays and opening on Saturdays. Where a rumour was circulating that a solicitor had retired from practice the Law Society declined to allow him to advertise that this was false. The man who decides to give up practice and seek paid employment is allowed to advertise for a job, and the chartered accountants have expressly permitted a firm to advertise the examination successes of its articled clerks. (64) An advertisement for salaried employment inserted by an architect in the general press must be anonymous. (65)

Certain professions do not disallow advertisements giving brief factual details of a firm, sometimes known as "card" advertisements. Among these are chartered surveyors and, according to Carr-Saunders and Wilson, patent agents. (66) The chartered surveyors' concession (which does not apply to quantity surveyors) allows, in addition to the name, address and telephone number of the firm, such descriptive phrases as "rating valuations and appeals"; "rent collections" and "surveys". Not allowed are phrases such as "Call in and discuss your housing problems with us". References to specialisation are only permitted where the member concerned is in fact a specialist; "otherwise they lose all significance". (67) In explaining the concession to the Monopolies Commission, the R.I.C.S. contended that "card" advertisements are "in essence an extension of the office plate". (68) In his presidential address, given in the centenary year of the Institution, Mr Oliver Chesterton criticised the concession and suggested it might be limited to advertising in recognised technical or professional journals. "I note with regret", he added, "a tendency for these card advertisements to be elaborated far beyond the spirit of the existing directions and I do not believe that the public should be subjected to the subtle pressure of the public relations man in fields where professional skill and integrity are concerned." (69)

The solicitors extend the rule against advertising to foreign news-papers and periodicals, and other professions would doubtless follow suit. It seems that the rule may indeed be more severe in its overseas application: Sir Thomas Lund states that "all personal advertisements of the solicitor which describe him as such are objectionable in the foreign press". (70)

## Press Reports

The attitude of the professions towards press publicity is slowly changing. The old dislike of publicity is giving place to a realisation of its value when not abused. The traditional attitude is exemplified by the doctors, barristers and solicitors. After somewhat grudgingly admit-ting that exception cannot reasonably be taken to publication in the lay press of a doctor's name in connection with a factual report of events of public concern, and that it is usually unexceptionable for a doctor's name to be included in a report of a social occasion, they go on: "Never-theless the name that is always occurring, sometimes in unlikely places, may well be suspect." Publicity-seeking medical men have long been the bane of the profession and the resentment of their colleagues is expressed by the B.M.A. with suitable restraint: "It is not beyond th' wit of man to manage to appear prominently and frequently in s ficient places for his name to become better known than would be ordinary sequel of good professional reputation. Ambition may s sede conscience and modesty." (71) The solicitors relaxed their somewhat in 1968, but the new version still reminds practitione "there are many things innocent in themselves which by the ma frequency of their doing may contravene the principle that s should not advertise". (72)

Professions which are beginning to welcome publicity incl architects and accountants. The R.I.B.A. encourages publi architecture and the work of members in contributing towards i and national newspapers increasingly carry news about build the architects who have designed them and, "although this so arouses dissatisfaction in members not so favoured" the welcomes this publicity provided the obligation to avoid oster self-advertisement is observed. (73) Similarly the Institute of Ch Accountants takes the view that while no member should active publicity for himself, it is in the interest of the public and the prof that appointments, awards and similar distinctions of members sl be suitably reported in the general press and that the report sh mention membership of the Institute. (74) In a relaxation of previ rulings, which was announced towards the end of 1968, the Institute gave members further encouragement in obtaining publicity within proper limits.

The traditional attitude of the professions towards publicity has been rather like that towards the attraction of business; if it comes at all it must come unsought. Thus what might be called "feeding the press" is frowned upon. A solicitor should not seek or inspire an interview with the press, except on his client's instructions and on that client's business. (75) A medical practitioner should not sanction nor acquiesce in anything which commends or directs attention to his professional skill. (76) Even the architects, who welcome publicity, prohibit a member from giving any monetary consideration as an inducement to the publication of descriptions of his work. (77) Chartered surveyors are allowed to supply the press with factual statements of property transactions and material for market intelligence. Where a doctor finds a press report commenting favourably on his professional activities or success, he is required by the B.M.A. to take action since "these statements cannot fail to place the named practitioner in a critical and embarassing situation, and this should not be allowed to pass unchallenged". (78) The action recommended is to send a latter of protest to the journal concerned, marked "not for publication".

The B.M.A. take the view that the appearance of a doctor's photograph in connection with any reference to medical subjects in the lay press is "a most undesirable form of publicity". (79) The Bar also frowns on the publication of photograph of members, though there is no objection to a barrister's portrait in robes appearing in an art exhibition. (80)

## Books and Articles

The health and progress of a profession depend upon its expertise being described and developed. Members are therefore encouraged to write textbooks, articles for the specialist press, and similar material. When they do so it is right that their names and qualifications should appear on the work. So far there is no difficulty. An infringement of the rule would however occur where an essential theme of the publication was the commendation of the skill and abilities of the writer himself. It is accepted that, in the words of the Privy Council in a medical case, "the hope that some legitimate meed of personal advancement will result may find its place among the motives of writing and may be the spur to command the industry that the task may require". (81) If however this natural feeling gets out of bounds and results in self-praise, the author will be in trouble.

M

Writing for a lay audience is a different matter. The professions do not encourage the transmission of their expertise directly to the general public, and self-diagnosis, self-medication and other forms of self-administered advice are considered dangerous. Nevertheless it is recognised that there is a legitimate public interest in professional doings, and that very often this can only be properly satisfied by a writer having professional qualifications. Strict rules are however laid down.

The professions differ on the question of whether the author's name and qualifications may appear together. Most of them now allow this, while discouraging mention of a firm's name as well. The Bar however continues to prohibit mention in the lay press of the professional qualification in addition to the author's name. Other rules usually applied include prohibition of any laudatory editorial reference to the author's professional status or experience, or of references to privately-owned institutions with which the author is professionally associated, or the entering into private correspondence with lay readers. A medical practitioner must not be a party to the publication in the lay press of medical articles of a sensational nature. (82) Irrespective of any specific rule, the General Medical Council "is conscious of the fact that certain contributions could not fail to promote the professional advantage of the author, who must shoulder the responsibility for any such result and be prepared if challenged to answer for it before a professional tribunal". (83) A barrister who writes for general publication any account of cases in which he has appeared is required to do so anonymously unless he has given up practice. (84)

### Broadcasting and Lecturing

The rules governing the transmission of views otherwise than through the printed word necessarily take a similar line. The enormous impact of television, with its attentive audience of millions, obviously gives great opportunities for self-advertisement. So far this does not appear to have caused serious difficulty.

In the early days of broadcasting anonymity was the rule. This has now been relaxed by all professions except the Bar. The B.M.A. have explicitly recognised that the policy of anonymity in all circumstances is no longer tenable, and do not now object to the announcement of a doctor's name. Where the circumstances of the broadcast specifically require it, mention may also be made of the branch of medicine in which the broadcaster specialises and any appointments held. A doctor engaged for a series of broadcasts is nevertheless advised to remain anonymous "lest the frequency of mention of his name should be held to be unethical". (85) Doctors are not allowed to appear as such in television advertisements, and other professions would no doubt follow this rule.

In a relaxation of rules made in 1968, the Law Society and the Institute of Chartered Accountants permitted members to broadcast under their own names and with mention of their professional qualifications. This is still forbidden by the Bar Council and the R.I.C.S., who require to be consulted in advance about such broadcasts, and to lay down conditions as to the manner in which members may be described. These restrictions do not apply to broadcasts on non-professional topics, provided membership of the profession is not mentioned.

The rules governing lectures and addresses are similar, though in some cases not quite so stringent. A barrister giving a lecture on a legal subject is allowed to describe himself both by name and qualification. Perhaps strangely, he is not allowed to give his qualification if the lecture is on a non-legal topic. (86) Doctors lecturing to a lay audience are advised to request the chairman beforehand not to make laudatory remarks in his introduction. (87)

## Advertising in Specialist Press

The editors of journals circulating wholly or mainly within a profession are usually aware of professional proprieties and careful to observe them. Furthermore a professional man knows very well that there is little to be gained, and much to be lost, from puffing himself in the professional journals. Clearly it is permissible to publish any advertisement in the specialist press which would be allowed in the general press (see page 160). In the specialist press greater latitude is allowed as respects the giving of information about the operation of a firm — particularly evidence of its growth, as by the opening of new branch offices. In some cases it is even permissible to advertise for work. The chartered accountants used to have a concession, designed to help new entrants to build a practice, whereby private practitioners seeking work were allowed to advertise the fact in the accountancy press. This concession was fully used, and the columns of the professional press contained many advertisements seeking part-time or sub-contract work. By no means all of these were by younger members attempting to start a practice, and the Institute came to the conclusion that the concession was being abused and withdrew. (88)

Some of the rulings given appear inconsistent and difficult to follow. Solicitors are told that advertising under a box number that a solicitor is prepared to undertake missions abroad as an agent for other solicitors is unobjectionable in the legal press. On the other hand a similar advertisement in the legal press that a solicitor is prepared to act as a London agent for country firms is held objectionable as offending against the rule regarding touting. (89)

## Advertising on Behalf of Clients

Where a person has obtained a professional adviser to handle certain of his affairs, it is very often necessary, in connection with that function, to publish advertisements carrying the name and address of the professional adviser. This presents an obvious loophole for obtaining publicity.

The professions recognise that nothing can be done to prevent a solicitor from advertising that his client wishes to become a naturalised citizen or to trace a beneficiary under a will, or a chartered accountant from announcing that his client wishes to acquire a particular type of business, or an estate agent from carrying out his function of informing the public of the properties in his books. In all such cases it is natural that the professional man's name and address, and professional qualifications, should appear in the advertisement. All the professions can do is require that they should not be given undue prominence or be embellished with unnecessary detail. Certain restrictions have been laid down however. It is "highly objectionable" for a solicitor to publish his name, address *and* description on an advertisement whereby a client offers specific property as security for a mortgage investment, or a specific fund as being available for investment. (90) It has also been held objectionable to have a solicitor's name on a poster offering a reward, though it is common practice for solicitors' names and addresses to appear on posters giving particulars of auction sales. (91)

Property sales are a special case, since their successful prosecution often involves lavish publicity. The agent's name cannot escape being associated with this, and there is little the professional bodies can do about it. The R.I.C.S. has advised its members that there should normally be only one board displayed on a property. Its appearance and the announcement on it should be "in good taste", and the board should at all times be kept in good order. Once the sale has been completed the board has served its purpose, but many agents like to keep the board in position adding the words "sold by" before their names. This of course is a pure and simple advertisement for the firm, rather than the property, and moreover gives the impression that the firm is a successful one. The R.I.C.S. has not felt able to ban this practice completely, but limits the period within which the board may be displayed in this condition to one month. Rules of this kind are not entirely in the interests of pure professionalism. It was noted by the Estates Gazette as long ago as 1908 that "there are few more certain methods of depreciating a street than to fill it with 'to let' boards". (92)

Unrestrained proliferation of sale boards can cause damage to amenity which lowers the price of property (and thus the commission obtainable by the agent) and also harms the reputation of the agent, whose name on the board proclaims him the obvious cuplrit.

Estate agents' permitted advertising is not limited to the requirements of clients themselves. An estate agent usually acts for the vendor of property, but if a prospective purchaser tells an agent that he is seeking a certain type of property the agent is allowed to advertise his requirements. In an attempt to limit this obvious loophole the R.I.C.S. and kindred bodies require an agent who publishes such an advertisement to disclose the name and address of the applicant if called on to do so. These advertisements are particularly awkward because not only do they give publicity to the agent but they also explicitly seek instructions. This arises because property owners answering the advertisement may be expected to place the expected sale in the hands of the agent publishing the advertisement. The R.I.C.S. defend the concession as being in the public interest because it assists applicants to be put in touch with vendors. (93)

Chartered surveyors are sometimes worried lest the permissive attitude of their institution towards advertising be looked at askance by other professions. They may take comfort from the fact that the Law Society, in its submission to the Monopolies Commission, found justification for estate agents' advertisements: "whereas a member of the public may obtain the services of any solicitor to act on the purchase of a property which he has already found, his normal way of finding a property is through the estate agent on whose books the property happens to be". (94)

## Advertising by Clients

Occasionally clients of professional people wish to publish advertisements which incidentally include the information that the professional person concerned is acting in the matter. This gives rise to the same possibilities of exploitation as advertisements by professional people themselves. While a professional man cannot directly control the advertisement published by his client, he has the ultimate sanction of refusing to go on acting. If he acquiesces in the publication of undesirable advertisements he will be held responsible by his institute.

Certain cases have given particular difficulty. The chartered accountants have been embarrassed by the long-standing practice of building societies publishing advertisements, often "flamboyant and unrestrained", which include the information that a specified firm of chartered accountants is acting as secretary or agent of the society. The standard of building society advertisements has steadily improved in recent years, and the problem has ceased to be pressing. (95)

Manufacturers of building components very often wish to puff their wares by stating that they have been used by specified architects. This is another case where inveterate practice has tied the hands of the professional body. The Architects Registration Council have felt compelled to allow an architect to permit the publication of his name in this way provided it is not ostentatiously displayed. The concession does not of course extend to soliciting by the architect for the use of his name, and an architect must not allow the advertiser to state in the advertisement for his product that it is *recommended* by the architect. (96)

The Law Society has ruled that it is undesirable for the name of the builder's solicitor to appear in advertisements for the sale of houses on an estate. There is however no objection to the name of the vendor's solicitor appearing in an estate agent's auction particulars, provided it is not given undue prominence. (97)

### Advertising for Staff

Plainly a thriving professional firm needs to recruit staff from time to time. The use of display advertising is becoming common for this purpose, and to attract staff of the desired calibre it may be desirable to describe the job and its opportunities in glowing terms. Here again there is an opening for blatant advertising of the firm itself and rules have been laid down to deal with this. Chartered accountants are required to observe precise rules governing the size of the advertisements (not exceeding two columns in width), the type to be used (of modest and uniform boldness), the sort of headings which may be employed and so on. (98) Croxton-Smith comments that the rules have worked very well "and the law of the jungle which prevailed a few years ago no longer operates". (99)

The R.I.B.A. forbids members to advertise for staff in the lay press by the use of display advertisements. Nor must they refer to the work of their practice "in fulsome terms designed to catch the attention of clients rather than potential staff". (100) The disciplinary committee of the Architects Registration Council has more than once published warnings that advertisements for staff in the lay press should be issued only with a box number, without mentioning the advertiser's name. The committee also objects to advertisements for staff containing photographs of buildings designed by the advertiser. (101)

### Advertisements by Consultancy Organisations

In certain fields the professions have been plagued by lay organisations set up to provide cut-rate consultancy services. In order to be able to function at all these bodies have to employ members of the profession concerned and to advertise their services. The professional bodies regard advertising of this kind, at least where the names of members of the profession are given, as being just as reprehensible as advertising by the individuals concerned.

A notable example of this type of organisation is the medical aid society. These grew up to meet a need caused by the shortage of doctors in general practice and, before the advent of the National Health Service, were common in many of the poorer districts. Readers of A.J. Cronin's *The Citadel* will remember the way these bodies operated, at least in South Wales. They would be run by a committee of mine managers and other prominent laymen, and would employ doctors on a salaried basis. Patients would be attracted by canvassing and advertising so as to provide a sufficient number to make the organisation financially viable. The employed doctors would be forced to accept far more patients than they could properly deal with. The General Medical Council reacted by forbidding registered practitioners to take employment with such bodies. Private practice still of course continues alongside the National Health Service, and there are today organisations in the form of provident societies which advertise their services. Mention of a doctor's name in such advertisements would carry the risk of disciplinary proceedings being brought against him.

Another type of consultancy organisation which has caused trouble to the profession concerned is the management consultancy company. Many such organisations follow the no-advertising rule of the professions, and little difficulty arises. It is a rule of the Chartered Accountants Institute however that a member may not be a partner, director or employee of any such company which does advertise its services. Even where the advertising is indirect, as by the insertion of advertisements for staff giving the name of the consultancy company in prominent lettering, members are discouraged from belonging to it and must certainly not allow their names to be used in connection with its advertisements. The Institute has not however felt able to prevent its members taking employment with other organisations which offer consultancy services and advertise, such as joint stock banks. The somewhat unconvincing reason given is that with such a body its accountancy services "are subsidary and incidental to its main business". (102)

## Advertising by Professional Bodies

As we have seen, some professional bodies (though not all) have in recent years come round to the view that the undesirability of advertising does not extend to advertisements on behalf of the profession as a whole. The professions have been treading gingerly in this matter, and have used the attraction of new entrants as a peg on which to hang much of their advertising. It seems somehow less objectionable to extol the virtues of a profession, and describe the services it can offer, in the context of advising young people on their future careers; and the chartered accountants in particular have taken advantage of this. The climate of opinion has already changed since Millerson, writing in 1964, remarked that associations consider direct canvassing for members "unethical", or "unprofessional". (103)

Many members of professional bodies are currently urging their institutes to embark on advertising campaigns, and often the only restraining factor is lack of finance. The justification is given by the Institute of Chartered Accountants in its submission to the Monopolies Commission, where it recognises that "it is important for the public to be informed of the services which its members can provide and that it is desirable in the interest of the public no less than of members generally that the use of these services should be encouraged". (104) *

* For an example of the way institutes, as well as individuals, can get into hot water over advertising see page 159

## CHAPTER 13

# THE FEE SYSTEM

Lord Bramwell once accused equity practitioners of complicating the law of mortgages through "love of fees". If he was right they were not true professional men, for these practise their profession "uninfluenced by motives of profit". (1) Laymen have not always found this sentiment convincing, as Hilaire Belloc showed with his physicians who "answered, as they took their fees, 'There is no cure for this disease.' ". The attitude is genuinely held however, at least by the majority of professional people, and stems from the fear that a relationship which is personal and often intimate may be vitiated by the passing of money. Barristers still call their remuneration an honorarium to which they can lay no legal claim, and wear on the backs of their gowns the vestigial remnants of the pocket into which golden guineas could be slipped unobserved. Fees then are only taken with reluctance, because everyone has to live. It follows that there can be no haggling, no taking a slice of the proceeds, no contingency arrangement of "no win no fee", and above all no unfraternal undercutting.

All kinds of reasons are advanced to justify rules against bargaining over fees. The true professional man is really only happy when doing the work of his profession; he dislikes wasting time arguing over money. Barristers leave such matters to their clerks. Most other professions get round the problem by laying down a scale of fees which provide a yardstick.

Some commentators ascribe dislike of bargaining to fears that dignity might be undermined. "For the consultant to descend to the market place," says Millerson, "might disturb the delicately-balanced superiority of his position". He goes on to give a more respectable reason: to quarrel over payment may destroy the ideal of public service. (2) The architects see a threat to trust, and they mean not only the client's trust in the competence and integrity of his adviser but the adviser's trust that the client will recognise his allegiance to high ideals and will pay fairly for his services. The R.I.B.A. describe how this trust would be eroded:

"Bargaining seems bound to make each party look narrowly

to their own foreseeable interests, and make each doubt that
the other can have more than his own interests in mind
when the bargain is made and the work is in progress. Price
competition seems bound to make the architect seek ways
of reducing costs that cannot be noticed by the client as
affecting his interests; and to make the client suspect that
competing prices reflect differing standards of service, while
hoping that somehow he can get a service adequate to his
own interests cheaper than is usual." (3)

It seems clear that bargaining with, say, architects would produce
different levels of fees for the same work. Its effectiveness would of
course depend on the relative strengths of the parties. Where the client
was a powerful local authority or commercial corporation, whose connection promised much, the architect would be in a weak position. With a
private client whose future requirements were likely to be small the
position would be reversed. This would inevitably produce varying
standards for the same type of work and firms would be tempted to
choose the most profitable level of operation. Institutes would tend to
concentrate on advising their members how to be most profitable,
instead of how to be most efficient. (4) The typical reaction of the
professional man to this prospect was expressed by the R.I.C.S. President
in 1968: "At a time when society is very consumer-conscious, the
suggestion appears to be that the client should be able to 'shop around'
for professional services in rather the same way as he shops around for
groceries. I am afraid the professions are not susceptible to the '3d off'
treatment . . . " (5)

The professions feel that the only way to avoid the dangers inherent
in the bargaining process is to insist on payment by fees arrived at in
the traditional manner. As the Architects' Code has it, a professional
man in private practice "is remunerated solely by his professional fees".
He is debarred from any other source of remuneration, and must not
allow his staff to receive such remuneration in his stead. (6)

The essence of the professional fee is that its amount, or at least
the basis for its calculation, is determined before it is earned, and is so
determined to the knowledge of the client; that it does not depend on
any contingency in order to become payable; that it is based on the
size of the task; and that it is not unfair to other members of the
profession. The rules by which these principles are secured will be considered in detail in the remainder of this chapter. Their essential basis
is indicated by the practice of barristers. In general a barrister must
not appear in court unless his fee has already been marked on his brief.

Counsel must be separately instructed and separately remunerated for each piece of work done, and cannot accept a fixed fee which will be the same for all cases. He must not, when taking a brief, agree that payment shall be postponed, or habitually accept a lower fee than would be allowed on taxation of costs. (7)

## Payment by Results

It might be thought that to pay a man according to the success of his efforts was sound and sensible. The professions do not think so. They feel this attaches the adviser too closely to the outcome of his advice, impairing his detachment and tempting him to devote more effort to causes likeliest to succeed. With lawyers it may encourage blackmailing actions in the name of men of straw. Most professions therefore have the rule laid down by the Chartered Surveyors: "No member shall offer to accept instructions on the basis that no charge will be made unless a successful result is attained." (8) Exceptions are occasionally allowed.

One consequence of the rule is that work made abortive by the abandonment of a project should be paid for in full. If this is not done the adviser is accepting some of the risk that the project will go off: in other words participating in a speculation. In condemning this practice the R.I.B.A. point out that it is likely to be an unwise course for an architect anyway. His work is seldom a major factor in determining whether a building project goes through, and the architect may in effect be dependent on financial and property management expertise outside his control. (9)

Impeccable though this reasoning may be, clients often want to pay by results, and object to paying for abortive work. The professions are not always able to resist this pressure. The ancient medical codes, embodied in the laws of the Visigoths or the Babylonian Code of Hammurabi, provided that the doctor whose "cures" led to the death of the patient should forfeit his fee. Today, the chartered accountants permit payment by results in the case of bankruptcies, liquidations and receiverships. (10) Chartered surveyors engaged in sales and lettings are permitted to charge a contingency fee, and this is the normal practice for all estate agents. The professional societies concerned with estate agency consider it to be of fundamental importance to the public that an agent unsuccessful in securing a sale or letting should not be entitled to a fee. In a submission to the Monopolies Commission on an enquiry into house agents' fees, these societies commented:

"To most people the sale of a house is the biggest kind of

transaction to which they are ever a party, and one in which the average person is not involved more than two or three times during his whole life. It is a serious step for the person affected to take; it often involves a good deal of personal upheaval and unforeseen expense; and it can in many respects be a worrying time for the person concerned. There is one substantial consolation to him during the whole period when he is arranging to move. He is not charged for the house agents' services unless the house is sold. He does not receive a bill in respect of services carried out on his behalf unless he has actually received a proportionately larger sum in respect of the house itself." (11)

## Suing for Fees

As mentioned above, barristers cannot as a matter of law sue for their fees. The weight of this limitation is effectively borne by the solicitors who instruct them however. It is a rule of etiquette of the solicitors' profession that the solicitor is personally liable for payment of Counsel's proper fees whether or not he has received money from the lay client with which to pay them. (12)

The only other restriction of this kind applies to doctors who are Fellows of the Royal College of Physicians. Here the limitation arises under a bye-law of the College, which provides that no Fellow shall be entitled to sue for professional aid rendered by him. The bye-law has statutory force.

Reader regards these rules as a "curious quirk" and seems puzzled by them. (13) They are merely a reflection however of the general reluctance of professional people to embark upon lawsuits with their clients. Nothing more destructive of the true professional relationship can be imagined, and such litigation is very rare. Most professionals would rather forego their fees than sue, even where it is clear that their relationship with the client in question is over in any case. Other clients and potential clients might well be put off by the spectacle of a public wrangle over fees, or indeed any other aspect of professional services.

An instance of the working of the "no suing" rule, and one which illustrates incidentally the comity of the professions, was mentioned in the 1967 report of the Medical Defence Union. An anonymous barrister was alleged to have consulted a doctor and then declined to pay his fees, relying on the rule mentioned above. The Chairman of the Bar Council protested that such conduct was most unlikely in a practising member of the Bar, and would be regarded by the

Bar Council as most unbecoming. (14)

## Overcharging

Some professions, though not all, regard overcharging as in itself reprehensible. Solicitors have been held guilty of professional misconduct in charging "grossly excessive" fees, but for this charge to stick there must be something more than a mere agreement to charge fees higher than those which would be allowed on taxation of costs. (15) If the client thinks the bill he has received from his solicitor is too high he can apply to have the bill "taxed" by the court. This is a process whereby a Master of the Supreme Court goes through the items in the bill to see that the charges conform to the scale. A similar procedure applies in the County Court. Without prejudice to this right of taxation the client may require his solicitor to obtain a certificate from the Law Society, certifying that the sum charged is fair and reasonable or, if it is not, what would be a fair and reasonable sum. This latter procedure is entirely free to the client, and he can be compelled to pay no more than the amount certified by the Law Society.

The Institute of Chartered Accountants does not take any disciplinary action on complaints of overcharging. Their reason is that it is open to an aggrieved client to challenge the fee charged by refusing to pay it and submitting the issue to examination by the court. (16) This overlooks the possibility that the fee might be fixed by a contractual agreement, which would necessarily have to be enforced by the court.

One argument in favour of fee scales is that by laying down a fixed rate they make overcharging more difficult. This depends on the type of scale however: a scale which determines fees according to the time spent on the work may in effect facilitate overcharging. The client may well have no means of knowing whether the time spent was reasonable, or was inflated by laziness or inefficiency.

It is not usually regarded as overcharging for a fee to be increased because of the greater experience and skill of the practitioner. Very great variations of fee are recognised at the Bar, and among consultant physicians, on this score. It is one of the criticisms of *ad valorem* fee scales that they disregard this factor.

## Minimum Fees

Few professions prescribe minimum fees, and only the architects do so through the whole range of their work. The R.I.B.A. maintains that the distinction between its own mandatory scales and the "recommended" scales of other professions is "a distinction without a difference", since all scales are treated in much the same way in practice. The Institute firmly believes that:

> "An explicitly negotiable fee system such as would result from a "recommended" scale would not work successfully; and the negotiable elements in the fee system have not worked well in the past. All the disadvantages in permitting price-bargaining and competition apply. If the obligation to [conform to the scale] were explicitly abandoned, it would have the effect of serving notice on clients that they could seek to negotiate fees with their architects with some hope of success, and the architect is ill-placed to negotiate fair terms with many of his clients." (17)

The minimum fee requirements of the Bar are in a different category. Whereas architects' fees are nearly always charged at the "minimum" rate laid down by the scale, the barristers' figures are a true minimum. They are inadequate for all except the most inexperienced counsel, and are usually exceeded in practice. The minimum fees are £3 5s 6d for a Q.C. and £2 4s 6d for a junior barrister. These figures were fixed in 1951. They were then intended to be the amount which inexperienced counsel could reasonably ask for the smallest item of work. (18) For many years it was a rule of the Bar that where a junior counsel appeared with a Q.C. he could not be paid less than two-thirds of the Q.C.'s fee, unless the latter amounted to more than 150 guineas. The rule was abolished in 1966.

The National Board for Prices and Incomes rejected the R.I.B.A. contention that there is no distinction between architecture and the other professions over fee scales. The Board attached importance to the fact that two of the other professions submitting evidence to them had made it clear that while their recommended scales were broadly followed in practice, they recognised that the parties in any individual case must have freedom of action. (19)

### The Role of the Institute

The present position under which most professional institutes regard it as part of their function to advise members generally as to the fees they should charge is of fairly recent origin. Moreover where such advice is given, as by the creation of a fee scale, it does not come out of the blue but is derived from the practice prevailing among individual firms before any general advice was laid down. In the case of the chartered surveyors, for instance, the professional institution refused to lay down any fee scale until as late as 1914. Until then it took the view that fees were the concern of individual surveyors, and that it would risk being confused with a trade union if it gave general advice to its members. Thompson, the historian of the surveyors' profession, holds that it was Lloyd George's land taxes which led the Institute to abandon its attitude of allowing members to charge what they liked. "Regarding the land taxes as revolutionary, the Institution itself took the revolutionary step of beginning to draw up a scale of fees to be charged under the land clauses of the Budget . . . " (20)

The Institution of Civil Engineers shared the surveyors' original views, and did not change its mind. It was on this ground that the civil engineers opposed attempts to obtain a statutory registration system for architects in the 1920s. The R.I.B.A. first issued a scale of fees in 1862.

The Institute of Chartered Accountants takes the view that fees are in general a matter for negotiation with the client. The Institute does not prescribe any fee scale, though this is mainly because it believes the nature of accountants' services does not lend itself to such treatment. The Institute has nevertheless become anxious, following an extensive enquiry, that "despite the pressure, engendered by competition, to improve efficiency and keep costs down, fees charged are often inadequate to make the rewards of professional practice . . . sufficiently attractive in competition with other occupations". (21)

Where members of a profession frequently carry out work for particular types of clients their professional institute will often negotiate a special scale of fees. The British Medical Association negotiates national agreements with life assurance companies in relation to medical examinations. The Bar Council similarly makes representation to the authorities concerned with the level of barristers' fees, for example in relation to criminal prosecutions. The Institute of Chartered Accountants negotiates with the Treasury on fees to be paid for government work.

What institutes are chary of doing is intervening where an actual dispute between client and practitioner has arisen. Since such a dispute could end in litigation it is obviously necessary to avoid seeming to predjudice the legal proceedings. Nevertheless informal advice is not infrequently given, and the availability of this can be a source of comfort to practitioners. One solicitor records how his client, the novelist Ursula Bloom, frequently sent him instructions in verse. He felt obliged to respond in the same manner, and included in his bill an item "to mental strain replying to your letters in verse". He adds "I have often meant to ask the Law Society what one could rightly charge in such abnormal cases. If it would sanction three shillings and sixpence or even one shilling a rhyme, I would turn poet and compose all my letters in verse." (22)

## Fee Scales

There are various types of fee scales, using the term in the broad sense as including not only "price lists" or percentage rates but any formula by which the amount to be charged can be calculated. The "price list" is a primitive form of scale. The Code of King Hammurabi, around 1700 B.C., laid down a fee scale of this kind which varied according to whether the patient was of high rank, a freeman or a slave. For opening with a bronze lancet an abcess in a freeman's eye, and healing it, the surgeon was entitled to five shekels of silver. For curing the broken bone of a slave, or a sickness of his bowels, a doctor was entitled to two shekels of silver. The hazards of medical practice in those times are indicated by the fact that a surgeon who treated an abcess in the eye of one of high rank and caused the loss of the eye was liable to have his hands cut off. If this mishap occurred with a freeman the surgeon had to forego his fee and give a slave to the patient. If the sufferer were a slave a penalty of half the fee was exacted. (23) In our own times the method of charging is usually based either on the value of the subject matter (*ad valorem*) or on the amount of time and trouble taken (*quantum meruit*). These are discussed in more detail below.

Whatever the mechanics of the scale, it will normally be designed to produce a certain level of income. When the surveyors adopted their scale in 1914 it was partly based on an unofficial scale for surveying work in compensation cases first produced over half a century earlier by the distinguished surveyor Edward Ryde. At a time when there was no means of distinguishing qualified and unqualified surveyors, Ryde's scale served to mark those who adopted it as "competent surveyors whose services were available at a stated tariff, men who would not exploit a particular situation by charging more, and men who sought employment for the quality of the service they offered rather than for its cheapness". Those who did not adopt the scale were thought of as men who depended on their cheapness for securing work, rather than a high level of skill. (24)

Factors governing the level of remuneration produced by a recommended scale include "what the market will bear", what is necessary to produce an economic return covering costs with a reasonable margin for profit, and the competitiveness of substitute providers of the service. The solicitors regard their scale, which is fixed by a statutory committee, as indicating "the proper economic level" for their charges. (25) The Bar Council, while not laying down a scale as such, pitch their recommendations at a level designed to produce a "fair" return. (26) The Prices and Incomes Board noted that a feature which occurs with some regularity in all forms of charging is that the charge is higher if the value of the work increases, even though no extra effort may be involved. This is of course a typical feature of the *ad valorem* scale. The Board considered that it could be explained by the fact that higher-value work involves greater responsibility and demands a higher level of insurance cover. (27)

There are a number of cases where certain items in fee scales are governed by statutory provisions, though the only cases where this applies widely are those of the solicitors and the medical profession.

According to the Prices and Incomes Board, solicitors are in a unique position in that their's is the only profession whose charges are subject to the control of an outside body. (28) This overlooks the extensive statutory controls on the remuneration of medical and dental practitioners. At least two-thirds of the total income of solicitors is determined by statutory bodies. In contentious matters, where litigation is involved, the scales of charges are regulated by Rule Committees. The system of charging in non-contentious business provides for remuneration in relation to sales and purchases of property, mortgages, leases, settlements and similar matters to be fixed by a committee consisting of the Lord Chancellor, the Lord Chief Justice, the Master of the Rolls and the President of the Law Society and one other solicitor. The main reason for this close control is that ever since the Statute of Gloucester 1278 there has been a rule in litigation that the unsuccessful party has to pay the reasonable legal costs of the successful litigant. This differs from most other legal systems, and the courts have always felt it a duty to ensure that the heavy burdens thus thrown on unsuccessful parties should not be greater than reasonable. Although nominally independent in the scales they fix, these committees are at the time of writing subject to political pressures. The Lord Chancellor indicated in 1968, for instance, that the advisory committee would not have a free hand in assessing fees but would be meeting to give effect to the recommendations made by the Prices and Incomes Board in its report on solicitors' remuneration. (29)

The statutory controls applying to medical and dental practitioners operate (with insignificant exceptions) only in the field of the National Health Service. They do not therefore govern fees paid by the patient. They are nevertheless framed in an attempt to reproduce so far as practicable conditions of private practice. Medical consultants in private practice can vary their fees to accord with their professional standing. In relation to Health Service work, where the remuneration comes from public funds, this is scarcely possible. By a system of "distinction awards" or "merit awards" an attempt has been made to bring the

N

cases into line. An almost entirely medical committee determines the amount of these awards and the persons to whom they should go. The Pilkington Commission, while finding it unusual for large sums of public money to be distributed to members of a profession on the advice of their colleagues, nevertheless approved the system. (30)

When the National Health Service was introduced in 1948 the Government imposed a scale of fees to be charged to private patients using Health Service hospitals. Like the Code of King Hammurabi this gave an exhaustive list of types of operation and the fee to be charged for each (though there were no "reverse" fees such as loss of the surgeon's hand). The scale was disliked by the profession, and was not rigorously enforced. (31)

## Ad Valorem Scales

Whenever the subject-matter of professional advice is a piece of property whose cost or value is readily ascertainable, the almost invariable practice both here and throughout the world is to base the fee for the advice on that cost or value. On the sale of a house, the price is of course a known figure and it is convenient to base the fee of the agent who sells it and of the solicitor who executes the conveyance on that figure. Other charges will also be based on the same figure – for example the fees of the Land Registry and the amount of stamp duty. If an architect designs a factory or cathedral the ultimate cost of construction will be a known figure, and again it is convenient to relate the architect's charges to this. The same applies to the charges of other professional people involved in the project, for example structural engineers and quantity surveyors. If an insurance broker arranges a policy, his fee will be related to the amount of the premiums or the value of the capital sum payable (though in practice it will usually be borne by the insurance company itself). If a literary agent negotiates a publishing agreement, his fee will be related to the amount of the royalties. Valuers, stockbrokers, mortgage brokers and many others proceed similarly. In all such cases it is generally accepted that the value of the property or rights involved is "the major factor in assessing fair remuneration for work and responsibility involved". (32)

Although the value of the subject matter is thus taken to be the determining factor in charges, it is usually recognised that the amount of effort, skill and time devoted to a transaction cannot be assumed to vary directly with the value of the subject matter. Many a solicitor has spent more trouble over the conveyancing of a small cottage with a troublesome root of title than he does over a dozen run-of-the mill conveyances of modern, semi-detached houses. An architect will not usually spend four times as much time, effort and skill in designing a £200,000 factory as he spends in designing one costing £50,000, though, for special reasons, he may do so where the subject matter is not a factory but a hospital. (33) Because costs do not normally increase in the same proportion as value, most professions include in their "ad valorem" scale differential rates which produce a tapering effect. The estate agent's scale, for example, provides for a fee of 5% on the first £500 of the sale price, 2½% on the next £4,500 and 1½% on the residue. So on the sale of a cottage fetching £1,500 the fee would be £50, but where a property fetched ten times as much the fee would be £287.10.0 and not £500.

The principle of *ad valorem* charging has consistently been upheld by the courts, though occasionally with reluctance. In 1966-7, at the request of the Lord Chancellor, the Law Society undertook a review of the method of charge for conveyancing. After consultation with local law societies throughout the country they came to the conclusion that the *ad valorem* system should be retained as being not merely in the interest of the profession (indeed alternative methods of charging would in some instances be more remunerative) but also in the interest of the public. (34) The Prices and Incomes Board, in its report on architects' fees in 1968, found that the *ad valorem* system had not operated to yield the profession excessive incomes, and did not recommend its abandonment. (35)

In a remarkably intolerant report published in 1969 the Monopolies Commission rejected all the arguments in favour of *ad valorem* scales for estate agency services. They did so on hypothetical grounds, without any evidence that the scales did not work well or were against the public interest. Indeed the Commission expressly found that estate agents' profits were not excessive. In a note of dissent one member of the Commission, the Hon. T.G. Roche Q.C., said it was "wrong and unwise" to condemn without evidence arrangements that were old established, working well and affording the public a reasonable service at a reasonable cost. (36)

A number of advantages are claimed for the *ad valorem* system of determining professional fees.

*Certainty.* The existence of a published *ad valorem* scale means that, if he knows the capital sum involved, the client can calculate the professional fee before he has committed himself to the transaction. He does not even have to approach any particular practitioner — the matter is a simple one of arithmetic. The capital sum may not be always known in advance, but its likely amount can usually be estimated. Another advantage of certainty is that it avoids subsequent disputes as to the amount of the fee, which are in themselves a cost item since they take time and trouble to resolve.

The importance of certain advance knowledge of the amount of a fee varies. Cases where it is obviously material include those of the man who is engaged in selling his house and buying another. Here the amount of cash that needs to be found, that is the difference between the net yield on the sale (sale price less fees, expenses and mortgage repayment) and the cash outlay for the purchase (purchase price plus fees and expenses, less amount raised on mortgage) is all-important and often needs to be worked out with considerable precision beforehand.

Again, a property developer needs to calculate precisely his outgoings and probable yield. Professional charges for architects, quantity surveyors, structural engineers, estate agents and solicitors may be a substantial element in this calculation and it is of assistance to the client to be able to work out their fees without even having to approach any of them first. In some countries attempts have been made to quantify the size of the job by different criteria. For example in Sweden an architect's client may choose to have charges based on the building's cubic capacity. This basis is unpopular however because clients often wish to fix a firm sum early in their negotiations, whereas the cubic capacity may not be known with any precision until late in the design stage. (37)

*Cheapness.* The *ad valorem* system saves the expense of keeping detailed records of time spent and work done by the practitioner. No time need be spent either in compiling or assembling and checking such data, and the public are saved from having to meet the administrative cost of this operation. An *ad valorem* bill can be easily and quickly prepared.

*Stability.* The system has a built-in regulator to cope with inflation, since the relevant capital sum usually increases at about the same rate as the general increase of prices under inflationary conditions. A fixed-rate fee would have to be constantly revised, with difficulty for the public in keeping informed about the current rate.

*Uniformity.* The Law Society claim that it is beneficial to provide uniformity in charges throughout the country for transactions of comparable value. (38) This is perhaps doubtful, since the economic cost of providing the service may well vary.

*Prevention of Overcharging.* As indicated above the *ad valorem* system tends to eliminate overcharging, provided the work is done properly. It is immediately obvious whether the bill submitted is higher than that regarded by the profession as appropriate. It is true of course that there may be good reasons for making a high charge in a particular case, as where unusual difficulties have been found in tracing a title to property. The public generally, says the Law Society, "knows very little of the work and the responsibility involved in conveyancing, and the factors which often cause substantial differences between one case and another, and if in respect of transactions of comparable value there were substantial variations in the charges made between one case and another, the public would find it difficult to understand or to accept the fact that there were good reasons for such variations". (39)

*Avoidance of discrimination.* The scale ensures that the amount of the fee will not be arbitrary, or discriminate between one client and another — for example by charging unusually high fees to a client whom it was desired to get rid of.

*Abortive Work.* Professional firms, like most businesses, have to devote a proportion of their time and overheads to dealing with prospective clients whose patronage does not come to anything. The *ad valorem* fee, like the sale price of goods, includes a contribution towards such abortive expenses. These must be met somehow, but it would be difficult to do this if fees charged to each client had to be calculated by reference solely to the work done for that client.

*Additional Work.* The client is relieved from anxiety lest the job prove unexpectedly difficult, with a corresponding rise in fees. Very often additional work will prove to be needed in order to do the job satisfactorily, but professional fees will not thereby be increased. This particularly applies to house sales, where the amount of effort needed by the agent varies enormously.

*Clients not Inhibited.* Where they know a scale fee is to be charged, clients will feel free to seek information or advice whenever they think it necessary in the course of the transaction. If each consultation were to be charged for separately clients would often be chary of incurring an extra fee.

*Co-operation between agents.* In some fields, there is a large amount of co-operation between practitioners. If one cannot secure the object desired by his client he will often have recourse to a colleague who can. The existence of a common scale fosters the co-operative spirit, since practitioners know exactly where they are in dividing work (and the resultant fee) between them. They also cease to be suspicious of undercutting.

The following are sometimes put forward as disadvantages of the *ad valorem* system.

*Variable Capital basis.* The *ad valorem* system is unsuitable where the work done bears no true relation to the capital sum. Thus a structural survey cannot appropriately be charged for by reference to the value of the premises surveyed. Although it is true that the more valuable property may be larger, and therefore involve more time and effort in the survey, this is by no means necessarily so. A thorough structural survey of a large, rambling, Victorian mansion worth £10,000 may take ten times as long as a survey of a recently-constructed house of twice the value.

Similar considerations might be thought to apply to fees for valuing a property, but in fact the *ad valorem* basis applies to such valuations. This may be explained on the ground that a time basis would seldom be appropriate, since accurate valuation depends much more on skill and experience than on time taken. The valuers' scale is sometimes criticised on another ground, namely that it encourages the valuer to place his valuation as high as possible, since this will inflate his fees. It is for this reason that the Institute of Chartered Accountants object to *ad valorem* charges for valuations carried out by accountants: "If in those circumstances members were to calculate their charges on a percentage basis their independence and objectivity might, however unjustifiably, be challenged. For example, an accountant reporting on profits for prospectus purposes could be embarrassed if it were thought that his fee was geared to the amount of profits stated in his report." (40)

Another criticism of this method of charging where the amount of the capital sum is under the control of the practitioner was voiced by the Prices and Incomes Board: "It could be said that the 'ad valorem' basis gives architects an incentive to design expensively, with only the ethical standards of the profession to protect inexperienced clients. Similarly cost increases caused by delay or error due to the architect himself will bring him more money." While mentioning this criticism, the Board appear to attach little weight to it. (41) The estate agents make a virtue of the fact that the capital sum, i.e. the price obtained on the sale, is to some extent in their hands. Here the incentives work the right way: the agent is encouraged to obtain the highest price possible since in doing so he increases his own remuneration.

*Uneconomic Work Encouraged.* Economists frequently criticise *ad valorem* scales on the ground that they distort the true economics of a transaction. There are many cases where the true cost of carrying out professional work is excessive in proportion to the value of the subject matter. It may even exceed that value. Under the scale, however, this true economic cost will be spread over many transactions and the fee charged in the troublesome case will be no higher. The professions defend this on social grounds. The widow with a modest investment in houses let at controlled rents is able to sell them, and receive some return, notwithstanding that the true conveyancing costs (as opposed to the scale fee) outweigh the economic value of the freehold. Whether the *ad valorem* scale is the right way to deal with such problems may be disputed, but at least it provides a simple and effective solution.

*Better-than-average Work Discouraged.* The practitioner who does an abnormally good job will get no extra reward for his pains under the *ad valorem* system. If he goes to a specialist consultant he will have to pay the latter's fee himself. (42) A man who does a poor job may scrape by and will receive the same fee. The answer to these points lies in the spirit and ethics of the profession — the true professional is uninfluenced by such considerations as these.

*Prices Rise before Fee Due.* If an interval elapses between the doing of the work and the time when the fee falls to be calculated, as for example between the design and execution of a building, the practitioner may benefit from a rise in prices during that period which inflates the capital sum (the cost of the building) and therefore the fee. The Prices and Incomes Board suggested that an architect's fee should be reduced in such circumstances, and it is difficult to resist this conclusion. (43)

## Quantum Meruit

The phrase *quantum meruit* ("as much as he has earned") is used to describe the method of calculating fees which basically depends upon the actual amount of work done, and the time taken. If the necessary data could be easily, cheaply and accurately assembled this might well be the best system — though it would still be open to abuse by those who needed an incentive to occupy their time industriously. "Fixing fees slavishly by reference to the time factor", say the Law Society, "has been tried and found wanting — notably by the accountants after many years' trial." (44)

Until 1883, when *ad valorem* scales were introduced for conveyancing, solicitors' charges were in all cases based solely on time taken (in the case of interviews or attendance at court) or the length of documents. Bills of cost were itemised on this basis, and were often very voluminous. In 1953 a true *quantum meruit* system was introduced for work other than conveyancing, entitling the solicitor to charge "such sum as may be fair and reasonable, having regard to all the circumstances of the case". Particular circumstances specified as relevant are the complexity of the matter, the difficulty or novelty of the questions raised, the skill, labour, specialised knowledge and responsibility involved on the part of the solicitor, the time expended by the solicitor, the value of any property involved, and the importance of the matter to the client. (45) This summarises the considerations applying to most professional fees charged on the *quantum meruit* basis. It can be seen that this basis lacks both the advantages and disadvantages of the *ad valorem* system. Since the former outweigh the latter, it seems right to conclude that the architects are right in saying that wherever possible the *ad valorem* method should be used. Uncertainty is cited by the R.I.B.A. as the main drawback of *quantum meruit*. "Clients are tempted to avoid the uncertainty by asking for quotations, which may be reasonable enough in exceptional circumstances but could not serve as a general method of charging." (46)

A drawback of the *quantum meruit* system peculiar to estate agency is that it would render the multiple agency system, as practised particularly in the south of England, impracticable. At present, vendors are free to go to as many agents as they like and know that they will only receive a bill from the one who is successful in selling their property. Under a *quantum meruit* system each agent would be entitled to charge for the time and effort he had put into the attempt to effect a sale, and the result could be very expensive.

## The Rule against Undercutting

Undercutters are never popular with their fellows. Augustus Hervey, later third Earl of Bristol, records how as a freebooting ship's captain in the Mediterranean during the mid-eighteenth century he followed the usual practice of carrying treasure and charging 1% on its value. Captains who undercut were unpopular, and Hervey prospered in charging the full rate. (47) The same unpopularity is felt today by those who undercut their professional brethren, though the matter is seldom taken beyond private expressions of disapproval. Carr-Saunders and Wilson, writing in 1933, found that there was no attempt by the Law Society to prohibit one solicitor undercutting another. (48) Their enquiries of the profession generally had failed to disclose any case of expulsion from the professional institute because of undercutting. (49) Shortly after the publication of Carr-Saunders and Wilson's book the solicitors did formally ban undercutting. The position about enforcement by extreme action seems not to have changed however. The R.I.B.A., for instance, reported to the Monopolies Commission that there had only been one case in the last ten years in which a member had been found guilty of undercutting. (50) This contrasts with the finding of the Prices and Incomes Board in 1968 that there had been many cases of undercutting by architects in various forms. (51) One explanation may be the extreme difficulty of collecting sufficient evidence to secure a conviction.

The statements of the rules against undercutting vary, but not significantly. The Solicitors' Practice Rules 1936, made under statutory authority, prohibit a solicitor from holding himself out as being prepared to do professional business at less than the scale. The prohibition is against *quoting* a reduced fee to one who is *not an existing client.* Once a client has been secured, therefore, the profession is not concerned with the fees he is charged: the rule is in other words directed to obtaining new business unfairly. The rule in a sense duplicates another rule, made at the same time, which is explicitly directed against unfair attraction of business. In 1951 the High Court upheld a finding under the latter rule that a solicitor had been guilty of unprofessional conduct where he let it be known that he was prepared to accept instructions from members of an organisation for which he acted at less than the proper scale of charges. (52) This illustrates that the holding out need not be to the person who becomes the prospective client; it is sufficient that the holding out was to an existing client, and as a result new clients were attracted. (53)

The consulting engineers express the rule in simple terms: "A member shall not knowingly compete with another member on the basis of professional charges." (54) The Architects Registration Council is even terser: an architect "must not compete with another architect by means of a reduction of fees . . ." (55) The R.I.B.A. reinforce this by requiring members to uphold and apply the scale of charges.

Rules against undercutting are difficult to frame and apply where the profession has no published scale. Despite this handicap the Institute of Chartered Accountants does regard as guilty of undercutting a member who has obtained professional work through having quoted *with that object* a fee lower than that charged by an accountant whom he has replaced. The Institute recognises that the mere charging of a lower fee is not necessarily discreditable, since "it may be a smaller firm, more conveniently situated geographically or even perhaps more efficient". Another indication of transgression, if it could be proved, would be where the business had been obtained by the quotation of a fee lower than the firm's normal fee. The Institute has resisted pressure by its members to rule that wherever a client changes his accountant the incoming accountant should seek an assurance that the change has not been made for the purpose of securing a reduction of fees. The conclusion was that it would be impracticable and contrary to the public interest to adopt this course. (56) The R.I.C.S. adopt a double-barrelled approach. No member must "undertake or offer to undertake work for charges which in the opinion of the Council would be unfair to other members". Not content with this, the bye-laws go on to prohibit members from attempting to compete with each other on the basis of fees with the object of securing instructions. (57)

Particular exception is taken by the professions to the practice of tendering. Many local authorities, filled with a praiseworthy desire to save on the rates and familiar with the system of tendering for building contracts, see no reason why outside professional consultants should not also tender. Thus firms of architects or valuation surveyors may be invited to submit quotations of their fees for a particular project in the same way that building contractors will later be asked to do for the same project. The proper course is for firms to decline to respond to this invitation, but the temptation to seek business in this way is sometimes difficult to resist and not resisted. The British Medical Association has been particularly vigilant in seeking to prevent members from responding to advertisements which in effect offer work to the practitioner who puts in the lowest bid. (58)

## Allowable Reduction or Waiver of Fee

The consultant professions recognise numerous exceptions to rules laying down scales of fees. The rules are not likely to be enforced where an established client is concerned, or where a reduction or waiver is made on grounds of poverty or other hardship. A barrister is allowed to waive his fee when acting for a personal friend, another member of the Bar or a charity. (59) A solicitor may, with the consent of his local professional society, charge a reduced fee where he acts for a near relative, an employee or in similar circumstances. (60) Where repetitive work is involved, as in conveyancing of similar houses on a building estate, or the client lightens the load, as in the case of building societies providing standard forms for mortgages, the solicitor may legitimately charge a reduced fee. (61)

The professions are frequently compelled to accept lower fees when working for public bodies. Here the client is so substantial and powerful that the individual practitioner can do little to resist, and his professional institute very often finds itself unable or unwilling to exert sufficient pressure to rectify the position. Surveyors who act for persons of unsound mind are thus expected by the Court of Protection to charge less than the scale fee. The architects have a long-standing grievance against the public sector: "the overall pattern has been marred by persistent attempts by some public authorities to buy private architects' services on special terms." The R.I.B.A. allege that a few public clients have unduly exploited the power given by their extensive patronage. "In some cases, public authorities seem even to have acted in bad faith." Between one fifth and a half of all local authorities required some form of reduction of fees from architects whose services were retained. The R.I.B.A. particularly object to the arbitrary manner in which these reductions are imposed, and the fact that they often have no reasonable relation to the work done by the architect. (62) The chartered accountants complain of Treasury scales indicating lower rates than members would normally expect to charge. (63)

## The Objection to Undercutting

Why do professional people feel so strongly about undercutting, while not feeling able to do anything drastic about it? Carr-Saunders and Wilson give the explanation that it is "indecent to undercut" and that the offender will cut himself off from friendly intercourse with his colleagues and perhaps be ostracised. (64) This is more a description than an explanation. The Law Society put its finger on the root cause when, in its submission to the Monopolies Commission, it remarked that the basic object of the rule was to maintain charges at a level which was not uneconomic. It is significant that the solicitors introduced their rule in the years following the depression of the early 1930s. The desperate search for work had led to vicious and severe undercutting, when work would be done for a fee ludicrously small and quite uneconomic merely because it was better than having no work at all. A number of professions suffered in this way and the memory still lingers among the older members.

The Monopolies Commission, in its 1969 report on estate agents, was indifferent both to the economic dangers of allowing unrestrained undercutting and to its effect on the sense of brotherhood and desire for cooperation within the profession. In a typical manifestation of current official opinion the Commission found no difference between price competition in professional services and in the supply of goods. They thus rejected, on doctrinaire grounds rather than concrete evidence, the whole basis of consultant professionalism and its philosophy. (65)

PART IV: TODAY AND TOMORROW

CHAPTER 14

# THE CODE IN TODAY'S WORLD

The treatment in Parts II and III of this book has been mainly confined to expounding the content and philosophy of professional ethics as prevailing in Britain today. The object has been to present in as complete and rounded a form as possible the corpus of professional ethics, giving the professions' reasons and justification for the rules as they exist. Only incidentally have current criticisms of these rules been dealt with.

We turn now to consider this corpus of rules through the eyes of its critics, who are mainly economists. This chapter also has the larger aim of debating whether in present conditions the professional ideal answers the purpose. This leads us to begin by looking again at the basic proposition given in Chapter 1 (page 15), and arguing the case for private practice as opposed to possible alternatives such as a state salaried service or the provision of professional advice by large commercial corporations. If the defence of private practice succeeds, individual practitioners must, unless they are to walk alone, combine to form professional institutes. We therefore briefly examine the case for these. This leads us to the concept of the code of ethics, and its modern utility as a system of regulation. We pass then to the content of the code, and in particular to those elements of it dealt with in Part III. Passing to the question of enforcement of the code, we conclude the chapter with an examination of the charge of monopoly.

## The Case for Private Practice

The justification of the consultant professions as at present organised depends on a justification of private practice as a vehicle for providing services of the kind under consideration in this book. There would be little point in attempting to defend the professional institutes and their code of ethics if the way of life that brought them into existence were found to be unsuited for present-day conditions. The professions may take some comfort from the fact that very few of their critics are opposed to private practice as such, even though they may advocate a salaried professional service in certain limited spheres. Though criticisms are levelled at many aspects of the current system its advantages, within the crucial field of health, rights and property, over any conceivable alternative are generally recognised by those who have studied the matter. Those who have not studied the matter, and this includes many in positions of authority as well as the general public, perhaps regard too lightly the virtues of private practice. In these conditions it might easily be whittled away unthinkingly. It is therefore worth spending some time in considering why this would be a disaster. Something has already been said on this head (pages 10-14, 18-20). Without duplicating that discussion, we proceed to indicate some of the main arguments. Before doing so we will look at evidence that the dangers just mentioned are not illusory.

Lewis and Maude pointed out in 1952 that private practice was becoming an ever smaller part of every profession. (1) The main reason is to be found in the tendency for large users of professional services to set up their own professional departments. Going back even earlier, we can trace the decline to the setting up of new organisations to carry out functions formerly left to private practitioners. The local government service is a prime example of this; before it came into existence in the nineteenth century much of its work was performed by solicitors and others in private practice. Similarly with the Civil Service itself – until the twentieth century most expert advice needed by departments of state was obtained by calling in outside consultants. On another aspect, the introduction of the National Health Service and the Legal Aid and Advice Scheme has involved large inroads by the state on private practice in several of the leading professions, though so far the essential nature of their operations has not been lost. State intervention is more marked in the medical field, and it is significant that recent surveys have shown that even where patients are dissatisfied with their treatment under the National Health Service they show no tendency to turn to private practice. (2) Even more ominous is the indifference of new entrants to the professions themselves. Lewis and Maude thought it "a sad sign that so many young people are content to accept the limitations, the frustrations, and the lack of adventure in the Civil Service, instead of taking a risk and hoping for the best". (3) Sir Robert Platt, in his book "Doctor and Patient", remarks that "although private practice can still be rewarding both financially and in experience, the young man of today does not particularly seek it, and often does not want it". (4)

The case for private practice in the field we are discussing mainly rests on the proposition that the qualities discussed in Part II of this book are of great importance, and are best provided on an individual basis. This is not susceptible of logical proof and no attempt will be made to provide it. The case must chiefly rest on the arguments in Part II and in general dislike of the British for the bureaucracy attendant upon a state service — which is the likely alternative. In perhaps extreme language, the point was made in a recent article by A.C. Thomas, a chartered surveyor, entitled "The Anger of the Patient Man". Thomas portrays the plight of the victim of bureaucrats, in this case rating officials, and his desire for the human touch:

> "He clings obstinately to the belief that officialdom could do more for him if it wished. Failing this, he yearns at least for some kind of human contact, for a voice that will say, 'Even if we cannot do anything, we know how you feel.' It is when he is denied this, and finds himself confronted with the official mind in all its pedantic, dessicated, impersonal, bureaucratic inadequacy, that the full Kafka-esque nightmare of our time takes hold of him, and he grapples naked with The Monster." (5)

The point was made with more subtlety by a medical consultant giving evidence to the Pilkington Commission. Comparing the treatment of patients within and outside the Health Service he said: "The slight difference in the handling is that . . . in an out-patients' session the patient listens to the doctor, whereas in a private practice the consultant listens to the patient." (6)

We now turn to consider some of the arguments for private practice additional to those emerging from the treatment in Part II of this book. We begin by saying a little more about clients' preferences. While the qualities discussed in Part II, such as competence, impartiality and integrity are undoubtedly the most important there are additional factors which should not be entirely dismissed. Only the relationship with a private practitioner can give the client or patient the feeling that his own convenience comes first. Appointments are made at a time to suit him: with a state service appointments are very often not made at all, and the public must await the convenience of the official. Though public service is staffed by many humane and courteous officials, the basis of the relationship is different and that is what counts. Even where the public official is quite free from the constraints normally found in employed service, as is the case with judges for example, the relationship with members of the public still lays stress on the convenience of the official. This explains the notorious reluctance of judges to institute a proper system of fixing dates and times for court hearings. With honourable exceptions, they tend to regard the waste of their own time which may arise under an appointments system from the unpredictability of court proceedings as much more important than the waste of the time of numerous professional people, witnesses and parties which arises where hearings are not arranged at fixed times. A state service moreover gives the client the feeling that he is one among millions, that his record sheet or dossier is kept available in some bureaucratic archive, and that if he is dissatisfied with his treatment he has no real alternative — even though his papers may be passed from one official to another (doubtless accompanied by a confidential report). A true second opinion becomes virtually impossible to obtain.

There are other, perhaps less worthy, motives behind a preference for private practice. Mencher gives one of the main reasons for the desire of many for private medical attention outside the health service as being a liking for what is believed to be the additional social status of private attention. He finds that the treatment of the private patient by those in the medical profession and in the publicity of provident societies "both subtly and directly caters to status satisfaction". (7) It is a truism that service provided as a right is undervalued by the recipient — particularly where its full economic cost is not represented in the charges (if any) made. Serious problems undoubtedly arise from the fact that many are unable to meet this full economic cost, and these are discussed below.

"Liberty means responsibility" said Bernard Shaw. He might equally have said that responsibility means liberty, and the man who is fully responsible enjoys the greatest freedom. The joys of being one's own master have been lauded throughout history. The more professional services are provided in private practice the more people can enjoy these benefits. It is fashionable nowadays to exalt the consumer as sovereign, but the economists and others who do so forget that most consumers are also producers — or at any rate members of the household of a producer. The satisfactions of individuals who are producers are just as important to social wellbeing as those of individuals looked upon as consumers. Indeed they are probably more important, since the work a person does is of more real concern to him than the goods and services he consumes.

Carr-Saunders and Wilson ended their book on the professions with a discussion of this point. After pointing out that the status of the freelance worker had long been envied, and that it had become customary to express regret for his relative decline in numbers, they went on to argue that it was not inevitable that a sense of dependence should accompany employed status. This only happened because the organisation (i.e. of the employer) had gained control. They appealed to workers to take it into their own hands to destroy the tyranny of these organisations, and instead build up the strength of their professional bodies. It is scarcely possible that such an idea could succeed, and it has not succeeded. A more fruitful course is surely for the professional institutes, while certainly not abandoning their members in employed service, to do all in their power to build up private practice so that its advantages become manifest to public and practitioners alike. The Joint Consultants Committee on the National Health Service concluded that private consulting practice is a means of attracting to medicine some of the most successful practitioners "who, without opportunities for private practice, might well decide to seek their fortunes elsewhere". (8) The Prices and Incomes Board reported that the personal and professional independence of a solicitor in private practice is "undoubtedly an important feature and is likely to play some part in a young man's choice of career". (9) Nevertheless, as mentioned above, there is much evidence that younger people especially are often inclined to eschew risks of private practice in favour of security. Lewis and Maude cite a young medical student who expressed a preference for salaried service on grounds, among others, that he desired regular hours of work. The authors comment: "He did not, in short, realise the deeper significance, or rewards, of general practice." They went on to suggest that only youngsters with actual experience of this could form a proper judgment, and that for this reason every medical student ought to spend some time working with a private practitioner. (10) The doctors have shown the way with the setting up of the Fellowship for Freedom in Medicine, which now has a large membership of private practitioners.

Other advantages of private practice which may be noted are as follows. The new entrant, and junior qualified man, has a wide choice of employer. If he falls out with one, and he may do so for good reason, he can find another. Where there is only one employer "an outspoken junior who feels himself frustrated may lose his keenness and fall into the pernicious habit of waiting for dead men's shoes, or he may seek employment abroad, or even become a "yes-man"." (11) Private practitioners have a flexible approach, and are quick to see openings for new services to be provided. They keep a profession dynamic and on its toes. In this way entire new professions emerge as the need for them arises.

The arguments of freedom and the like might be held by some to go by the board in times of economic stringency if private practice were shown to be wasteful or inefficient as a means of providing professional services. Measured in economic terms, the professions are a substantial element in the national life — the solicitors alone receive nearly £200,000,000 a year in gross fees. (12) No evidence has been adduced tending to show that private practice is in itself a wasteful method, as opposed to say a state service. Most experience indicates that the cost of providing any service where the stimulus of personal profit or loss is lacking, and elaborate steps have to be taken to provide staff pensions and other benefits and avoid the slightest risk of abuse, is very high. The risk-taking private practitioner has to be something of a business man, or he will not survive. His counterpart in official employment need not worry about this. Professional firms, unlike industrial concerns, are not capital-intensive and can work efficiently on a small scale and with little equipment.

A vital factor is that the freelance professional, having no subsidy to draw on, is compelled to charge clients (taken as a whole) the full economic cost of services provided. Private practice avoids the distortions in the economy involved where true economic cost is heavily disguised. A vivid illustration of this is given by current American experiments in town planning. The new town of Columbia, Maryland, which will house over a hundred thousand people, was planned in every detail by a private enterprise company without any government aid, finance or powers. As the Estates Gazette remarks, this necessarily means that the city is "firmly based on economic common sense". The journal goes on to comment that the entrepreneur "has an incentive which statutory planners lack; he pays for his mistakes and reaps the rewards of his success". (13) Unexpected support for this thesis comes from the Prices and Incomes Board report on architects. Understandably reluctant to state specifically that architectural departments of local authorities were often uneconomic, the Board threw out strong hints to this effect. While not feeling able to say outright that local authorities should give more work to private architects, the Board used a circumlocution which might be thought to bear this meaning: "It remains open to question therefore whether there might not be advantage in placing a greater proportion of public design work with private practice." (14)

If private practice is indeed able to supply a service more cheaply, recent taxation policy has been devised to offset this. Particularly effective in this respect is Selective Employment Tax, introduced in 1966. This marked the final departure from the old idea that the professions should be shielded from the full force of tax policies essentially designed for commercial activities.* The Selective Employment Tax

* An example of this policy was the exemption of the professions from Excess Profits Tax when it was imposed by the Finance (No. 2) Act, 1939 — see s. 12.

O

was specifically aimed at labour-intensive services, and professional services in particular. As introduced, it imposed on them a weekly tax of 25s. for each employed male, or 12/6d. for females. Within 3 years these rates were twice increased, to nearly double. Manufacturing industries not only do not bear the tax, but actually receive a premium out of the proceeds.

Four reasons were advanced by the Government to justify the tax. First, services had hitherto been lightly taxed as compared with manufactured products. Second, there was a need to restrain consumer demand for services. Third, there was a need to encourage economy in the use of labour in services and thereby make more labour available for the expansion of manufacturing industry. Fourth, services were less advantageous to the economy than manufactured products and were, therefore, to be discouraged. It is worth spending a little time in examining these reasons.

As to the first reason, why should it be assumed that services, especially professional services, should be taxed at all? It is acceptable course that the profit or net income yielded to the supplier of the services should rank for taxation in the ordinary way, and so it always has done. But S.E.T. is not a tax upon profits; it is an extra expense added to the cost of providing the service. Unlike purchase tax, it is not borne directly by the consumer – though of course the consumer has to pay in the end.

The second reason is also puzzling. Professional services are rendered in circumstances where the need for them plainly exists. One may say in relation to motor-cars, refrigerators, and other consumer durables, that people can very often do without them. But professional services are not in this category. Usually a person is compelled to make use of these services by force of circumstance. If he needs legal advice, he needs it, whether he likes the idea or not. If he is ill he needs a doctor. If he has land which is being compulsorily acquired or on which betterment levy has become payable, he must have professional advice. The idea that the demand for professional services is something which can be increased or damped down at a touch of the economist's finger on the button would be comical were it not so serious.

On the third point, the need to encourage economy in labour, one might have thought that constantly-increasing wage and salary levels were a sufficient inducement to any employer to economise on labour as far as possible. As originally introduced, the tax had the effect of something like a 6% or 7% wage increase for the employer. It did not however save him from a similar real wage increase at the same time. While admittedly reinforcing the encouragement to limiting the labour force, it did so in a way which increased costs in the same way as ordinary wage rises but did not have the compensating advantage of encouraging staff to work better.

The last reason for the new tax, namely that manufactured products were to be preferred to services, was again mystifying. Many professional services help to swell invisible exports. Only a relatively small proportion of manufactured products are exported, whereas the tax premium is payable to all manufacturers.

The new tax was a severe blow to private practice. It operated unfairly, since if a manufacturing concern employed its own professional staff, such as accountants, solicitors and doctors, it would receive a tax premium for them and their ancillary workers. If the manufacturing company went to a private firm for professional advice however it would have to pay its share of the cost of S.E.T. This was a clear inducement to commercial companies to set up their own professional departments.

Finally in this discussion of the virtues of private practice, we deal with two financial aspects. These are the provision of capital and the problem of the client, or would-be client, who cannot afford to pay. These might be taken to represent weaknesses in the private practice system, and corresponding advantages for public provision of consultancy services.

Some professional services need expensive capital equipment if they are to be provided in a comprehensive and up-to-date fashion. This is particularly true of medical and dental care and engineering services. We have seen how the partnership system hampers capital formation, and the exceptions that have been made to it for this reason (pages 68, 102). The previous discussion indicates where incorporation can be justified by the need to raise capital for expensive equipment, and to provide a method of withdrawing and transferring shares in the firm (under proper safeguards). There is no objection of substance to incorporation in itself. The real objection is to limitation of liability, but this can be met by requiring firms to maintain adequate professional indemnity insurance. The possible effect on the personal relationship with the client is more serious, and great care is needed to ensure that incorporation does not have this result. It can be done however, and there is no necessity from incorporation in itself for the firm to be any larger or the way it does its business any less personal.

It cannot be said that private practice, in its essentials, cannot exist in corporate form. This is recognised by the Law Society in their submission to the Monopolies Commission, though this still betrays the usual confusion between incorporation and limited liability. The Law Society say that it would clearly be against the interests of the public that solicitors should be able to practice through *limited* companies and thus be able to restrict their liability to their clients. That this is not clear, provided proper insurance safeguards are insisted upon, has already been demonstrated. The Law Society say there would be less objection to allowing practice through *unlimited* companies, but this would not benefit the public. The implication is that there would be *some* objection to unlimited companies, but the nature of this is not specified. (15) The professions will need to heed Lord Butler's warning, given in 1968, that at least in technical fields professional teams of specialists will be required in the future, who may "for a number of reasons have just cause to seek incorporation". Lord Butler went on to imply that professional rules preventing incorporation would need to be adapted to meet the challenge of the future. (16)

The social problem of the impoverished client is real, difficult and serious. It applies mainly within the field of individual health or rights — where advice is needed in relation to property funds are usually available to pay for it, often out of the income or proceeds of the property itself. In Britain much has been done since the Second World War to meet the problem of poverty in relation to health and rights — principally in medical and legal services. It has been done furthermore without abandoning the principle of private practice, a most praiseworthy achievement. Both the National Health Service and the Legal Aid and Advice Service proceed upon the basis that the private practitioner continues to advise patients or clients who come to him under the state system in the same way as those who come to him privately. The only difference, in theory at least, is that his fee comes not from the client but the state. In practice, as one might expect, stresses and strains appear in this admirable arrangement.

The Health Service differs from the Legal Service in being universal. There is no means test and the stigma attaching to poverty is avoided. The relationship of patient and practitioner is subtly different under the Health Service and in purely private practice, however, and studies reveal that private patients come mainly from what an American commentator has been pleased to call "the upper income or class range of the socio-economic spectrum". (17) The ethical consequences of this have worried some members of the medical profession. Either paying patients are to receive better treatment, which involves discrimination and "queue-jumping", or they are not to receive value for their money. The dilemma is acute. There can be no complete solution, and most people will sympathise with the Guillebaud Committee who in 1956 condoned inequalities provided that they did not get out of hand: "While appreciating the reasons why some have objected to the provision of pay-beds, we do not ourselves feel that the objections are strong enough to warrant the abolition of pay-beds in the hospital service. If there is any 'jumping of the queue' it cannot amount to very much when account is taken of the relatively small number of pay-beds at present provided in hospitals." (18)

More disquiet is felt about the Legal Aid and Advice scheme. The administration of this is more in the hands of the profession than is the case with the Health Service, and its availability depends on lack of capacity to pay. The system of partial contributions to legal costs means that charges are to some extent "tailored" to match financial resources. Yet there are many complaints that the lower-paid section of the community lacks assistance, particularly legal advice, that it should have. The truth is that such advice, if it is to be efficient, is very expensive to produce. The law grows ever more voluminous and complex, with corresponding increases in the skill and time needed to give advice. The problem is being studied by the Law Society and by the Legal Aid Advisory Committee, and research at the London School of Economics is being financed by the Ford Foundation. Inevitably some are advocating the provision of a state salaried legal service, perhaps on the model of the neighbourhood law firms set up in some parts of the United States. The Society of Labour Lawyers produced a report in December 1968 recommending this course, and the Times was misguided enough to suggest that experiments on these lines should be carried out. If however it is accepted that private practice provides the most effective organisation for the provision of advisory services, it is wrong that people should be offered a second-class service because they are poor. Nor should the grave dangers to the citizen involved in the loss of lawyers' independence be underestimated. The citizen often needs legal protection against the state, because it is the state which is threatening his rights. How can this be equated with a system under which he would seek advice from another department of the state, staffed by lawyers? The suggestion has only to be raised to be dismissed (one would think), yet there is talk of "experiments". Even if limited experiments appeared to work, this would only be because they were operated by lawyers trained under the present independent system, and were conducted on a small scale. They would certainly not indicate the type of legal service which would be provided in years to come by salaried departments staffed by practitioners who had known no other master but the state. Far better surely is the provision of advisory services by private practitioners paid, so far as necessary, from public funds but otherwise enjoying their traditional independence. To the objection that solicitors are reluctant to set up offices in the poorer areas, the Society of

Conservative Lawyers has countered with a proposal for state subsidies to encourage them to do so. (19) The University Grants Committee has shown that independence and state aid are not incompatible. They are difficult to achieve however; and state subsidies should be a last resort for professional people.

## Institutes and the Code

Going forward on the premise that the system of private practice should be preserved and strengthened, we need spend little time on justifying the existence of professional institutes. No one has suggested that private practitioners should not band together in this way, and the existence of the institutes has not been challenged. Forming a focal point for the teaching, examination, and development of professional expertise, they perform an obviously useful function. In maintaining the tone and spirit of the profession, and providing for social intercourse among its members, they serve a hardly less valuable purpose. Their function in relation to the professional code is more debatable. but before looking further at this aspect we ought to consider the financial viability of the institutes.

The cost of operating professional institutes, even at the current level of activity, is formidable. The R.I.C.S., with a qualified membership of less than 20,000, finds it necessary to employ a staff of 120 and maintain a headquarters building on an expensive site in Parliament Square, Westminster. With an annual budget approaching £400,000, it has no financial resources apart from what is provided by its own members. Other institutes are similarly placed, and the situation is an anxious one. If the professions are to accomplish the tasks expected of them they need an injection of new finance. Development and research in the field of professional techniques, the compiling and use of comprehensive statistics, educating the public in the nature and availability of professional services, and above all coping with the growing flood of Government-inspired activities – all these call for increased funds.

The last-mentioned item alone has in recent years taken up a great deal of the time of institute staffs. The Government rightly looks to the professional bodies for advice and information in the framing of new legislation. Bodies such as the Monopolies Commission and the Prices and Incomes Board conduct enquiries which demand a great deal of time and trouble from the professions. If the professions are unable to make an adequate response to these demands not only does the national interest suffer by the preparation of measures inadequately reflecting the viewpoint of the professions, but the professions themselves may be seriously harmed. What is the remedy? Institutes can be relied on to extract as much money from their own members as the latter are able and willing to give. Rises in subscription rates have been very steep in recent years, and alternative sources must be found.

The public purse should pay its share. It would be right for the tax-payer to finance that part of the professional organisation which is called into being to meet demands made by Government and public bodies. If civil servants and others do not find, in dealings with the institutes, officials of equal number and calibre to themselves backed by organisations as effective as their own, their work is inevitably handicapped. The cost of providing these things should be borne by the state out of money raised from the professions themselves through Selective Employment Tax and other imposts. The professions have not asked for this assistance and would perhaps fear loss of independence if it were provided. Adequate safeguards could be found however, and where so much is taken in taxation the arguments against looking to the state for "aid" are inevitably weakened. The neatest solution might be for each institute to put in a bill annually for fees to cover costs incurred in meeting public responsibilities.

The other potential source of financial help is the large business organisation which relies heavily on professional advice. Even if only out of self-interest, industry and commerce ought to see the need for safeguarding and developing the professional institutes who foster the qualities they gladly pay for as employers. They, and others, should bear in mind the wise words of Lord Butler quoted at the beginning of this book. As bulwarks of individualism, the professional institutes deserve the support of all who base their affairs on private initiative.

Having concluded that private practice is desirable, and with it the existence of professional institutes, we turn to the question of whether the concept of a code of conduct can also be supported. The idea of a code, as we have seen, is ancient and universal. Lord Reid, in the 1968 case of *Dickson* v. *Pharmaceutical Society,* described the prevalence of the code:

> "In every profession of which I have any knowledge there is a code of conduct, written or unwritten, which makes it improper for members of the profession to engage in certain activities in which ordinary members of the public are quite entitled to engage. Normally this is regarded as a domestic matter within the profession." (20)

This being so, the onus is clearly on those who wish to see the abolition of the practice of laying down rules of conduct to justify their con-tention. Discussion is hampered by the crude and sketchy nature of the arguments brought against the code as a concept. The current stick with which to beat it is that it is "restrictive". Some commentators indeed seem to think it sufficient to damn the code if they point out that it imposes restrictions. Knox and Hennessy, concluding a discussion of the "contractor" rule, argue that mere publicity of the existence of the rule, debate of its damaging consequences (unspecified) and "not least, attempted public defence of the indefensible" would cumulatively discredit restrictions of this kind in the professions. (21) The "contractor" rule has in fact been modified, as we have seen, but its essence remains. Since its purpose is solely to safeguard the independence, and therefore the integrity, of professional advisers, talk of "discredit" is indeed strange.

The mere existence of a code, never mind its content, necessarily involves "restrictions". A rule without a restriction is an impossibility, and it is ironic indeed that in an age when governments are loading more and more official restrictions on the citizen (presumably with his consent, or even approbation), the term should be regarded as sufficient in itself to condemn the professional code.

The professional code expresses the collective mind of the profession. Many of its principles, as we have seen, are not spelt out in written rules but are to be collected from pronouncements and rulings of professional bodies. The views professional people have about right and wrong behaviour would not disappear overnight if written formulations of the code disappeared. It follows that the strong influence a body of people have upon individuals in their number, particularly newcomers, would go on operating. The conduct of barristers, for example, is much more affected by what their brethren would think than by what is written in the handbook on etiquette at the Bar. The Bar is small enough for word to get round very quickly of any falling short. Senior members believe in straight speaking on these occasions, and the chambers system helps in this. The head of the chambers will regard himself and all under his roof as implicated to some extent if the conduct of any member is called in question.

Discussion should therefore turn not on the existence or otherwise of a code, since in some form it must exist, but on the rules comprised in it and the sanctions for their breach. Here the critics are on firmer ground. We do not need to go to enemies of the professions for disquieting statements. Millerson, in his measured and objective book *The Qualifying Associations*, finds it necessary to say: "Associations show greatest concern over competition: firstly, in terms of finding work; secondly, with the method of payment. Very little emphasis appears to centre on service to clients, or on any duty to expose professional incompetence." (22) The extent to which this comment is justified varies, but there are few if any professional bodies which can afford to ignore it completely. Another pertinent factor is the extent to which the code is enforced, particularly those aspects of it concerning the public and dealt with mainly in Part II of this book.

## A Free Grab for Business?

When people talk about the "restrictive practices" of the professions they usually refer to the rules described in Part III of this book, mainly regulating internal relations of professional people. As we have seen, these rules are almost entirely directed to the ways in which new business is sought. Is there any place for these rules in the world today? Before examining the arguments of those who wish to see the rules cut down or abolished let us attempt to summarise the way the professions would defend them.

We start with the position that the rules exist, and presumably exist by the will of at least the majority within each profession — otherwise there would be little difficulty in altering them. If the state considers that they must be altered in the near future it will have to act therefore through parliamentary powers. This will infringe the autonomy of the professions, which has long been respected by the law. It will overturn rules which have been recognised by Government departments, and are observed by many professions in countries overseas as well as at home. Parliamentary repeal of rules against touting, canvassing, advertising and undercutting will overnight expose individual practitioners to the full rigours of cut-throat competition; in self-defence they will be forced hastily to adopt the methods of the commercial world. Distracted from their proper function, they will put at risk the individual qualities which first induced them to take up a profession. Courtesy, modesty, dignity and detachment — these qualities may not survive. Self-respect and peace of mind may be imperilled.

The change may well destroy the solidarity and the fraternal spirit which led to the setting-up of professional institutes, and are fostered by them. Co-operation between professionals, the shouldering of the burden of training new entrants and helping lame dogs, the habit of making the fruits of experience available to colleagues, and striving to keep up the expertise and tone of the profession — all these may be fatally damaged. Some may feel there is no longer any point in keeping up the expensive equipment of a professional institute at all. The individual would lose his protection against the powerful client, and the very existence of private practice might be imperilled. All the qualities discussed in Part II of this book on which the client depends would then rely for their continuance not on the vigilance of the professional institutes but on the qualities of individual practitioners. Such qualities could not survive unimpaired in the heat of a battle for business with no holds barred. Inter-professional rivalries would spring up, with those trained in one set of techniques casting longing eyes at areas of other professions where the pickings looked good.

Would public confidence and trust in professional advisers survive this change? Competing bids for their business, with derogation of fellow-practitioners and advantage being taken of the client relationship to seek new business would hardly sustain confidence. To choose a consultant on the basis of the skill of his advertising agency and the amount of his publicity spending, rather than on the advice of a disinterested, informed third party could scarcely profit the public. It would also diminish the incentive to build up a practice through sheer hard work and the development of professional skills. The costs involved and the loss of revenue due to undercutting, would necessitate a reduction in the quality of service. Practitioners might, as in past times, find themselves working for much less than the economic cost of providing the quality of service they were trained, and are accustomed, to provide. In the long run, no one would benefit.

This gloomy picture shows what could happen. It might turn out to be overdrawn, but no one can be sure. Why, say the professions, run the risk? It could only be justified by criticism of such weight and cogency as to compel action, whatever the hazards. Let us now look at the criticisms that are currently being made against the restrictions on methods of seeking business and consider whether they are indeed of this irresistible character. Before doing so however we might spend a moment considering a doctrine familiar to lawyers — onus of proof. Most criticisms seem to assume that the onus is on the professions to justify their rules because they amount to "restrictive practices". As we have shown however, and as is indeed obvious, there cannot be rules without restrictions, and there can hardly be professional associations without rules. Since the critics do not attack the existence of such associations they are illogical if they attack rules as such. Furthermore these are not merely the rules currently in existence, but rules which have marked the essence of professionalism for a very long time. The presumption is therefore on their side, and the onus is on their critics to prove them wrong. Where a system has been operating for a long time, and grew up under conditions of free enterprise, there must, as the R.I.B.A. point out, be "a strong presumption that it meets society's needs and that radical change in it might be difficult to achieve". (23)

It can be confidently stated that the critics have totally failed to discharge the onus of showing this presumption to be false. A straight-forward and effective way of showing it to be false would be to establish, after proper investigation, that professional rules led to practitioners being overpaid. Yet, after carrying out investigations in the case of solicitors and architects, the Prices and Incomes Board concluded in 1968 that in neither case was the profession, on balance, receiving greater remuneration than was proper. This must mean that those who seek to drive charges down by making the professions more competitive are seeking to get the work done for less than a fair reward. The only long-term consequence of this would be the disappearance of the independent professions, since their continued operation would become uneconomic. As most criticisms are put forward on economic grounds, this is indeed a strange conclusion.

The basis of economic criticism of the professions is that their rules inhibit competition and therefore deny the public the economic advantages which competition is said to bring. The fallacy is that because competition is restricted in one direction, namely the seeking of business, it is restricted generally. Even in economic terms, unrestrained competition has not always been found beneficial — indeed a large part of the apparatus of government during the past hundred years has been devoted to imposing restraints on capitalist competition for the public advantage. Within the field of sale of goods and property, a host of statutory restrictions now shield the public from the full force of competition. Indeed the whole emphasis on protecting the consumer, which is the rationale of most economists attacking the professions, comes down to restraint on what may be permitted of competitive traders striving for business.

The case of the professions in no way depends, however, on attacking competition as such. They believe that in the vital realm of health, rights and property what really matters is not price-cutting but adequacy of service. If the practitioner depends solely on the quality of service he renders in order to build up his practice he has the strongest possible incentive to do the job to the best of his ability. If his ability is insufficient, he will go under. The go-ahead practitioner can devote his skill and energy to improving the service he offers. He may do this by employing staff of good quality, by having offices in a location convenient to clients and ensuring that the appearance, lay-out and equipment of the office are up to date and efficient, and by developing in their full variety the services offered to clients. If he fails to do all these things, the opening will be there for a rival to prosper at his expense, and sooner or later this will happen. Nor is limitation of competition on the price level a peculiar feature of the professions.

As Harris and Seldon point out in "Advertising and the Public", there are many commodities such as soap, detergent, cars, chocolates, radios, petrol and cigarettes where competition is vigorous but takes place in quality or other features rather than in price. (24)

When we come to examine in detail the economic criticism of professional restrictions we find ourselves in a difficulty. The criticisms are made in fragmentary form and consist largely of mere assertion. The points made are ill-selected, and a comprehensive case has to be built up from a number of sources and even then seems incomplete. We give below a summary of the arguments which have recently been put forward by economists supplemented by additional points that seem worthy of inclusion if a complete case is to be presented.

We begin with Professor Lees, since he has been the most vocal of the economist critics. His onslaught takes the form of setting up Aunt Sallies in the shape of arguments said to be used by the professions in defence of their practices and then attempting to knock them down. This is a curious form of attack, dictated by Lees' self-confessed failure to carry out more than a superficial examination. After asking why the professions maintain restrictions on charges, advertising and touting, Lees comments:

> "There has been no systematic treatment of this question but from the sparse literature and numerous pronouncements by the professions themselves, two main justifications seem to be claimed. First, that overtly competitive activities are inconsistent with the achievement and maintenance of the social status of a professional man. And secondly, that these activities reduce the confidence of the consuming public in the quality of professional services. In technical language, the claim is that restriction of overt competition generates a producer surplus, taken as psychic income in the form of status, and raises the total demand for the services of the group, to the advantage of consumers as well as to members of the group." (25)

Lees does not say which professional associations advance these reasons. As can be seen from Part III of this book they amount to a very inadequate statement of the justifications put forward by the professions. Indeed the first or "status" argument is not one which any self-respecting professional body would put forward as a justification in itself. It is not surprising then that Lees finds little difficulty in demolishing it. We may dismiss it here with the simple reminder that it is not necessarily wrong, and is certainly human, for people to mind about whether society shows respect for their work by according it (and them) high prestige.

Lees finds the second justification, that restrictions on competition avoid loss of confidence, "essentially empirical" and "extraordinarily difficult to test against the facts". (26) This difficulty certainly makes itself felt in Lee's discussion of this point, and his argument is somewhat obscure. At one point he seems to be saying that there would be a positive gain to clients if practitioners came to be regarded more like "tradesmen" and less like "professional men", though how this would increase confidence in their advice is not specified. In truth it is not possible for such criticism to go beyond asserting that no harm would come of abolishing the rules. This is mere guesswork, but it can be said, as Lees does, that doctors in Switzerland and dentists in the United States advertise and are not noticeably mistrusted by patients. (27) Again it can be said, as Lees does not, that bodies depending on public confidence, such as banks and insurance companies, advertise in Britain without noticeable damage to that confidence. This argument deserves careful consideration.

Advertising by insurance companies has a long history. The nineteenth-century advertising agent Samuel Deacon was impressed by the vigorous advertising of the Royal Insurance Company. Urging more conservative insurance companies to follow suit, Deacon said that when they did advertise their manner was so apologetic as to recall the impoverished gentleman, reduced to crying fish in the streets, who exclaimed: "I hope to goodness no one hears me". (28) This complaint is still heard today; Harris and Seldon comment that banks and insurance companies "are often inhibited from using advertising at all or on a scale necessary to make it effective, and they use it in a decorous manner that prevents it from attracting much attention". (29) In another recent work, "Advertising in Action", the same authors examine the recent growth of the Eagle Star Insurance Company. They find it to be among the fastest-growing, and most enterprising insurance companies, and add: "What part has current press and television advertising played in all this? The evidence suggests the answer is: 'Not much.' " The company believe that advertising is ineffective in bringing new business. Its recent advertising campaign has not yielded good results. The authors conclude that this is a view shared by other insurance companies, for not many advertise extensively or regularly. (30) Banks have until recently shown a similar disinclination to advertise, assisted no doubt by the fact that Farrow's Bank, which failed in 1920, had before closing its doors engaged in a big press campaign. Harris and Seldon comment: "This indifference or hostility developed no doubt partly because the training of bankers emphasised personal service to customers whose affairs were strictly private ... " (31) Going on to describe the recent burst of bank advertising in Britain, these authors find difficulty in assessing the effectiveness of the various campaigns. They conclude that the drive for business would be much more effective if competition between banks extended to interest rates or opening at more convenient times. As it is, banks' services are so similar in all respects as to leave the advertiser little to build upon.

Another activity where judicious advertising has not been held to have prejudiced public confidence is the sale of spectacles by opticians. This is of questionable value as an analogy, since it is contrary to true professionalism for the consultant to gain financial benefit from the fact that his advice tends in one direction rather than another. The practice under which the same firm conduct eye testing of patients and promptly sell spectacles to those held to need them is a blot on professionalism and should be discontinued. Baster, writing in the 1930s, criticised opticians' advertising for creating new conventions to increase sales, for example that propriety demands a minimum of four pairs of spectacles per person: "One pair, in tortoiseshell and nickel, for business, one pair framed in gold, for evening wear, gold-mounted pince-nez for full dress, and a fourth pair, framed in pure tortoiseshell, 'for sport or relaxation'." (32) Denys Thompson, also writing in the 1930s, indicts lyrical advertisements from another source with claims to professionalism, advertising agencies. These describe how copywriters, inspired by the merits of Goodyear tyres or Hoover cleaners, work far into the night, and have not finished even on leaving the office:

> "One of the lay-out men has just left his drawing-board and
> is going down in the lift. Under his arm he carries a tissue
> pad. A new idea is stirring in his mind. It will be roughed
> out in pencil before morning comes. Weeks, may be months
> from now you will see it in print, a finished advertisement
> for Hoover."

This advertisement was intended to convince prospective clients of the advertising agency that their work would be in dedicated hands. No information about success or otherwise is available. (33) In America this kind of approach has even been tried in a sphere where confidence is all-important, the church. Not content with neon signs flashing an invitation to worship, the publicity adviser offers sage counsel to the minister:

> "It may be that you have the reputation of having stale

goods; maybe you are foolishly stressing side lines. It may be the first assistant sales manager is out of harmony with the Sales Manager, the Holy Spirit, and therefore all the salesmen, the members, are demoralised and don't know what they are selling; or have quit their job and are just hanging around blaming the preacher and their fellow-members for the fact that the church doesn't go." (34)

Denys Thompson condemns advertising by religious bodies as leading them to lose sight of spiritual functions: "Advertising in such a case is an inherently unsuitable method; it may rouse some momentary public attention and produce some emotionally-moved converts, but when the emotion has cooled, so will devotion." (35)

We may conclude that the onus of proving the professions wrong in fearing loss of confidence through advertising has not been discharged. Indeed such evidence as there is tends on the whole to the conclusion that there may well be a sound basis for their fears. The Consumer Council, in its evidence to the Monopolies Commission, suggested that where confidence in the practitioner is important − "among doctors and other medical professions, perhaps" − there was a case for banning advertising, at least where it involved claims to medical superiority. The Council felt this might not apply in the case of architects, surveyors or solicitors. This was apparently on the ground that here confidence in the practitioner does not matter − a strange conclusion. (36)

Lees states that two propositions, both "very odd", seem to follow from the argument that professional restrictions on competition improve public confidence. These are that competition necessarily reduces quality, and that prohibiting advertising raises demand. The first of these points is highly important, and must therefore be examined closely. The second is a mere debating point and easily got out of the way. In saying that public confidence would be reduced by the sight of trusted advisers outbidding each other in advertising claims, the professions are not necessarily arguing that this would lead to a reduction in demand for their services. The public cannot do without their services, and the total demand might not lessen. The argument is that the public need advisers they can trust. If these are not available they will have to make do with what is. They can only suffer thereby, even if the suffering is confined to what Professor Lees would no doubt describe as their "psychic income".

In dealing with the question of cheapness and efficiency we enter the heart of the controversy. Lees states that the claim that competition reduces quality is not borne out by what happens to products generally in competitive conditions, citing findings of the Restrictive Practices

Court in relation to Scottish baking, transformers and linoleum. Are these really analogous to professional services, where the product cannot, at the time of buying, be inspected, tasted, prodded or weighed? If quality is to be maintained and, as seems clear, the current remuneration of the consultant professions is not excessive cheaper services could only come through increased output without corresponding increase in costs. Would uninhibited advertising bring this about? The spur to efficiency is very keen now, and professional firms are continually being squeezed out of business by economic pressures. The Robson Morrow Report on architects' practices in 1956-65 found that productivity in private architects' offices had increased by about 4% per annum over the period. (37) This rate is higher than that of industrial productivity over the same period, and can probably be paralleled in other professions. The only concrete suggestion whereby advertising could improve productivity is made by Knox and Hennessy in their report on restrictive practices in the building industry, where they say that the ban on advertising accentuates the irregularity of building work by making it impossible for surveyors, engineers and architects to secure a continuous flow of work "instead of alternations of over-full, medium and underemployment". (38) It is not clear that advertising is the best way of dealing with this problem. (39)

We may conclude that if an all-out drive for business does lead to reduced charges for professional services, this will not be against a background of correspondingly reduced costs. On the contrary, costs would rise because of additional expenditure on getting business, particularly of course on advertising. Rival firms mounting opposing advertising campaigns of the same intensity are likely to find at the end of the day that they are still in the same relative position, with their costs heavily increased to pay for the campaign. (40)

Baster gives the possibility of deadlock in competitive advertising as one reason why the professions restrict advertising "and so save themselves from internecine strife, and their clients from the wastes of mutually-destructive publicity."(41)

Samuel Courtauld once remarked that most competitive advertising was a costly extravagance, and the American advertising world is said to hold the view that some 90% of advertising efforts are failures. The English Gallup Poll director, Dr Durant, recently argued that advertising was becoming less effective, pointing out that the costs of advertising for each one thousand actual readers had risen by 180% between 1951 and 1961. (42)

If costs then increase, and charges (and therefore income) are reduced, can we really believe, with Professor Lees, that there would be no tendency for quality of service to decline? The Prices and Incomes Board said in one report that "quality in professional work depends on professional standards", and in another that standards depend primarily on the rigour of the tests applied to the granting and taking away of qualifications. (43) If they are insufficiently remunerated, professional people will either be forced out of private practice or will lower their standards to enable costs to meet income. No other conclusion is possible. Some outsiders might gain satisfaction from the former contingency. Knox and Hennessy for example find there are "unnecessarily large numbers of firms" in the building professions. (44) But can we be sure that the public will really gain from the loss of individualism and personal service consequent on reduction in the number and inflation in the size of firms? Harris and Seldon point out that reducing the number of firms through advertising leads to "oligopoly" and that in an oligopolistic market there is little price competition "because no producer can reduce his price without the others following suit, in which cases all would end by charging prices too low to make production profitable". While oligopoly has some advantages in commercial production where the economics of scale can be fully exploited, there are corresponding disadvantages which alone are operative in the case of the professions. These include "higher costs of management as organisation becomes complex in larger firms, higher selling costs (including those of advertising), higher prices, barriers to the entry of new firms with new ideas and methods because of the high cost of breaking into the market, and a possibly dangerous concentration of economic power". (45)

We conclude this examination of the economics of professional restrictions by looking at certain other objections which can be dealt with more concisely. Professor Lees and others complain that the rules against touting, advertising and undercutting operate in favour of firms already established and prevent newcomers using what are "the normal competitive devices of new entrants". This argument cuts both ways, since if newcomers enter a field where costs are inflated by the need to indulge in large-scale advertising they will need more initial capital or bridging finance to cover the period before fees begin to flow in. Harris and Seldon point out that in a number of industries "advertising has been used with the intention of stopping or discouraging new competitors". The American economist, Gideonse, alleged that advertising entrenched monopoly by setting up a financial barrier to the competition of new and small firms. (47) The Prices and Incomes Board suggested to the R.I.B.A. that young architects might be permitted to charge a lower fee to assist them in starting a practice. After saying that there was "a certain sentimental attraction" in the proposal, the R.I.B.A.

P

proceeded to demolish it with pitiless logic. The work that ought to be done for a client remains the same, whoever does it, and this would be a court's view if the architect were sued for negligence: "The standard of service he has given will be gauged by the court in terms of what a reasonable architect would have done; not in terms of what a reasonable *young* architect would have done, nor in terms of what he was paid." The cost of doing the work could only be less if the young architect were more efficient. This is unlikely, and would hardly be a reason for rewarding him with lower fees. (48)

Lees criticises a statement by the President of the Law Society that new charges proposed were a fair remuneration for the work involved on the ground that absence of competition prevented us from knowing whether this was so or not. (49) It is an extraordinary illustration of the length to which some present-day economists are prepared to take the regression to laissez-faire principles that it should automatically be assumed that the price level produced by unrestricted competition is necessarily "fair". If this argument were sound the real cause of concern would be the remuneration of those paid from public funds, such as most doctors and dentists. Here, as the Pilkington Commission pointed out, the only standard of comparison possible is with professional people in private practice. (50)

We conclude therefore that there should *not* be a free grab for business, or at least that no case has been made out for coercing the professions, against their will, into relaxing current rules. This is not to preserve a monolithic position. Professional bodies reflect very accurately the current feelings and beliefs of their members, and these are influenced by general shifts of opinion. There have been considerable relaxations of professional rules in recent times, and there is a strong, and perhaps growing, element within the professions who would like to see further relaxations. This particularly arises where members of professional bodies are in direct competition with unattached practitioners operating without any restriction other than that imposed by the general law, as in the field of estate agency and surveying. There is a natural tendency for the young enthusiastic newcomer to feel impatient of rules which seem to him to operate as a handicap in building up his business. Certain it is that the justification for such rules will have to be clearly and powerfully put across if they are to survive these pressures.

Other factors tending to relaxation of the no-advertising rule are the tax advantages of advertising and the thought that, by becoming free-spending advertisers, the professions could secure a better press. Neither reason is particularly worthy, but for completeness they ought to be described.

The tax advantages arises from the fact that advertising expenditure is treated by the Inland Revenue as a trading and not a capital expense. This means it can be allowed against income in computing profits for income tax purposes. It nevertheless, if seriously embarked on, may have an effect in building up a capital asset, namely the goodwill of the business. In other words capital can be built up by payments which are fully allowed for tax purposes — an unusual situation.

As for getting a better press by heavy advertising, Harris and Seldon point out that a firm that advertises often and generously is more likely to receive frequent and favourable mention in the editorial columns than one that does not. "To suppose otherwise would be to doubt the effectiveness of advertising and to deny human nature." (51) Political and Economic Planning have reported that there is undoubtedly a tendency to tone down or suppress news which seems likely to annoy advertisers or potential advertisers. (52) Denys Thompson cites a memorandum to sub-editors which appeared in a national newspaper office: "Don't pass anything detrimental to Bread. To say that bread is fattening, for instance, is detrimental." (53)

We may conclude that it unless it is fairly proved that the public interest is harmed the professions should be left to govern their own affairs. As Durkheim said in his *Professional Ethics and Civic Morals,* a system of ethics is not to be improvised. "It is the task of the very group to which they are to apply."(54) The advertising practitioners have themselves testified to the truth of this, by laying down their own code of ethics. Unless this too is to be abolished it makes unrestricted advertising virtually impossible — there are always some rules, and not alone those of the state.

Is the public interest harmed by restrictions on advertising? The only allegation that carries any conviction relates to the inadequacy of information as to professional services.

It is plainly in the interests both of the public and the professions that the former should be fully aware of the variety of professional services available. This is certainly not the case at present, and the professions must take responsibility. Few people, if any, could give a comprehensive list of the services available from the consultant professions. Some professional bodies, such as the Law Society and the R.I.C.S., have produced explanatory leaflets but these are not generally available. The public is therefore going without advice which it needs to have. One example may be given. A surprisingly large number of people owning substantial property die each year without having made a will, presumably through ignorance of the consequences. The result is that intestacy procedure has to be followed, involving delay and additional expense to the relatives. We have seen above that professional institutes are aware of the need to publicise services, but are hampered by lack of funds. A modest attempt to help in this direction will be found in Appendix II to this book, which describes the services available from members of the consultant professions and uses material supplied by the professional bodies themselves.

Having identified a need, and the service required to meet it, the prospective client needs to locate a source from which it may be obtained. If advertising by firms were unrestricted he might scan the columns of his local paper and pick out the most glowing advertisement. It is unlikely that this would turn out to have been inserted by the most able practitioner. Knox and Hennessy criticise the no-advertising rule on the ground that it "drastically limits specialisation by making it almost impossible for architects and surveyors to publicise their specialisms". (55) Is this justified?

Those who would like to see individual firms free to publish advertisements describing in detail the services they offer argue that such advertisements would be merely informative and could do no harm. Students of advertising have shown however that there is no such thing as a merely informative advertisement; even the plainest set of assertions has a persuasive effect. (56) Denys Thompson quotes a blistering page from Baster:

> "The major part of *informative* advertising is, and always has been, a campaign of exaggeration, half truths, intended ambiguities, direct lies, and general deception. Amongst all the hundreds of thousands of persons engaged in the business, it may be said about most of them on the informative side of it that their chief function is to deceive buyers as to the real merits and demerits of the commodity being sold." (57)

Hartley Withers, in *Poverty and Waste,* remarked that it was the glory and boast of the skilful advertiser that he could make people buy things they did not want. (58)

If a member of the public needs a run-of-the-mill service which can be adequately rendered by any qualified practitioner, he may be satisfied to seek one out in a directory or even by walking the street till he finds one. This might apply to swearing an affidavit or receiving an inoculation, but it hardly extends to affairs in which skill and judgment may make all the difference to success. Nevertheless the facilities for finding practitioners to do the more humdrum tasks ought to be improved. Directories might be more elaborate, names of firms perhaps more prominently displayed. There is a case for allowing all professions to adopt the "card" advertisement system in local papers which is followed by the "land" professions. If the "card" advertisement is looked on as no more than an extension of the brass plate, and contains a limited amount of strictly factual information, it can do no harm.

For weighty advice on matters of substance there is surely no doubt that the public should use the traditional method, and seek recommendations from those who are in a position to know. It is this system, and only this, which produces the result best both for the public and the profession by securing an expanding connection for the practitioner who, on pure merit, earns it, and denying it to everyone else. Those who doubt this should ponder the words of Walter Raeburn, an experienced barrister, in reviewing Michael Zander's book *Lawyers and the Public Interest*. Commenting on Zander's advocacy of uninhibited advertising and contingent fees, Raeburn says:

> "Once the Bar were well and truly in the rat race, few could survive who refrained from coaching witnesses, letting in illicit evidence, concealing vital documents and all the other tricks of the shady advocate. There are some things with which decency cannot compete." (59)

In most, if not all, professions the reward of merit is not merely an enlarged practice but the ability to charge higher fees. There is thus no restraint (other than taxation) on the incentive to succeed, and the public benefits.

### Who Should Fix Charges?

There has been much recent criticism of the way the consultant professions determine the fees they charge clients. A favourite target is the *ad valorem* scale, and the relatively few objections to it have been magnified, while its more numerous advantages are played down (see pages 181-185). Criticism is also levelled at professional institutes for promulgating scales, rather than leaving fees to be determined at random by individual practitioners or fixed by some outside body. Complaints have been made about inadequate statistical information, and over all has been the vexed question of how the Government's prices and incomes policy should operate in relation to the professions. Despite all this questioning, no proof has emerged that the professions are being overpaid — if anything the evidence tends the other way.

Professor Lees attacks the *ad valorem* basis of charging on a number of grounds, none of them original. The advantage of certainty he dismisses with the statement, given as usual without supporting evidence, that "it is quite clear that consumers choose not to have fixed prices". The advantage of stability, arising from the fact that the scale automatically keeps pace with inflation, is also dismissed. Lees regards inflation-free incomes as bad: "At best, they weaken resistance to rising prices and, at worst, positively promote them". How, if the practitioner's income is not to keep pace with inflation, he is to retain his ability to practise is not revealed.

The fact that low-price but costly transactions are "subsidised" is also attacked. With the relentless logic of the academic economist, Lees says that "there is nothing in this argument at all", and that it involves an unjustified interference with economic forces. It amounts to a transfer of income from those who are paying more than the economic cost of, say, their conveyances to those who are paying less. No one knows the amount of this "transfer", but it is probably insignificant. Nevertheless, says Lees, it is no part of the business of lawyers to promote social justice. "That is the task of government." The Consumer Council are also critical, but in less extreme terms. Their's is the language of one who cannot make up his mind: "We are not convinced of the validity of the social arguments for scale fees – that certain transactions would be very expensive if charged according to work done – nor is it clear why the professions should set themselves a social task of this kind." (60) Despite his onslaughts, Lees concludes that *ad valorem* scales are probably justified on the ground of low administrative costs. He admits that there is no evidence one way or the other about this, and this whole argument therefore peters out in a conclusion that things should probably be left as they are. (61)

The Prices and Incomes Board report on remuneration of solicitors, issued in 1968, bears out this conclusion. While the Board proposed variations in the amount of the scale fees for conveyancing, and felt that the *ad valorem* system produced in levels above £20,000 a charge higher than could be justified by the work involved, they concluded that the basic principle had not been shown to be at fault. The effect of their recommendations was to reduce the total revenue of the profession from conveyancing, but to counterbalance this by increasing fees for county court work. The Board repeated criticisms made by the Pilkington Commission in 1959 about the lack of information concerning professional earnings. They recommended that statistics should be compiled by the Government, and kept up to date. No reason was given why such information should not be collected by the professional body concerned, rather than the Government. This is clearly a task the professions would do well to take on – otherwise they will in time find it being done by some state organisation. (62)

The criticisms of rules against undercutting have been dealt with in the discussion above on seeking business. The question of undercutting is separable from the general question of how fees should be determined. As currently operated, the restriction on undercutting is of very limited effect, and usually applies only to a fee deliberately reduced in order to attract a new client. We confine ourselves here to the general problem of how, in the interest of the public and the professions, fees ought to be calculated under modern conditions.

The position is complicated by the existence of a "prices and incomes policy", which has been followed by successive Governments (though in somewhat different form) for several years and seems likely to be with us for some time to come. If Governments aim to exercise a close influence, or even control, over all incomes the professions can scarcely hope to be exempt. The most they can do is to ensure that the machinery of the prices and incomes policy, and especially the Prices and Incomes Board itself, is not used as a *primary* means of determining fees. It is beyond the scope of this book to debate the utility of a prices and incomes policy, but it can be confidently asserted that it should operate over and above the normal professional machinery for calculating fees. The professions would do well to resist to the utmost the suggestion, made by the Prices and Incomes Board in 1968, that the Board should itself become the body by which fee scales are from time to time revised. (63)

No more will be said here about the best basis of calculation for fees, whether *ad valorem, quantum meruit,* or any other. Whichever method is used, there is general agreement that it ought to be so operated as to produce a reasonable income for the practitioner. The Prices and Incomes Board describe as reasonable an income which is "sufficient to attract into the business and retain the required human capital and [to secure that] the services of the profession are rendered in the most economical way". (64) One need not quarrel with this criterion, if it be accepted that the standards of the profession must also be maintained. The Bar Council seek an income comparable with that of other professions "having regard to the risks inherent in intense competition and in individual responsibility" and to the need to make provision for retirement. (65)

If these are the guide lines for the level of remuneration, what is required to put them into effect? Some would argue that this should be left to the unrestricted competition of the market. We give reasons below for the rejection of this view. Assuming it is rejected, what remains?

There remains the need of the client for guidance as to the fee he should expect to pay, and the need of the practitioner for guidance as to what level of fees would be regarded as reasonable by his colleagues and the public generally. The question is how this guidance ought to be given, and no single answer is possible. We start from the position however that the person or body who is to decide what level of fees is necessary to conform to the desired criteria, and what technique is to be used for calculation, must be one having the fullest knowledge and experience of the factors involved. In other words no one can determine fees properly who lacks a thoroughgoing knowledge of the working of the profession, the current intake of new members and the numbers leaving practice before retiring age, the likely changes in techniques which will affect costs, the opportunities for more efficient performance, and so on. Those best equipped with this knowledge are the members of the profession themselves, and it follows that the professional institute is therefore best able to give the necessary guidance. The only argument that could be produced against leaving the matter to the professional institute is that it could not be trusted to apply the criteria fairly. Or, putting it more mildly, that at least in the case of the "closed" professions the public ought to be allowed some external check on the fairness of guidance given by the professional body. This is the system in the case of solicitors. Their professional body, the Law Society, keeps a watchful eye on fee levels, and when a change is thought necessary will make representations to the appropriate Rule Committee. The Bar does not have this system, but the work of a barrister is so variable that little is possible in the way of guidance by the professional body. Most fees are moreover controlled by the system of taxation of costs, and by fee scales laid down for particular courts. The Chairman of the Bar Council complained in November 1968 that the county court scales had not changed since 1956, fees for prosecutions and interlocutory work had remained static and fees for undefended divorces had been effectively reduced by the transfer of this work to the county court. (66)

Can it be said that where the profession is not "closed" there ought to be no interference with recommendations of the professional body, subject always to the overall operation of the prices and incomes policy? The Prices and Incomes Board, at least, may not think so. They have severely criticised the R.I.B.A. for presuming to give guidance to its members and the public generally by laying down fee scales. The Board seems to have confused the issue of whether such scales should be mandatory (which is certainly debatable) with whether they should be issued at all. Because they clearly do not consider it right for observance of the R.I.B.A. scale to be compulsory for members, the Board have suggested that all guidance on fees should be given by a new independent body. The grounds for this suggestion are curious. One is that only a minority of R.I.B.A. members are principals in private practice, and therefore directly concerned with fees. "We see no necessity", say the Board with breathtaking presumption, "for the power and prestige of the premier professional body to be used in the defence of the interests of a minority of its members". They go on to suggest that the R.I.B.A.'s functions relating to fees should be surrendered to an external body on which the Government, local authorities, the professions concerned with building and client bodies should be represented. (67) It is not surprising that a sister professional society, the R.I.C.S., should have commented that it seemed extraordinary that any organisation would presume to succeed the professional society as the arbiter of such matters. (68)

While it would be quite wrong, and totally unjustified, to deprive a professional body like the R.I.B.A. of the right to issue guidance about fee levels, there may be a case for setting up an independent body representing clients whose purpose would be to comment on scales recommended by the professional institute. The justification for this in the case of the R.I.B.A. would be that, while not a "closed" profession, architecture is so closely identified in the public mind with the R.I.B.A. that the very pre-eminence of that body produces some of the characteristics of such a profession. The need for a "client's watchdog" is doubtful however. The Government, considered as a client, is well able to take care of itself. The local authorities have powerful representative bodies of their own, such as the Association of Municipal Corporations. The smaller client may need some protection but while the Prices and Incomes Board continues it seems pointless to duplicate its operation. Here it is apposite to point out a remarkable discrepancy between two reports of the Prices and Incomes Board issued in the same year, 1968. While the report on solicitors, issued in February, rejected the idea of establishing an independent body to review earnings and charges from time to time on the ground that "the multiplication of bodies of this kind cannot be conducive to the establishment of a single coherent prices and incomes policy" (69), the report on architects issued three months later suggested the establishment of just such a review body for architects. (70) This is how the fate of our great professions is nowadays determined.

In the third category of case, where the profession is neither "closed" nor dominated by a single institute, there seems no case for interfering with the normal right of the various professional bodies to make recommendations about fees. Again this is subject to overriding considerations such as the prices and incomes policy, upon the merits of which we cannot embark in this book. It is as well to remind ourselves however that even so extreme a critic of the professions as Professor Lees pauses in his

attack to point out that: "There are profound objections to the regulation of prices by the state, not least that prices may be set wide of the
competitive mark and regulation may continue after it has outlived
its usefulness." (71)

## Blowing off the Dust

The recent spate of criticism of the professions began with an article
in The Times on 24th January 1966, headed "Blowing the Dust from
the Professions". This was a summary of Professor Lees's criticisms. The
journal of the Chartered Surveyors quickly came out with a spirited
reply under the heading "Into Whose Eyes?", and other professional
journals followed suit. It was indeed all too easy to pick holes in Lees's
analysis, though this did not prevent its having a damaging effect. It is
simple for the uninformed to poke fun at professional rules, and to
demand with an injured air that each and every one of them should be
solely designed for the benefit of the public. The welfare of the profession
itself can easily be shown by demogogic commentators to be an unworthy
aim. That they thus deny human nature troubles them not. It is easy,
again, to sneer with the Prices and Incomes Board at "tradition" (72)
as though the beliefs and ideals handed down by previous generations
were invariably outweighed by the musings of those who only desire
to be "forward-looking".

However justifiable, irritation with its critics should not blind the
professions to the need for periodic re-examination of its rules. Nor does
it. The Bar Council, for example, began in 1962 a thorough reappraisal
of its practices in order to discard those which were no longer justifiable, and this has led to a number of important changes. The R.I.C.S.
speedily responded to the suggestion by the Banwell Committee that
the "contractor" rule should be examined (see page 86), and as we
have seen the Law Society, the R.I.B.A. and the Institute of Chartered
Accountants have all recently examined and relaxed their rules on
advertising. This activity is essential, if expensive in terms of administrative cost. It is furthermore necessary to make known results of such
examinations and to be ready with comprehensive defences of rules
which are to be retained. Again, expense is involved.

Every reader of this book will have his own ideas about which
professional rules constitute "dust" which should be blown off.
Some may select the minute rules about the size and lettering of
nameplates; others may choose the proliferation of designations in
some professions and the misleading nature of some of these. It
may be felt that some rules reinforcing the demarcation between

professions need relaxing. It should be possible, for example, for a lay client to brief a barrister direct where the intervention of a solicitor is obviously unnecessary — as where a company employing a barrister as legal adviser wishes to take counsel's opinion (see page 94). Barristers, it might be thought, should not always insist on clients coming to them for conferences or be regarded as letting the side down if they disregard this rule. Rules against incorporation may, as suggested above (page 106-7), need to be modified. Many more examples could be added, but it is not the purpose of this book to presume to tell the professions what improvements they should make in their rules. What is certain is that no professional body can afford to neglect its defences. If it is not ready with a full and detailed justification, based on historical grounds but also taking account of modern conditions, for every so-called restriction which it retains, it is likely to meet continued criticism and ultimate state interference.

## Keeping up to the Mark

Another point on which the professions need to look to their defences concerns the enforcement of standards. We have discussed this question already (page 50ff.). It partly concerns the content of the code, particularly in relation to incompetence by a practitioner, and partly the extent to which its observance is insisted on.

The gravamen of the charge against the professions is undoubtedly that they pay too much attention to rules designed for their own protection and too little to disciplining practitioners who fail in their duty to the public. This is the constant refrain of commentators, both friendly and hostile.

We have in Part II of this book set out principles of professional practice which the public are entitled to see observed. Where they are not observed the public may justly expect something to be done about it by the profession. This may mean that clients should be encouraged, where they feel a sense of grievance, to put in a complaint to the appropriate disciplinary body. They should be told what the standards of conduct are, so that they may see whether they have been transgressed (books on professional ethics published by the institutes have hitherto been designed mainly for the information of their own members). The titles and addresses of disciplinary bodies should be included in standard works of reference, and the public given information about the procedure for lodging a complaint. The practice under which bodies such as the British Medical Association decline to pass on complaints to the General Medical Council should be discontinued. The institutes should no longer use the possibility of court proceedings as a justification for inaction; at least they should ensure that when court proceedings are complete the disciplinary body looks into the matter. Investigation by non-statutory bodies may be hampered by lack of powers available to courts, for example to compel the attendance of witnesses. There might be a case for giving such powers, under appropriate safeguards. The example of the Institute of Chartered Accountants should be followed in giving full information to members about the nature of charges in disciplinary cases, the results of proceedings and the penalties imposed. Perhaps the practice of the General Medical Council should be imitated, and hearings conducted in public. Certainly the public should be kept informed about disciplinary action. Loss of confidence owing to publication of professional misdemeanours would be outweighed by knowledge that the profession believed in its standards to the extent of enforcing them rigorously.

An increase in the number of investigations and the publicity given to disciplinary proceedings would add to the already burdensome expenses of the institutes. Who should pay? The obvious answer is the erring practitioners themselves, in the form of costs and fines.

So far as concerns keeping practitioners up to the mark by making changes in the code, two points need to be stressed. One concerns the need to make adequate professional indemnity insurance mandatory, and to back this by fully developed accounting rules. The other is the treatment of serious cases of incompetence as misconduct. The professions' oft-repeated claim that their rules operate directly or indirectly for the public's good would be much better received if they were seen to take account of this need of the public's to be protected against incompetent practitioners. Where instances of widespread incompetence come to light, as for example in the case of some solicitors engaged in legal aid work whose standards were criticised by the Widgery Committee (73), the professional body needs to take swift and effective action. It is not suggested of course that proceedings for incompetence should be brought in other than clear cases. Practitioners should not be harassed by the threat of proceedings over what amount to genuine differences of professional judgment, rival theories of some aspect of professional expertise or mere witch-hunting. Much professional advice turns on the attribute of judgment. Only in extreme cases can an error of judgment be held culpable on professional grounds.

Professional rules are unlikely to be obeyed unless they are known and understood by those to whom they apply. Apart from the need, mentioned above, for greater publicity within the profession for disciplinary proceedings there is also a vital need for proper training of new entrants in what is expected of them. Other professions might profitably study the R.I.B.A.'s practice of teaching and examining in rules of professional conduct.

Even if all these things were put into effect there would still, on the evidence of current enforcement statistics, be many breaches of rules which would be likely to go unpunished. This may be because the difficulty of securing evidence, and the time and expense of proceedings, are held not to justify formal action. Alternatively it may be because formal action has not seemed appropriate anyway. Many breaches of rules against advertising, touting or undercutting go unpunished. Since these primarily concern the profession itself it is for the professional body to take action or not, as it thinks fit. It is never healthy however to have in the rule book injunctions which are allowed to be broken with impunity. This weakens the respect paid to other more essential rules. One answer would be to put rules for which formal sanctions are considered inappropriate into a different category – perhaps regarding them as mere "etiquette". Breaches of etiquette would be visited by informal signs of the profession's displeasure – a rebuke from a senior member, perhaps, or a warning letter from the secretary of the institute. Rules of this kind have the great advantage that they are beyond the reach of outside busybodies, and are wholly in the hands of the profession itself.

## The Complaint of Monopoly

The consultant professions, or many of them, are accused of monopoly by their enemies, and not infrequently by their friends. The term is freely employed by economists such as Professor Lees, by students of the professions like Carr-Saunders and Wilson, by the Prices and Incomes Board, and even by journals catering for the professions. Yet it is nowadays a pejorative expression, raising visions of unscrupulous extortioners preying on society. Lees distinguishes two forms of monopoly. A legal monopoly is said to exist where the state has by law prohibited persons outside the profession from providing the services in question. An effective monopoly exists where, although the state has not gone thus far, the profession is in a comparable position for other reasons, for example because the majority of clients, or perhaps a monopoly client, declines to give business to unqualified practitioners. Lees identifies thirteen professions as being either legal or effective monopolies, of which eight are connected with medicine. (74)

Before going further we must ask ourselves whether, notwithstanding this wide use of the term monopoly in relation to the professions, it is a correct use of language. Dictionaries define the term as an exclusive right or privilege enjoyed by a particular person or body. By means of this right or privilege, in classical economic theory, the person or body will make profits exceeding those obtainable where there is no monopoly. Where demand is inelastic this may be done simply by raising prices; in other cases the method is to lower quality (and therefore costs) without lowering the price. Either way the public is exploited in a way not now considered justfiable.

Is this the case with the professions or any of them? By a confusion of thought it is supposed to be so. There is a professional body, usually a body corporate, and in the case of the legal "monopoly" at least it will usually be this body which has secured from the state the passing of laws prohibiting outsiders from practising. Is it then a monopolist? A little reflection will show that it is not. The professional services are not provided by the professional body, but by individual practitioners. The body itself cannot exploit the rights it has secured, since remuneration for professional services will pass straight to the practitioners. They are a host of individuals whose economic ends are their own and no one else's. Restrained only by the rules and traditions of their professional brotherhood, they are each in active competition with one another. Their resources are not pooled, their work is not carried out in concert and their rewards are not shared. This is individualism, not monopoly.*

What then do Lees and others complain of when they refer to monopoly? Treating a profession as comprising all who are capable of exercising its arts, we can say that the complaint is against the unification of the profession. Unification, if effective, means that all practitioners agree, through an elected council, on what attainments qualify for practice, and what rules members should observe.

What complaints are levelled against unification masquerading as monopoly? Lees makes a halfhearted suggestion that practitioners gain

---

*The Institute of Chartered Accountants showed its understanding of the real meaning of monopoly when defending to the Monopolies Commission the rules against poaching of clients by firms offering management consultancy services. Admitting that the rule protected small firms unable to provide these services themselves, the Institute said that such protection was in the public interest because "the encouragement of the large number of small firms within the profession operates to prevent conditions favouring monopoly from developing".

the reward of the classical monopolist. But after raising the hypothesis that professional incomes contain an element of monopoly rent, he admits that not only is there no evidence that this is so, but "there is no chance of testing the hypothesis." (75) Owing to absence of information "we cannot even make a start towards an answer". (76) Some pages later we find the professor has forgotten his depression (and indeed his conclusion) and is asserting that as a result of unification or "monopoly" consumers "lose out in the form of higher costs and prices". (77) A few pages later still we find, without evidence, that "the public are paying barristers too much". (78)

Hopefully, another horse is tried. If the unified group assumes power to control entry, it might artificially restrict the number of entrants in order to give monopoly advantages to those already qualified. As we have shown, there is no evidence that this is done, and Lees does not succeed in producing any. That horse won't run. Lees is thus reduced to general grumbles that "monopoly" reduces competition; at one point he says, clearly wrongly, that it eliminates competition. (79) It is not surprising that the professor concludes that the problem of monopoly "seems less serious than is commonly supposed", and that where it exists there appear to be strong safeguards.

Although it is easy to explode such inconsistent and unsupported criticisms of professional unification, their very persistence shows that more is required. The best defence is to demonstrate real and substantial advantages, and not merely repel criticisms. That advantages exist, and are indeed substantial, has been amply demonstrated by Emile Durkheim, founder of the French school of sociologists. In *Professional Ethics and Civic Morals*, first published in 1950, he explains the social importance of professional groups and their codes. So valuable are they that he would see counterparts established in every field of industry and commerce: "no reform has greater urgency". (80) Where institutes exist they enjoy a comparative autonomy "since each alone is competent to deal with the relations it is appointed to regulate". (81) They can only be formed by bringing together individuals of the same profession. Without them there is in the field of morality between workers at the same task a vacuum. A system of morals is always the affair of a group and can operate only if this group protects its constituent members by its authority. Durkheim holds that the state itself is unfitted for this task "and its intervention, when not simply powerless, causes troubles of another kind". (82)

In a remarkable series of passages, Durkheim sets out the claim of professional ethics to rank higher than blind economic forces. They confirm the thesis of this book, and are of such importance as to demand extensive quotation. After showing that the moral crisis from which European societies are suffering springs from the growth of economic and industrial activity, he continues:

"A form of activity that promises to occupy such a place in society taken as a whole cannot be exempt from all precise moral regulation, without a state of anarchy ensuing. The forces thus released can have no guidance for their normal development, since there is nothing to point out where a halt should be called. There is a head-on clash when the moves of rivals conflict, as they attempt to encroach on another's field or to beat him down or drive him out. Certainly the stronger succeed in crushing the not so strong or at any rate in reducing them to a state of subjection. But since this subjection is only a *de facto* condition sanctioned by no kind of morals, it is accepted only under duress until the longed-for day of revenge. Peace treaties signed in this fashion are always provisional, forms of truce that do not mean peace to men's minds. This is how these ever-recurring conflicts arise between the different factions of the economic structure. If we put forward this anarchic competition as an ideal we should adhere to − one that should even be put into practice more radically than it is today − then we should be confusing sickness with a condition of good health. On the other hand, we shall not get away from this simply by modifying once and for all the lay-out of economic life; for whatever we contrive, whatever new arrangements be introduced, it will still not become other than it is or change its nature. By its very nature, it cannot be self-sufficing. A state of order or peace amongst men cannot follow of itself from any material causes, from any blind mechanism, however scientific it may be. It is a moral task.

From yet another point of view, this amoral character of economic life amounts to a public danger. The functions of this order today absorb the energies of the greater part of the nation. The lives of a host of individuals are passed in the industrial and commercial sphere. Hence, it follows that, as those in this *milieu* have only a faint impress of morality, the greater part of their existence is passed divorced from any moral influence. How could such a state of affairs fail to be a source of demoralization? If a sense of duty is to take strong root in us, the very circumstances of our life must serve to keep it always active. There must be a group about us to call it to mind all the time and, as often happens, when we are tempted to turn a deaf ear. A way of behaviour, no matter what it be, is set on a steady course only through habit and exercise. If we live amorally for a good part of the day, how can we keep the springs of morality from going slack in us? We are not naturally inclined to put ourselves out or to use self-restraint; if we are not encouraged at every step to exercise the restraint upon which all morals depend, how should we get the habit of it? If we follow no rule except that of a clear self-interest, in the occupations that take up nearly the whole of our time, how should we acquire a taste for any disinterestedness, or selflessness or sacrifice? . . .

It is therefore extremely important that economic life should be regulated, should have its moral standards raised, so that the conflicts that disturb it have an end, and further, that individuals should cease to live thus within a moral vacuum where the life-blood drains away even from individual morality. For in this order of social functions there is need for professional ethics to be established, nearer the concrete, closer to the facts, with a wider scope than anything existing today . . . A system of ethics, however, is not to be improvised. It is the task of the very group to which they are to apply. When they fail, it is because the cohesion of the group is at fault, because as a group its existence is too shadowy and the rudimentary state of its ethics goes to show its lack of integration. Therefore, the true cure for the evil is to give the professional groups in the economic order a stability they so far do not possess." (83)

Durkheim sees the *content* of the code as a set of rules laying down for each individual what he should do so as not to damage collective interests and so as not to disorganise the society of which he forms a part.

"If he allowed himself to follow his bent, there would be no reason why he should not make his way or, at very least, try to make his way, regardless of everyone in his path and without concern for any disturbance he might be causing about him. It is this discipline that curbs him, that marks the boundaries, that tells him what his relations with his associates should be, where illicit encroachments begin,

Q

and what he must pay in current dues towards the maintenance of the community." (84)

Durkheim demonstrates how working groups lacking a system of
ethics deprive their members of the guidance needed to prevent anti-
social sins. In a vital passage he dismisses the argument of classical
economists that this moral anarchy is a privilege of economic life:

"But from what source could it derive such a privilege?
How should this particular social function be exempt from
a condition which is the most fundamental to any social
structure? Clearly, if there has been self-delusion to this
degree amongst the classical economists it is because the
economic functions were studied as if they were an end
in themselves, without considering what further reaction
they might have on the whole social order. Judged in this
way, productive output seemed to be the sole primary aim
in all industrial activity. In some ways it might appear that
output, to be intensive, had no need at all to be regulated;
that on the contrary, the best thing were to leave individual
businesses and enterprises of self-interest to excite and spur
on one another in hot competition, instead of our trying to
curb and keep them within bounds. But production is not
all, and if industry can only bring its output to this pitch
by keeping up a chronic state of warfare and endless dissatisfaction amongst the producers, there is nothing to
balance the evil it does. Even from the strictly utilitarian
standpoint, what is the purpose of heaping up riches if they
do not serve to abate the desires of the greatest number,
but, on the contrary, only rouse their impatience for gain?
That would be to lose sight of the fact that economic functions are not an end in themselves but only a means to an
end; that they are one of the organs of social life and
that social life is above all a harmonious community of
endeavours, when minds and will come together to work
for the same aim. Society has no justification if it does
not bring a little peace to men — peace in their hearts
and peace in their mutual intercourse. If, then, industry
can be productive only by disturbing their peace and unleash-
ing warfare, it is not worth the cost." (85)

The same theme is taken up later, in language that must surely
remind the most severely practical economist that economic man has
other attributes as well. The individual, says Durkheim, finds decided

advantage in taking shelter under the roof of a collectivity that ensures peace for him; he knows that anarchy is painful:

> "He too suffers from the everlasting wranglings and endless friction that occur when relations between an individual and his fellows are not subject to any regulative influence. It is not a good thing for a man to live like this on a war footing amongst his closest comrades and to entrench himself always as though in the midst of enemies. This sensation of hostility all about him and the nervous strain involved in resisting it, this ceaseless mistrust one of another — all this is a source of pain; for though we may like a fight, we also love the joys of peace; we might say that the more highly and the more profoundly men are socialized, that is to say, civilized — for the two are synonomous — the more those joys are prized. That is why, when individuals who share the same interests come together, their purpose is not simply to safeguard those interests or to secure their development in face of rival associations. It is, rather, just to associate, for the sole pleasure of mixing with their fellows and of no longer feeling lost in the midst of adversaries, as well as for the pleasure of communing together, that is, in short, of being able to lead their lives with the same moral aim." (86)

Pure economic forces are amoral — the tincture of morality, essential to social wellbeing, can arise only within groups. As religious groups decline, those of the professions assume greater, not less, importance. For many people today professional ideals form the only system of group morality with which they are in contact.

To attack the homogenity of a profession, to accuse if of "monopoly" because it aims to comprehend all who practise its specialty, is to attack the potent source of social morality which Durkheim would extend throughout the sphere of labour and employment. To break the cohesion of natural groupings in the cause of marginally greater economic effectiveness might well prove one of the social disasters of the twentieth century.

## CHAPTER 15

# LOOKING AHEAD

If the argument of this book is accepted the consultant professions are seen as far more than mere providers of services to be bought and sold in the market place. They set an example, and give a tone to society the effect and influence of which is far-reaching. Even if they are looked on solely as providers of services, however, their importance is growing. Within the vital field of health, rights and property there is an increasing demand for advisory services. This is illustrated by the growth in numbers of practising professionals. The number of architects grew by 50% between 1950 and 1966 (1) and in the six years ending in the latter year the number of practising barristers grew by 17%. (2) This rate of growth is expected to continue, and may well be inadequate to meet the real needs of the public. If the professions grow in numbers and importance, so will the significance to society of the way they are organised and operate. If, as we contend, this way is not only the most satisfactory for the immediate purpose but also has valuable social side-effects, it follows that society needs to ensure that conditions are right for its future wellbeing.

Because the professional system we have described is right and natural we need not be surprised to find it extending to other fields. Wherever there is scope for consultancy services concerning health, rights or property we may expect to see the continued development of new consultant professions organised on similar lines to those of long standing. This is an evolving process. In comparatively recent times professions such as accountancy and surveying have, on the lines of older professions, established themselves firmly. We may expect the process to continue as new specialisms are evolved to meet new needs. Since the process is imitative there is a responsibility on the older professions to ensure that the example they set is in every way the best possible. They will thus spread the social good of professionalism widely through society, benefitting many others as well as themselves.

Some consultants may continue to stand aloof from professional organisations. Although their role as consultants is increasing, economists have so far declined to form a professional organisation. Their current influence in matters of finance and property is of course immense but the objects of setting up a professional institute, notably the pooling of ideas and experience and forging of an agreed set of principles, are not attempted. Perhaps this is why economists so often fail to agree, and why their advice does not always have the effect intended.

The prospective expansion of British professional practices is not limited to Britain itself. The major professions have long acted as training grounds for students from the Commonwealth, most of whom return to their own countries on qualifying. They often retain membership of the British institute — the Institute of Chartered Accountants has for example more than 5,000 overseas members. It is natural that British professional ideas, thus exported, should take root in the developing countries of the Commonwealth. They are fostered by numerous Commonwealth associations of which the constituent members are autonomous professional bodies. Such associations flourish in the fields of medicine and architecture, and an association is currently being set up for surveyors. Other professions, such as law, have organisations which are international and not merely Commonwealth in ambit.

To help improve the effectiveness, the standards and the prestige of the professions in the Commonwealth, and particularly in the underdeveloped countries, the Commonwealth Foundation was established in 1966. The governments of the Commonwealth, in setting up the Foundation, agreed to provide it with an annual income of a quarter of a million pounds. This is used to make grants, particularly to organisations in the newer Commonwealth countries. Part of this money has been used to set up lectureships to encourage the spread of professional ideals. Another proposal is to create professional centres in developing countries. These are designed to meet the problem that emergent professional groups in these countries lack finance and have only small memberships. They are therefore unable to afford the necessary premises and secretarial services. The professional centres will each consist of suites of offices to be shared by all professional bodies willing to take part. Staff will also be employed on a shared basis. The first two centres are planned at Kampala and Port-of-Spain. (3)

The exporting process is not of course limited to ideas and methods. Many British firms are establishing branches on the continent of Europe and elsewhere. Despite many difficulties the value of British professional ideals is coming to be appreciated in Europe. The advantages of this in economic terms and prestige are obvious, and it is a trend to be encouraged. To help on this process within the field of construction, the British Overseas Engineering Services Bureau was set up in 1967 on the initiative of the Association of Consulting Engineers. The Bureau promotes the overseas work of British consultants. Its main function is to ensure that the possibility of employing British consultants is considered by foreign clients, and to recommend firms to those clients. Half the administrative costs are met by the Board of Trade.

A further aspect of the importance of healthy professions lies in their peripheral advantages to the public. Campaigning by professional bodies for social improvements can have a decisive effect. The British Medical Association can claim the credit for the introduction of compulsory registration of births, marriages and deaths and the introduction of universal vaccination. (4) The setting up of the British Standards Institution, which has been of inestimable value to industry, can be traced to the initiative of the engineering profession. (5) Facilities such as professional libraries are often made freely available to the public. This is the case, for example, with the R.I.B.A. library – one of the two largest architectural libraries in the world, with a stock of over 70,000 books and 500 current periodicals, not to mention the world's largest collection of architectural drawings. (6) Firms themselves often make wide-ranging contributions; the quantity surveying firm of Munk and Dunstone have done pioneering work of great value in computers. The public work of individual practitioners in serving on Government committees and similar bodies is of undoubted importance. In the long run, all such contributions to the public welfare depend ultimately on the health of the professions.

## The Institutes and the Future

Being convinced of the rightness of their cause, and the importance of their success, how should the institutes seek to bring this about? They certainly need to take every opportunity to allay hostility and soothe public disquiet. In face of growing egalitarian pressures this will not be easy. Some commentators have stigmatised the professions as a socially divisive, institutionalised elite. Their members are accused of being superior beings addicted to ritual and mystery. Other attacks have come from the realm of business. Lord Campbell of Eskan, in a speech in 1966, criticised the tendency of the professions to behave as "a sort of priesthood apart from the hurly-burly of the business or political world". He went on to ask for more competition between consultants and less prudishness about advertising. These criticisms are easy to make and difficult to counter effectively. This is particularly true when, as not infrequently happens, they come from professional people themselves. People who are disgruntled with their profession often rush to attack it in print; those who regard their profession with approval are usually too busy practising it to sing its praises. As Mr. Arabin found in *Barchester Towers:* "It is so easy to condemn; and so pleasant too; for eulogy charms no listeners as detraction does."

There is certainly a need for professional people, fully instructed about the content and justification for their code, to adopt a positive, rather than a defensive posture. In order to convince others it is first necessary to convince oneself. While it is part of the professional nature to see things objectively and judicially, and to avoid extremism, this should not be carried beyond the process of making up one's mind. Once there is conviction, it needs to be acted upon.

An extraordinary illustration of the tendency of professional people to undervalue themselves was contained in proposals for the redevelopment of the Whitehall area of London, published in 1965. Prepared by a distinguished team of architects, led by Sir Leslie Martin, the plan at one point recommended the removal of two professional institutions which had occupied their sites near Parliament Square for around a hundred years on the argument that such bodies were of insufficient importance in the national life to warrant their occupation of such a position. That professional men should have reached this conclusion is startling. Lack of self-confidence in the importance of one's role in affairs does not lead to success in convincing others.

The professions must learn to react more positively to attacks. Under recent public interference, some of it intolerable, their leaders have grumbled but not spoken out. The attitude of the solicitors and architects, for example, to wide-ranging proposals (based on obviously inadequate information and experience) from the Prices and Incomes Board was one of pained but dignified reproach. This got them nowhere. Contrast the reaction of university teachers to a similar report affecting their future. Immediately on the publication, in December 1968, of the Board's report on university teachers' pay, which included a suggestion that the remuneration of lecturers should vary according to students' estimates of their ability, the Vice-Chancellor of Liverpool University announced his resignation in protest. Other protests quickly followed. Professor Andrew Young, of Ulster University, declared that the report was a fundamental attack on the autonomy and freedom of the universities and should be considered in a spirit of contempt. The Association of University Teachers secured an interview with the Minister responsible for education, who gave an undertaking that the Government would not accept the objectional features of the report. By its immediate and violent response the academic world reduced the report to the level of importance it deserved. (7)

We have considered the need to publicise professional services, and the staffing and financial difficulties this involves. The burdens could be lessened by concerted action. Hitherto, owing to the tradition of exclusiveness of the professional bodies, moves have generally been made in isolation, are very often duplicated, and undoubtedly lose their force and effectiveness by dispersion, with its concomitant of scattered timing and feeble impact.

In this book we have treated rules of conduct operated by the consultant professions as a single code, on the premise that while there are of course individual variations these are minor in comparison with the common ground. If this is right it justifies, indeed demands, unified action by the professions in relation to the code. The common features, which predominate, could be reduced to a single formulation. This basic code, being the same for all, could be explained and defended very much more easily. Individual institutes could adopt the basic code with minor variations (if really deemed necessary), and could add additional rules of their own. The cost of disciplinary proceedings could be reduced by having a common procedure and a shared staff to administer the common code. It might be necessary to have different tribunals, so that each accused could be judged by his peers, but even this could be dispensed with at least in some cases. There seems no obvious reason why an accountant found guilty of toutingsor undercutting should be dealt with differently from an architect or a solicitor.

There are many other matters which could be dealt with on common lines with a saving of money and a gain in efficiency. Proposals for legislation affecting the professions, particularly on taxation, could be examined jointly and representations to government made with one voice. Sometimes a professional body seeks to promote legislation. If it does so in isolation its effort will be weakened and may not succeed. Or, if it succeeds, other professions who would equally have benefited may be excluded. This happened in the case of legislation to deal with the situation caused by the decision in *Brown* v. *Inland Revenue Commissioners*, (8) where the court held that a professional firm was not entitled to retain interest on money held in its client's account. The principle of this was not challenged, but legislation was required to remove certain practical difficulties. A bill was promoted in Parliament by the Law Society, and passed; but it applied only to solicitors. Other professions equally affected by the decision have not shared in the remedy. The ineffectiveness of separate representations was illustrated when Selective Employment Tax was introduced in 1966. Although each professional body made strong protests to the Government they were unco-ordinated. The arguments were not always the same, and the Government were easily able to disregard them.

Other matters of common concern arise from the fact that a private firm has much the same problems in financing itself, organising its offices, handling clerical and administrative staff and coping with rating, tax and planning problems, whatever the nature of the practice carried on by it. Advice to practitioners on these problems could be given on a uniform basis.

Another field in which the consultant professions could co-operate more closely is that of public relations. Between them, the institutes employ a considerable number of staff engaged in various aspects of public relations and there would be an obvious increase in effectiveness if, on points concerning the professions generally, the public relations resources could operate collectively rather than making individual, and possibly even inconsistent, forays.

The professions have banded together in one way or another in a number of countries. On the continent of Europe there are professional groups recognised and even sponsored by governments. In Australia attempts are currently being made to set up a Council of the Professions. This is by extension of the New South Wales Council of the Professions which has been in existence some years. In the Republic of Ireland there was set up in 1966 a Federation of Professional Associations.

It is suggested that the institutes in Britain would do well to establish a Council of Consultant Professions. This should not detract from the autonomy of the individual institutes. It would be a body with advisory functions, coupled with executive duties under authority granted by the constituent bodies. It would need to have a permanent staff and premises. Just as the Confederation of British Industries operates effectively without detracting from the independence of member companies, and the Trades Union Council serves, rather than is served by, the independent unions, so the Council of Consultant Professions could operate as a valuable adjunct, in no way diminishing the self-determination of the professional institutes. Where any clash threatened between two institutes, as in the case of "demarcation" disputes, the Council could mediate with advantage.

In their submission to the Monopolies Commission the Consumer Council suggested that professional bodies tended to impose rules on their members which did not operate in the public interest, and that a Government department should be set up to deal with this, headed by a registrar of professional societies. The registrar would supervise conditions of entry and the rules and disciplinary procedures of professional bodies. This function is to some extent performed in relation to chartered bodies only by the Clerk of the Privy Council, and it therefore seems unnecessary to establish a new department. It would be better to extend the jurisdiction of the Clerk of the Privy Council, if really considered necessary, so that it embraced all professional bodies. It is suggested however that this step would not be required if a Council of Consultant Professions were set up. This could operate in the same way as a unifying factor, and could include independent members who would draw attention to rules which seemed to be operating adversely to the public interest. It would have the great advantage that control would remain, where it belongs, in the hands of the professions. The Council would no doubt consult from time to time, if so required, with an appropriate Government department and in practice the public interest would be fully safeguarded.

Apart from its other advantages, the setting up of a Council of Consultant Professions would demonstrate to the public the concern of the institutes that their house should be put and kept in order. In this respect it might be compared to the establishment in 1946 of the Retail Trading-Standards Association. This voluntary body, set up by retailers and manufacturers, played a prominent part in dealing with traders in false trade descriptions. It proceeded by issuing warning notices, and even launching prosecutions against offenders. It has published codes for its members on such merchandise as fabrics, clothing, furniture and domestic hardware. (9)

## The State Intervenes

The constant carping at the professions, ill-founded though most of it is, has had its effect. Public sympathy has been forfeited, even though undeservedly. A climate of opinion has been brought into being against the professions, so that a defence of the code is described by headline writers as "clinging to restrictive practices". Editorial writers rebuke institutes for presuming to stand up for their practices. Authors of books are rude in chapter headings.* Any stick will do to beat the professions with.

It was in these circumstances that the Government decided to refer the question of professional restrictions to the Monopolies Commission. This was done under powers conferred on the Board of Trade by the Monopolies and Mergers Act, 1965, s.5, under which the Board can require the Commission to submit a report on the general effect on the public interest of practices of a specified class which are commonly

---

* Chapter XV of *Lawyers and the Courts* by Abel-Smith and Stevens (London, 1967) severely critises recent efforts by the Bar Council to increase remuneration. It is headed "The Barristers' Trade Union in Action". Yet these authors would think a trade union a worthy body if representing manual workers. Is this snobbery?

adopted as a result of, or for the purpose of preserving, conditions of monopoly, or of any specified practices which appear to the Board to have the effect of preventing, restricting or distorting competition in connection with the production or supply of goods or services. The reference was made on 30th January 1967 and at the time of writing the report has not yet appeared. The professional practices covered by the reference include practices regulating entry, fees, incorporation or partnership, terms of service and advertising. In announcing the reference the Government indicated in Parliament that it was intended to be followed by legislation, where the need for this was indicated.

The terms of reference of the Monopolies Commission preclude an all-round examination of the professions: the Commission are directed to concentrate on so-called restrictive practices only. As this book has attempted to show, the practices of the professions need to be seen as a whole. Their true operation cannot be assessed by looking at so-called restrictive practices in isolation — this is bound to produce a distorted view. Distortion is also likely to result from entrusting the examination of professional practices to a body whose very name seems to some extent to prejudge the issue. As we have shown above the word "monopoly" is inappropriate in relation to the professions. To begin an examination of this kind on the assumption that conditions of monopoly are likely to exist, and using techniques hitherto employed in relation to commercial companies, is to start the enquiry with a bias from which it might easily not recover. Whether the Commission succeeds in overcoming this obstacle has yet to be seen.

At the time of writing, the outcome of State intervention remains in doubt. So far, despite a large dose of socialisation, the medical, dental and legal professions have retained their essential nature. The operations of State boards and commissions have not yet proceeded to the extent of taking autonomy from any professional institutes. Danger flags are fluttering in the breeze however. One delusion may prove critical. It is the delusion that because standards of conduct are now high they will remain so although their supports are forcibly dismantled. The code of professional ethics is not scaffolding to be removed from a building now complete. It is the steel framework integral to the structure.

# NOTES AND REFERENCES

The following abbreviations are used in the notes and references —

"A.C.E. Code". Professional Rules and Practice of the Association of Consulting Engineers, London, 1965.

"*Advertising and the Public*". *Advertising and the Public*, by Ralph Harris and Arthur Seldon, Institute of Economic Affairs, 1962.

"A.R.C.U.K. Code". Architects Registration Council of the United Kingdom Code.

"Baster". *Advertising Reconsidered – A Confession of Misgiving*, by A.S.J. Baster, London, 1935.

"B.M.A. Submission". Statement by the British Medical Association to the Monopolies Commission, 1967-68.

"Boulton". *Etiquette at the Bar*, by W.W. Boulton.

"Carr-Saunders and Wilson". *The Professions*, by Sir A. Carr-Saunders and P.A. Wilson, Frank Cass & Co. Ltd., London, 1933 (second imp. 1964).

"Chartered Accountants' submission". Statement by the Institute of Chartered Accountants in England and Wales to the Monopolies Commission.

"Croxton-Smith". *Professional Ethics*, by C. Croxton-Smith, Institute of Chartered Accountants in England and Wales, London, 1965.

"Denys Thompson". *Voice of Civilization – An Enquiry into Advertising*, by Denys Thompson, London, 1944.

"Durkheim" *Professional Ethics and Civic Morals*, by Emile Durkheim, translated by Cornelia Brookfield, Routledge & Kegan Paul, 1957.

"Hodgkinson". *Debit Experience Account,* by Norman J. Hodgkinson, The Estates Gazette Ltd., London, undated.

"Knox and Hennessy". *Restrictive Practices in the Building Industry,* by Frank Knox and Jossleyn Hennessy, Institute of Economic Affairs, 1966.

"Law Society's Submission". Memorandum of Evidence by the Council of the Law Society to the Monopolies Commission, September 1968.

*"Lawyers and the Courts". Lawyers and the Courts,* by Brian Abel-Smith and Robert Stevens, Heinemann, 1967.

"Lees". *Economic Consequences of the Professions,* by D.S. Lees, The Institute of Economic Affairs, 1966.

"Lewis and Maude" *Professional People,* by Roy Lewis and Angus Maude, Phoenix House Ltd., London, 1952.

"Lund" *A Guide to the Professional Conduct and Etiquette of Solicitors,* by Sir Thomas Lund, C.B.E., The Law Society, 1960.

*"Medical Ethics" Medical Ethics,* British Medical Association, London, 1965.

"Mencher". *Private Practice in Britain,* by Samuel Mencher, G. Bell & Sons, London, 1967.

"Millerson". *The Qualifying Associations,* by Geoffrey Millerson, Routledge & Kegan Paul, London, 1964.

"Pilkington Report". Report of the Royal Commission on Doctors' and Dentists' Remuneration 1957-60 (Cmnd. 939).

"Reader". *Professional Men,* by W.J. Reader, Weidenfeld & Nicholson, London, 1966.

"R.I.C.S. and Associates' Submission". Memorandum of Evidence to the Monopolies Commission by the Royal Institution of Chartered

Surveyors, the Chartered Land Agents Society, the Chartered Auctioneers' and Estate Agents' Institute, the Incorporated Society of Auctioneers and Landed Property Agents and the Valuers' Institution, 31st January 1968.

"R.I.C.S. Charters". The Royal Institution of Chartered Surveyors Royal Charters and Bye-Laws 1958, amended 1964 (published by the Institution).

"F.M.L. Thompson". *Chartered Surveyors,* by F.M.L. Thompson, Routledge & Kegan Paul, London, 1968.

"Turner". *The Shocking History of Advertising,* by E.S. Turner, Penguin Books, 1965.

## CHAPTER 1. Elements of Professionalism

1. Millerson, pp. 1-10.
2. Lewis and Maude, p. 54.
3. Millerson, p. 10.
4. Originally framed by G.W. Higgin in an article in the R.I.B.A. Journal for April, 1964.
5. Lewis and Maude, p. 137.
6. Carr-Saunders and Wilson, p. 3.
7. Reader, p. 8.
8. Reader, p. 9.
9. Carr-Saunders and Wilson, p. 3.
10. Lewis and Maude, p. 109.
11. Lewis and Maude, p. 121.
12. Reader, p. 40.
13. [1968] 3 W.L.R. 286.
13a. Diaries and Letters 1945-62, p. 269.
14. Lewis and Maude, p. 108.
15. Estate Agents Bill, 1965, Clause 10, as amended.
16. R.I.C.S. and Associates' Submission, p. 19.
17. Hodgkinson, p. 21.
18. Reader, p. 60.
19. Lewis and Maude, p. 26.
20. Carr-Saunders and Wilson, p. 430.
21. Carr-Saunders and Wilson, p. 143.
22. Reader, p. 113.
23. Reader, p. 123.
24. Reader, p. 117.
25. Fortnightly Review II (New Series) p. 177n.
26. Carr-Saunders and Wilson, p. 73.
27. The Hairdressing Act, 1964.
28. Mencher, p. 9.
29. Millerson, p. 7.
30. Pilkington Report, para. 142.
31. Law Society's Submission, p. 7.
32. Millerson, p. 8.
33. Millerson, p. 153.
34. Mencher, p. 73.

## CHAPTER 2. Consultant Professions

1. See a 13th century work cited by F.M.L. Thompson, p. 5.
2. A.C.E. Code, p. 4.
3. *Cordery on Solicitors*, 6th ed. p. 489.
4. Lees, p. 35.
5. *Ibid.*
6. Carr-Saunders and Wilson, p. 82.
7. R.I.B.A. Submission to Monopolies Commission, 1967, p. 4.
8. R.I.C.S. Charters, p. 23.
9. A.C.E. Code, p. 4.
10. Millerson, pp. 221-245.
11. Carr-Saunders and Wilson, pp. 7-233.
12. [1957] 2 Q.B. 567, per Devlin J.
13. *Allinson* v. *General Council of Medical Education and Registration* [1894] 1 Q.B. 750.
14. *Medical Ethics*, p. 35.
15. *Hughes* v. *A.R.C.U.K.* [1957] 2 Q.B. 561.
16. *Marten* v. *Royal College of Veterinary Surgeons* [1965] 1 All E.R. 949.
17. Lund, p. 120.
18. Lund, p. 123.
19. *Medical Ethics*, p. 35.
20. Lund, p. 117.
21. *Medical Ethics*, p. 42.

## CHAPTER 2. (contd.)

22. Lund, p. 117.
23. *Sivarajah* v. *General Medical Council* [1964] 1 All E.R. 504.
24. *General Medical Council* v. *Spackman* [1943] A.C. 627.
25. *Medical Ethics*, p. 35.
26. *Hughes* v. *A.R.C.U.K.* [1957] 2

Q.B. 558; *Marten* v. *Royal College of Veterinary Surgeons* [1965] 1 All E.R. 949.
27. Croxton-Smith, p. 49.
28. *Medical Ethics*, p. 43.
29. B.M.A. Submission to Monopolies Commission, p. 28.

## CHAPTER 3. Competence: the Giving of the Hallmark

1. B.M.A. Submission to Monopolies Commission, p. 13.
2. 14 and 15 Henry 8 c. 5.
3. R.I.B.A. Submission to Monopolies Commission, para. 47.
4. Cmnd. 3529, para. 50; Cmnd. 3653, para. 45.
5. Association of Consulting Engineers' Code, p. 3.
6. The Times, 10th October, 1967.
7. Carr-Saunders and Wilson, p. 382.
8. Croxton-Smith, p. 27.
9. Resolution of 27th December, 1881.
10. *Ethical and Legal Obligations of Dental Practitioners*, 1964, p. 7.
11. R.I.B.A. Submission to Monopolies Commission, para. 7.
12. Reader, p. 35.
13. Carr-Saunders and Wilson, p. 375.
14. Reader, p. 56.
15. Carr-Saunders and Wilson, p. 374.
16. R.E. Megarry, *Miscellany-at-Law*, p. 49.
17. Carr-Saunders and Wilson, p. 61.
18. British Medical Journal, 5th October, 1968; The Daily Telegraph, 5th October, 1968.
19. Carr-Saunders and Wilson, p. 395.
20. *The High Girders*, by John Prebble, p. 211.
21. *The High Girders*, by John Prebble, p. 210.
22. Report by Bernard L. Clark & Partners, p. 4.
23. "The Structural Engineer", September 1966, p. 288.
24. "Building", 17th March, 1967.
25. Medical Defence Union, annual report for 1967.
26. *Examples of Law-Making*, Oxford 1962, p. 99.
27. Lund, p. 61.
28. Lund, p. 121.
29. [1960] 2 All E.R. 391.
30. Solicitors Act, 1965, 6, 11, 12, 13.
31. Lund, p. 3.
32. Cmnd. 3529.
33. Dentists Act, 1957, 36-40.

## CHAPTER 4. Humanity: A Personal Relationship

1. *Confessions of an Uncommon Attorney*, p. 24.
2. *Confessions of an Uncommon Attorney*, p. 68.

## CHAPTER 4. (contd.)

3. Hodgkinson, p. 12.
3a. *Demand and Need for Dental Care,* by Nuffield Foundation Hospital Trust, Oxford, 1969.
4. *Medical Ethics,* p. 1.
5. *The Healers,* by K. Pollack and E.A. Underwood, p. 55.
6. *The Healers,* by K. Pollack and E.A. Underwood, p. 55.
7. R.I.C.S. Submission to Monopolies Commission, paras. 58, 59.
8. R.I.C.S. Submission to Monopolies Commission, para. 57.
9. Lewis and Maude, p. 56.
10. Bar Council Submission to Monopolies Commission, p. 32.
11. Boulton, p. 50.
12. Lund, pp. 32, 71.
13. I.C.A. Submission to Monopolies Commission, Appendix B.
14. Croxton-Smith, p. 9.
15. *Medical Ethics,* p. 2.
16. Reader, p. 149.
17. Carr-Saunders and Wilson, p. 294.
18. *The Spirit of a Profession,* by John A.F. Watson, p. 11.
20. Lund, p. 57.
21. R.I.C.S. Submission to Monopolies Commission 1968, para. 61.
22. B.M.A. Submission to Monopolies Commission 1967, p. 10.
23. *Medical Ethics,* p. 2.
24. Bar Council Submission to the Monopolies Commission, pp. 2, 27.
25. Bar Council Submission to the Monopolies Commission, p. 6.
26. Boulton, p. 17.
27. *Medical Ethics,* p. 10.
28. R. Hine, pp. 46-7.
29. Lund, p. 70.
30. Boulton, p. 4; R.C.P. Bye-Law 160.
31. Partnership Act, 1890.
32. Lund, p. 48.
33. Limited Partnership Act, 1907.
34. Boulton, p. 60.
35. "English Accountancy", p. 55.
36. R. Hine, p. 112.
37. *Chartered Surveyors: The Growth of a Profession,* p. 234.
38. Bar Council Submission to Monopolies Commission, O. 18.
39. *Economic Consequences of the Professions,* p. 38.

## CHAPTER 5. Discretion: The Secure Confidant

1. *The Beaux' Stratagem,* III, iii.
2. Carr-Saunders and Wilson, p. 394.
3. Carr-Saunders and Wilson, p. 106.
4. H.A. Clegg, British Medical Journal 1958, Supplement 1, p. 342.
5. Lund, p. 96.
6. *Medical Ethics,* p. 1.
7. *Medical Ethics,* pp. 2, 3.
8. *Medical Ethics,* pp. 6, 7.
9. Boulton.
10. Lund, pp. 96-104.
11. Lund, p. 99.
12. Croxton-Smith, p. 41.

R

## CHAPTER 5. (contd.)

13. *Medical Ethics*, p. 7.
14. *Medical Ethics*, p. 18.
15. Sunday Times, 18th August, 1968.
15a. Evening Standard, 19th December 1968.
16. Lund, p. 97.
17. Boulton, p. 34.
18. Lund, pp. 97-8.
20. Boulton, pp. 70-2.
21. Lund, pp. 103-4.
22. Boulton, pp. 33, 35.
23. Carr-Saunders and Wilson, p. 423.
24. Lund, pp. 99, 113.
25. Lund, p. 86.
26. Lund, p. 101.
27. Lund, p. 86
28. *Medical Ethics*, p. 7.
29. Carr-Saunders and Wilson, p. 424.
30. Croxton-Smith, p. 42.
31. Lund, pp. 98-9.
32. *Observations* by Dr Willoughby (1863), pp. 135-6.
33. *Mrs Grundy, Studies in English Prudery*, p. 184.

## CHAPTER 6. Impartiality: No Axe to Grind

2. Reader, p. 1.
3. A.C.E. Code, p. 7.
4. Boulton, p. 35.
5. Boulton, p. 35.
6. Boulton, p. 28.
7. Croxton-Smith, p. 43.
8. Lund, p. 87.
9. Hodgkinson, p. 63.
10. Lund, p. 58.
11. A.R.C.U.K. Code, p. 10.
12. A.C.E. Code, p. 6.
13. *Medical Ethics*, pp. 20-21.
14. R.I.C.S. Charters, Bye-Law 21.
15. *Medical Ethics*, p. 20.
16. *Medical Ethics*, p. 20.
17. *Medical Ethics*, p. 23.
18. *Medical Ethics*, p. 21.
19. Boulton, p. 13.
20. R.I.C.S. Charters, Bye-Law 21.
21. A.R.C.U.K. Code, p. 10.
22. A.C.E. Code, p. 6.
23. Banwell Report, p. 5.
24. The Architects' Journal, 8th November, 1967, p. 1145.
26. Pilkington Report, p. 186.
27. Boulton, p. 14.
28. Lund, p. 32-3; Law Society Submission to Monopolies Commission, p. 19.
29. A.R.C.U.K. Code, p. 10.
30. I.C.A. Submission to Monopolies Commission, Appendix B.
31. R.I.C.S. Charters, Bye-Law 21.
32. B.M.A. Submission to Monopolies Commission, 1967-8, p. 5.
33. Report on Remuneration of Solicitors (Cmnd. 3529), p. 22.
34. *Medical Ethics*, pp. 10, 20.
35. Lund, p. 28.
36. I.C.A. Submission to Monopolies Commission, Appendix B.
37. Carr-Saunders and Wilson, p. 247.
38. Lund, p. 35.
39. B.M.A. Submission to Monopolies Commission, p. 5.
40. *Medical Ethics*, p. 15.

## CHAPTER 6. (contd.)

41. Institute of Chartered Accountants' Fundamental Rule 3.
42. R.I.C.S. Charters, Bye-Law 21.
43. I.C.A. Submission to Monopolies Commission, p. 24.
44. Law Society's Submission to Monopolies Commission, p. 18.
45. Mencher, p. 70.
46. Bar Council's Submission to Monopolies Commission, p. 27.
47. A.R.C.U.K. Code, p. 12.
48. Lund, p. 108.
49. Boulton, p. 16.
50. Boulton, p. 32.
51. Lund, p. 111.
52. Boulton, p. 34.
53. Solicitors Act, 1957, s. 33.
54. Boulton, p. 6.
55. Bar Council Submission to Monopolies Commission, p. 18.
56. Bar Council Submission to Monopolies Commission, p. 5.
57. *Medical Ethics*, p. 15.
58. Bar Association Submission to Monopolies Commission.
58a.*Lawyers and the Courts*, p. 209.
59. Estates Gazette, 21st September, 1968, p. 1165.
60. R.I.B.A. Submission to Monopolies Commission, p. 37.
61. Lund, p. 113.
62. Cmnd. 3529, p. 17.
63. Pilkington Report, p. 4.
65. The Times, 5th December, 1966. For subsequent correspondence see issues for 8th, 9th, 13th, 16th and 20th December.

## CHAPTER 7. Responsibility: Answerable in Full

1. Croxton-Smith, p. 61.
2. A.R.C.U.K. Code, Principle V.
3. *Medical Ethics*, p. 3.
4. Boulton, p. 6.
5. Boulton, p. 19.
6. Hodgkinson, p. 25.
7. Hodgkinson, p. 7.
8. *The Seven Lamps of Advocacy*, by Judge Parry (Fisher Unwin 1923), p. 23.
9. Croxton-Smith, p. 54.
10. R.I.C.S. Charters, Bye-Law 21.
11. "Accountancy", June 1961, p. 383.
12. Lund, p. 59.
14. Lund, p. 92.
15. Architects Registration Act, 1931, s. 17.
17. Carr-Saunders and Wilson, p. 450.
18. R.I.B.A. Submission to Monopolies Commission, p. 34.
19. Croxton-Smith, p. 33.
20. A.C.E. Code, p. 7.
21. R.I.C.S. Charters, Bye-Law 21.
23. Law Society's Submission, pp. 15, 31.
24. "Accountancy", June 1961, p. 383.
25. [1967] 3 W.L.R. 1666.
26. Law Society's Memorandum, p. 8.
27. *Professional Indemnity Insurance*, by Peter Madge, Butterworth, 1968.

## CHAPTER 8.  Integrity: "Sans Peur et Sans Reproche"

1. A.C.E. Code, p. 7.
2. Reader, p. 159.
3. *History of Accounting and Accountants,* by R. Brown, Blackwood, Edinburgh, 1905, p. 197.
4. St. Luke, Chapter 16, verse 10.
5. Lund, p. 133.
6. Reader, p. 159.
6a. F.M.L. Thompson, p. 155.
7. Daily Telegraph, 10th September, 1968.
8. *Ralston* v. *Ralston* (1930) to K.B. 238 at 245.
10. Re Weare [1893] 2 Q.B. 439.
11. Lund, p. 52.
12. *Ethical and Legal Obligations of Dental Practitioners,* 1964, p. 4.
13. Lund, p. 51.
14. Law Society's Submission, p. 18.
15. Lund, p. 58.
15a. The Times, 16th November 1968.
16. Lund, p. 59.
17. *Confessions of an Uncommon Attorney,* by R. Hine, p. 27.
18. *Medical Ethics,* p. 2.
19. *Confessions of an Uncommon Attorney,* by R. Hine, p. 82.
20. A.R.C.U.K. Code, pp. 3, 8.
21. Lund, p. 54.
22. Lund, p. 133.
23. Hodgkinson, p. 53.
24. Hodgkinson, p. 26.
25. Lund, p. 54.
26. Boulton, p. 5.
27. *The Seven Lamps of Advocacy,* by Judge Parry (Fisher Unwin 1923), p. 32.
28. Bar Submission to Monopolies Commission, p. 2.
29. "Accountancy", October, 1964.
30. Carr-Saunders and Wilson, p. 232.
31. Lund, p. 1.
33. Hodgkinson, p. 64.
34. A.R.C.U.K. Code, p. 6.
35. A.C.E. Code, p. 7.
36. Lund, p. 58.
37. Lund, p. 58.
39. Lund, p. 59.
40. Croxton-Smith, p. 43.
41. Carr-Saunders and Wilson, p. 64.
43. *Medical Ethics,* p. 37.

## CHAPTER 9.  Professional Solidarity

1. *Dickson* v. *Pharmaceutical Society of Great Britain* [1968] 3 W.L.R. 286, 298.
2. *Dickson* v. *Pharmaceutical Society of Great Britain* [1968] 3 W.L.R. 286, 298.
3. *Medical Ethics,* p. 2.
4. Dentists' Code, p. 9.
5. Consulting Engineers' Code, p. 6.
6. R.I.C.S. Bye-Laws, Bye-Law 21 (1).
7. R.I.B.A. Journal, April 1968, p. 158.
8. *Medical Ethics,* p. 5.
9. Bar Council's submission, p. 7.
10. Lund, p. 81.
11. Lund, p. 122.
12. Law Society's submission, p. 16.
13. *Medical Ethics,* p. 26.
14. *Medical Ethics,* p. 21.

## CHAPTER 9. (contd.)

15. Venereal Diseases Act, 1917, Cancer Act, 1939 and Pharmacy and Medicines Act, 1941.
16. Consulting Engineers' Code, p. 6.
17. Lund, p. 81.
18. *Precepts of Hippocrates,* Loeb Series, Vol. 1.
19. *Medical Ethics,* p. 3.
20. *Medical Ethics,* p. 6.
21. Lund, p. 73.
22. A.R.C.U.K. Code, p. 9.
23. Dentists' Code, p. 5.
24. Boulton, p. 20.
25. Lund, pp. 78, 79.
26. Lund, p. 88.
27. National Association of Estate Agents' Code, para. 11.
28. Dentists' Code, p. 10.
29. Dentists' Code, p. 8.
30. Royal College of Physicians, Bye-Law 158.
31. *Medical Ethics,* p. 12.
32. *Medical Ethics,* p. 14.
33. Dentists' Code, p. 13.
34. Lund, p. 77.
35. Lund, p. 73.
36. *The Elements of the Common Law,* preface.
37. Bar Council submission, p. 21.
38. *Medical Ethics,* p. 15.
39. *The Healers,* p. 55.
40. Dentists' Code, p. 10.
41. Lund, p. 85.
42. R.I.C.S. Bye-Laws 1958, No. 21 (3).
43. Law Society's submission, p. 18.
44. R.I.C.S. submission, p. 23.
45. Boulton, p. 46.
46. Royal College of Physicians, Bye-Law 159.
47. *Medical Ethics,* p. 3.
48. A.R.C.U.K. Code, p. 8.
49. Consulting Engineers' Code, p. 6.
50. *Medical Ethics,* p. 15.
51. Croxton-Smith, p. 40.
52. Dentists' Code, p. 10.
53. *Medical Ethics,* p. 8.
54. Dentists' Code, p. 6.

## CHAPTER 10. Attraction of Business

1. Law Society submission, p. 17.
2. Quoted Turner, p. 54.
3. Bar Council submission, p. 33.
4. Reader, p. 193.
5. Bar Council submission, p. 8.
6. Quoted Reader, p. 191.
7. Lewis and Maude, p. 107.
8. *Dickson* v. *Pharmaceutical Society of Great Britain* [1968] 3 W.L.R. 311.
9. R.I.C.S. submission, p. 18.
10. Bar Council submission, p. 2.
11. *Medical Ethics,* p. 10.
12. Law Society submission, p. 17.
13. R.I.C.S. submission, pp. 19-21.
14. British Optical Association Code of Conduct (issued in 1963).
15. *Advertising and the Public,* p. 241.
16. Lund, p. 3.
17. General Medical Council submission, p. 4.
18. Dentists' Code, p. 13.

## CHAPTER 10. (contd.)

19. Lund, pp. 23-25.
20. Lund, p. 22.
21. Law Society's submission, p. 16.
22. Boulton, p. 88; for instances of abuses by unscrupulous practitioners see Lawyers and the Courts, p. 149.
23. Lund, p. 26.
24. Lund, p. 27.
25. Lund, pp. 28-32.
26. Croxton-Smith, p. 21.
27. Bar Council submission, p. 32.
28. Croxton-Smith, p. 10.
29. Bar Council Annual Statement 1967, p. 36.
30. *Confessions of an Uncommon Attorney*, p. 49.
31. Lund, p. 88.
32. Boulton, pp. 11, 51.
33. Boulton, p. 51.
34. "Accountancy", March 1967, p. 213.
35. F.M.L. Thompson, p. 156.
36. Chartered Accountants' submission, p. 24.
37. Boulton, p. 12.
38. Boulton, p. 12.

## CHAPTER 11. Touting and Canvassing

1. Turner, p. 85.
2. Consulting Engineers' Code, p. 6.
3. A.R.C.U.K. Code, Principle III.
4. Solicitors' Practice Rules 1936, Rule 1.
5. Lund, p. 3.
6. R.I.C.S. submission, p. 9.
7. Boulton, p. 50.
8. "Accountancy", October 1964.
9. Dentists' Code, p. 27.
10. Chartered Accountants' submission, p. 28.
11. Bar Council submission, p. 21.
12. *The Ethical Basis of Medical Practice*, 1951, p. 80.
13. Lund, p. 7.
14. Lund, p. 69.
15. Solicitors' Practice Rules, 1936, Rule 4.
16. Lund, p. 37.
17. *Lawyers and the Courts*, p. 196.
18. R.I.B.A. submission, p. 42.
19. R.I.C.S. Bye-Laws, Bye-Law 21.
20. R.I.C.S. submission, p. 10.
21. "Accountancy", December 1964.
22. "Accountancy", December 1964.
23. Lund, p. 21.
24. Dentists' Code, p. 6.
25. Croxton-Smith, p. 13.
26. "Accountancy", December 1964.
27. Boulton, p. 53.
28. Boulton, pp. 53-4, note (h).
29. Lund, p. 10.
30. Lund, p. 10.

## CHAPTER 12. Advertising

1. [1957] 2 Q.B. 559.
2. See, e.g., *Carr* v. *Inland Revenue Commissioners* [1945] 2 A.. E.R. 163; *Allinson* v. *General Council of Medical Education & Registration* [1894] 1 Q.B. 750.
3. A.R.C.U.K. Code, p. 6.
4. *Medical Ethics*, p. 31.
5. Boulton, p. 50.
6. *Medical Ethics*, pp. 24, 25.
7. *Conduct at the Bar*, by Lord Justice Singleton, London 1933, p. 22.
8. *Advertising and the Public*, p. 18.
9. *Advertising and the Public*, p. 22.
10. *Advertising and the Public*, p. 17.
11. Turner, p. 132.
12. Quoted Turner, p. 19.
13. Turner, p. 161.
14. Turner, p. 161.
15. Turner, p. 161.
16. See Denys Thompson, pp. 17, 36.
17. Baster, p. 61.
18. *Advertising and the Public*, p. 11.
19. Quoted Turner, p. 76.
20. Turner, p. 20.
21. I am obliged to Mr F.M.L. Thompson for this quotation from pages 25-6 of *The Surveiors Dialogue*.
22. Turner, p. 49.
23. Carr-Saunders and Wilson, p. 112.
24. Quoted Reader, p. 160.
25. Law Society's submission, p. 20.
26. *Medical Ethics*, p. 31.
27. Law Society's submission, pp. 19-20.
28. Cited Lees, p. 5.
29. B.M.A. submission, pp. 13, 14.
30. Law Society's submission, p. 20.
31. Quoted Lees, p. 6.
32. Lewis and Maude, p. 61.
33. Bar Council submission, p. 34.
34. Carr-Saunders and Wilson, p. 433.
35. *Medical Ethics*, p. 25.
36. Bar Council Annual Statement for 1967, p. 31.
37. Boulton, p. 52.
38. Bar Council submission, p. 33; Law Society's submission, p. 33.
39. *The House of the Arrow*, by A.E.W. Mason, London (undated, but apparently about 1920), p. 21.
40. *Medical Ethics*, p. 25.
41. Boulton, p. 52.
42. Dentists' Code, p. 28.
43. Cf. Lund, p. 9.
44. *Medical Ethics*, p. 10.
45. *Medical Ethics*, p. 10.
46. Lund, p. 9.
47. Dentists' Code, p. 7.
48. Dentists' Code, p. 22.
49. Croxton-Smith, p. 22.
50. Lund, p. 9.
51. Lund, p. 9.
52. Croxton-Smith, p. 21.
53. Lund, p. 10.
54. *Medical Ethics*, p. 11.
55. R.I.B.A. submission, p. 42.
56. R.I.C.S. Directions to Members on Advertisements, Etc., May 1961.
57. A.R.C.U.K. Code, p. 7.
58. *Medical Ethics*, p. 11.
59. Architects' Journal, 30th October 1968.

## CHAPTER 12. (contd.)

60. Estates Gazette, 14th December 1968, p. 1251.
61. Cf. Lund, p. 13.
62. Croxton-Smith, p. 19.
63. Lund, p. 12.
64. See Lund, pp. 15, 16; "Accountancy", October 1964; R.I.C.S. Directions to Quantity Surveyors, March 1962.
65. A.R.C.U.K. Code, p. 7.
66. Carr-Saunders and Wilson, p. 62.
67. R.I.C.S. Directions to Members, May 1961.
68. R.I.C.S. submission, p. 14.
69. Estates Gazette, 16th November 1968, p. 752.
70. Lund, p. 16.
71. *Medical Ethics*, p. 30.
72. Law Society's submission, p. 37.
73. R.I.B.A. submission, p. 43.
74. "Accountancy", October 1964.
75. Law Society's submission, p. 37.
76. *Medical Ethics*, p. 31.
77. A.R.C.U.K. Code, p. 7.
78. *Medical Ethics*, p. 29.
79. *Medical Ethics*, p. 30.
80. Boulton, pp. 66-7.

81. *Medical Ethics*, p. 41.
82. *Medical Ethics*, p. 26.
83. *Medical Ethics*, p. 26.
84. Boulton, p. 56.
85. *Medical Ethics*, p. 28.
86. Boulton, p. 57.
87. *Medical Ethics*, p. 26.
88. Croxton-Smith, p. 12.
89. Lund, pp. 14, 15.
90. Lund, p. 18.
91. Lund, p. 22.
92. Estates Gazette for 21st November 1908, p. 909.
93. R.I.C.S. submission, p. 14.
94. Law Society's submission, p. 33.
95. Croxton-Smith, p. 20.
96. A.R.C.U.K. Code, pp. 8, 10.
97. Lund, p. 18.
98. "Accountancy", October 1964.
99. Croxton-Smith, p. 13.
100. R.I.B.A. submission, p. 42.
101. Knox and Hennessy, p. 39.
102. Croxton-Smith, p. 34.
103. Millerson, p. 197.
104. Chartered Accountants' submission, p. 6.

## CHAPTER 13. The Fee System

1. *Medical Ethics*, p. 3.
2. Millerson, p. 41.
3. R.I.B.A. Journal, April 1968, p. 157.
4. See R.I.B.A. Journal, April 1968, p. 158.
5. Estates Gazette, 16th November 1968, p. 752.
6. A.R.C.U.K. Code, p. 3.

7. Boulton, pp. 43, 45.
8. R.I.C.S. Bye-Laws 1958, Bye-Law 21 (8).
9. R.I.B.A. Journal, April 1968, p. 163.
10. Croxton-Smith, p. 31.
11. Memorandum dated 31st May 1968, submitted to the Monopolies Commission by the Nine Societies Committee.

# CHAPTER 13. (contd.)

12. Lund, p. 72.
13. See Reader, p. 37.
14. The Times, 12th October 1967.
15. Lund, p. 65.
16. Chartered Accountants' submission, p. 21.
17. R.I.B.A. Journal, April 1968, p. 158.
18. Bar Council submission, p. 15.
19. Report on Architects' Costs and Fees, Cmnd. 3653, p. 15.
20. F.M.L. Thompson, p. 311.
21. Chartered Accountants' submission, pp. 7, 20.
22. *Confessions of an Uncommon Attorney*, p. 85.
23. *The Healers*, p. 14.
24. F.M.L. Thompson, unpublished M.S.
25. Law Society's submission, p. 14.
26. Bar Council submission, p. 16.
27. "Remuneration of Solicitors", Cmnd. 3529, p. 14.
28. "Remuneration of Solicitors", Cmnd. 3529, p. 1.
29. Daily Telegraph, 9th September 1968.
30. Pilkington Report, p. 72.
31. Mencher, pp. 49-51.
32. Law Society's submission, p. 34.
33. Cmnd. 3653, p. 26.
34. Law Society's submission pp. 12, 36.
35. Cmnd. 3653, p. 25.
36. Monopolies Commission: Report on the Supply of Certain Services by Estate Agents. H.M.S.O. 1969.
37. Cmnd. 3653, p.25.
38. Law Society's submission, p.35.
39. Law Society's submission, p.35.
40. Chartered Accountant's submission, p.21.
41. Cmnd. 3653, p.25.
42. See *Lawyers and the Courts.* pp. 213-4.
43. Cmnd. 3653, p.25.
44. *Know What It Costs You.* published by the Law Society, p.2.
45. Solicitors' Remuneration Order 1953.
46. R.I.B.A. Journal, April 1968, p. 159.
47. Cited Reader, p.9.
48. Carr-Saunders and Wilson, p.27.
49. Carr-Saunders and Wilson, p.452.
50. R.I.B.A. submission, p.33.
51. Cmnd. 3653, p.15.
52. Law Society's submission, p.17.
53. Lund, p.34.
54. A.C.E. Code, p.6.
55. A.R.C.U.K. Code, p.8.
56. Croxton-Smith, pp.24,31-2
57. R.I.C.S. Bye-Laws 1958, Bye-Law 21 (7).
58. See Carr-Saunders and Wilson, p. 432.
59. Boulton, p.47.
60. Lund, p.35.
61. Law Society's submission, pp.14. 35.
62. R.I.B.A. Journal, April 1968, pp. 163-4, 166.
63. Chartered Accountants' submission, p.7.
64. Carr-Saunders and Wilson, p.453.
65. Monopolies Commission: Report on the Supply of Certain Services by Estate Agents. H.M.S.O. 1969.

CHAPTER 14. The Code in Today's World

1. Lewis and Maude, p. 262.
2. Mencher, p. 45.
3. Lewis and Maude, p. 257.
4. Cited Mencher, p. 90.
5. Estates Gazette, 9th November 1968, p. 652.
6. Cited Mencher, p. 74.
7. Mencher, p. 38.
8. Cited Mencher, p. 70.
9. Cmnd. 3529, p. 9.
10. Lewis and Maude, p. 182.
11. Cited Lewis and Maude, p. 130.
12. Cmnd. 3529, p. 10.
13. Estates Gazette, 2nd November 1968, p. 525.
14. Cmnd. 3653, p. 31.
15. Law Society's submission, p. 31.
16. "Chartered Surveyor", June 1968, p. 607.
17. Mencher, p. 35.
18. Report of the Committee of Enquiry into the Cost of the National Health Service (1956) para. 419.
19. "Rough Justice", Conservative Political Centre, 1968.
20. Dickson v. Pharmaceutical Society of Great Britain [1968] 3 W.L.R. 292.
21. Knox and Hennessy, p. 54.
22. Millerson, p. 165.
23. R.I.B.A. Journal, April 1968, p. 159.
24. Advertising and the Public, p. 84.
25. Lees, p. 23.
26. Lees, p. 24.
27. Lees, p. 27.
28. Cited E.S. Turner, p. 87.
29. Advertising and the Public, p. 185.
30. Advertising in Action, p. 31.
31. Advertising in Action, p. 21.
32. Baster, p. 80.
33. Denys Thompson, p. 41.
34. Quoted Baster, p. 11.
35. Denys Thompson, p. 119.
36. Consumer Council's submission to the Monopolies Commission, p. 3.
37. R.I.B.A. Journal, April 1968, p. 165.
38. Knox and Hennessy, p. 43.
39. For other suggestions see The Architect and His Office, published by the R.I.B.A. in 1962.
40. Cf. Baster, p. 105.
41. Baster, p. 105.
42. Advertising and the Public, pp. 82, 95, 131, 153.
43. Cmnd. 3529, p. 16; Cmnd. 3653, p. 16.
44. Knox and Hennessy, p. 42.
45. Advertising and the Public, p. 73.
46. Lees, p. 27; Knox and Hennessy, p. 45.
47. Cited Advertising and the Public, p. 70.
48. R.I.B.A. Journal, April 1968, p. 161.
49. Lees, p. 42.
50. Pilkington Report, p. 4.
51. Advertising and the Public, p. 142.
52. Cited Turner, p. 195.
53. Denys Thompson, p. 145.
54. Durkheim, p. 13.

## CHAPTER 14. (contd.)

55. Knox and Hennessy, p. 43.
56. See *Advertising and the Public*, p. 74.
57. Denys Thompson, p. 22.
58. Cited Baster, p. 70.
59. Sunday Telegraph, 10th November 1968.
60. Consumer Council's submission, p. 3.
61. Lees, pp. 41-45.
62. Cmnd. 3529, pp. 8, 9, 25, 27.
63. Cmnd. 3529, pp. 25, 26, 28.
64. Cmnd. 3529, p. 27.
65. Bar Council submission, p. 3; see also Cmnd. 3715, p. 38.
66. Law Guardian, November 1968, p. 29.
67. Cmnd. 3653, p. 32.
68. "Chartered Surveyor", August 1968, p. 66.

69. Cmnd. 3529, p. 25.
70. Cmnd. 3653, p. 32.
71. Lees, p. 22.
72. Cmnd. 3529, p. 13.
73. Widgery Report, p. 82.
74. Lees, p. 13.
75. Lees, p. 15.
76. Lees, p. 17.
77. Lees, p. 31.
78. Lees, p. 39.
79. Lees, p. 8.
80. Durkheim, p. 30.
81. Durkheim, p. 7.
82. Durkheim, p. 30.
83. Durkheim, pp. 11, 12, 13.
84. Durkheim, pp. 14-15.
85. Durkheim, pp. 14, 15, 16.
86. Durkheim, p. 24-25.

## CHAPTER 15. Looking Ahead

1. R.I.B.A. submission, p. 27.
2. Bar Council submission, p. 14.
3. Commonwealth Foundation, first progress report.
4. Carr-Saunders and Wilson, p. 100.
5. Millerson, p. 210.
6. R.I.B.A. submission, p. 5.
7. See The Times, 20th December 1968, and subsequent issues.
8. *Brown* v. *Inland Revenue Commissioners* [1965] 44 A.T.C. p. 399.
9. *Advertising and the Public*, p. 209.

# SERVICES PROVIDED BY CONSULTANT PROFESSIONS

The following descriptions of the services which are obtainable by the public from practitioners have been kindly supplied by the professional bodies concerned.

## Actuaries

Actuaries advise mainly in the field of monetary problems involving future payments, the assessment (using suitable mathematical techniques) of the probabilities of those payments having to be made, and their equivalent value at other points of time having regard to the operation of compound interest. That is, in essence, the solution of problems which a businessman might recognise as discounted cash flow but with an appropriate allowance for any uncertainty attaching to the payment of the sums discounted. Whilst any problem of this fundamental nature is one on which the advice of an actuary may be sought, such problems have hitherto most usually been seen to arise in connection with the operation of life assurance companies, industrial and commercial pension funds and friendly societies, the valuation of reversions and life interests under trusts and the apportionment of trust funds between the interested parties. Advice may also be sought on statistical and operational research problems, on investment matters and on all problems arising in connection with pension funds in addition to the assessment of their financial position. Actuaries are called upon in the course of their career to advise on administrative problems as well as problems of finance.

Institute of Actuaries,
Staple Inn Hall,
High Holborn,
London, W.C.1.
Tel; 01-242 9175

## Architects

The architect's job is to advise a client on his building needs and to design buildings to meet them, in time and for the right price.

Some firms specialise: in hospital design, housing, factories, shop-fitting, or the care and restoration of historic buildings, for example. Others offer special knowledge of landscaping, town-planning, engineering in all its branches, contract management, acoustics, or the design of components for building, though the great majority of private firms can take on most commissions. The scope of the collective service offered by the profession is constantly changing in response to the public's demand, which may range from a domestic alteration job to a major feasibility study for a development with wide social and economic implications worth millions of pounds.

The architect's normal design service includes analysing his client's requirements, preparing the contract documents, obtaining tenders, letting and administering the building contract, supervising the work on site and settling the final account. He will apply for planning and building regulations consents and will guide his client through the mass of legislation that now governs building. Throughout, he will exercise control over the project's cost and timing, and when employed privately will thus act as an independent agent safeguarding the client's interests. Architects also advise on how best to exploit a site or an existing building; will carry out level, measured and structural surveys; and act as expert witnesses, technical assessors, and arbitrators in cases of dispute.

If a project requires the services of other specialists, say a structural, heating or electrical engineer; a valuation, land or quantity surveyor; or any other consultant, the architect is responsible for co-ordinating the work of the full design team. He thus stands as designer, in a special and central position synthesising the client's and user's needs and the complex variety of skills needed to produce a finished building.

Royal Institute of British Architects,
66 Portland Place,
London, W.1.
Tel; 01-580 5533

### Barristers

The professional services supplied by members of the Bar of England and Wales consist of services in relation to litigation, civil and criminal, in courts, tribunals, and inquiries of all kinds, and of the giving of advice (including the drafting of documents) on legal matters.

The barrister acts, with minor exceptions, on the instructions of a solicitor and renders his services on his own account as an individual.

The services in relation to litigation include the drafting of written pleadings and advising on evidence, but the primary service is that of advocacy, the actual conduct of the case in Court. Barristers have a right of audience in the superior courts which include the House of Lords, the Supreme Court, the Assize Courts, the Crown Courts and the Courts of Quarter Sessions.

Members of the Bar are available, as consultants, to solicitors who seek their opinion on the more difficult cases which may require much legal research. There are, within the Bar, sections of specialists, some of whom may do little court work but spend their time giving advice on their special branch of the law and drafting the often very difficult documents which may be required.


General Council of the Bar of England and Wales,
Carpmael Building,
Temple,
London, E.C.4.
Tel; 01-353 4649


### Chartered Accountants

Chartered accountants engaged in the practice of public accountancy provide independent auditing; the preparation of financial accounts; tax advice; planning and negotiations; financial advice, management consultancy; investigations; reports for inclusion in prospectuses; the financial aspects of company reconstructions and amalgamations; share and business valuations; evidence before tribunals as expert witnesses; members of Government Committees; liquidations, receiverships and insolvencies; executorships and trusteeships; company secretarial activities and commercial arbitrations.

This variety of work is performed for an equally variegated clientele: practitioners' clients include businesses ranging from the multi-million-pound international group to the corner tobacco shop; they include individuals whose annual earnings run into six figures, and those who are looking for an executor to an estate which will barely reach four figures. The practitioners' firms themselves reflect, in their size, the variety of their functions.

Institute of Chartered Accountants in England and Wales,
56 Goswell Road,
London, E.C.1.
Tel; 01-253 1090

## Chartered Surveyors

The chartered surveyor is qualified by examinations and experience in one of the five main branches of the profession, i.e. General Practice, Quantity Surveying, Agricultural Surveying, Mining Surveying and Land Surveying.

The surveyor in GENERAL PRACTICE is concerned in the management, development and valuation of land and buildings and is expert in one or more of the following:

(i)  *Valuation and Estate Management,* which includes the valuation of all types of property for purchase, sale or letting, for national or local taxation and for compulsory purchase, and the management of all forms of urban property on behalf of public and private owners.

(ii)  *Town and Country Planning*, where he advises private owners on aspects of planning which affect their property, including procedures for obtaining planning permission for development, or on the owner's position where permission is refused. He also advises on all forms of land use and on the economic problems of planning and development.

(iii)  *Building Surveying.* This includes expert advice on the maintenance, repairs, improvement and extension of buildings and on problems involving building law, including public health and building regulations.

(iv)  *Estate Agency.* The chartered surveyor may act as an estate agent and, on behalf of clients, sells and purchases and lets houses, shops, offices, factories and almost any type of land or building; he can also arrange mortgages and advises on the market value of properties.

(v)   *Finance.* Advice on the best method of financing developments or acquisition of property, both for developers and owner occupiers.

The QUANTITY SURVEYOR acts as a building economist and advises building owners and architects on the probable costs of building schemes and on the cost of alternative designs. He advises on procedures for arranging building contracts and he is an essential member of the design team with the architect and other consultants. He prepares bills of quantities and, where appropriate, negotiates contracts with buildings; forecasts costs and prepares valuations for payment to the builder as the work proceeds. He is responsible for the measurement and valuation of variations in the work during the contract, and for the preparation and agreement of the builder's final account.

The AGRICULTURAL SURVEYOR renders professional service and advice to all interests in rural property. He advises on the purchase, sale, development and management of land used for agriculture and forestry. These functions include advice on the letting of land to tenants, the equipment of farms and transactions arising out of compulsory acquisition of land.

The LAND SURVEYOR carries out geodetic, topographical large-scale engineering and development surveys. He compiles and produces maps and plans resulting from these surveys. The Hydrographic Surveyor carries out all aspects of the survey of oceans, seas, inland waterways and harbours and compiles and produces nautical charts.

The MINERAL SURVEYOR carries out surveys of mines and mineral workings and prepares all necessary plans and sections which, in some cases, are required by law. He advises on problems resulting from the movement of ground due to mining operations and his specialist knowledge enables him to value minerals and manage mineral estates.


Royal Institution of Chartered Surveyors,
12 Great George Street,
London, S.W.1.
Tel; 01-930 5322

## Consulting Engineers

The Consulting Engineer's more useful service is to design and supervise the construction of engineering works.

The Consulting Engineer will first discover by such discussion as is necessary his client's general requirements. He will then examine those requirements and determine their technical practicability and economy and work out in broad terms means or alternative means by which, and at what cost, the client's wishes could be satisfied.

When the client has approved an outline project the Consulting Engineer will develop a design in detail and document his work so that contractors can prepare and submit competitive tenders for carrying out the work. The Consulting Engineer then examines the tenders and advises the client on the selection of that to be accepted.

Once the contract is let the Consulting Engineer undertakes responsibility for the supervision of the construction, for making sure that the specified materials are used, that the design is followed and that the workmanship is of the necessary standard. During the progress of the work and on completion the Consulting Engineer issues certificates authorising payments to the contractor and (within the terms of the contract) settles any differences which may arise between his client and the contractor. He finally certifies that the project is complete.

The above describes the Consulting Engineer's part in the concept, design and supervision of construction of a capital project. In addition he is qualified to investigate and report on any engineering problem within his field of work and to inspect materials and plant during manufacture and on site. He is also able to advise on causes of mishaps and to recommend remedial measures or to act as an arbitrator in disputes, or to assist the Courts as an expert witness on matters within his experience.

Association of Consulting Engineers,
Abbey House,
2 Victoria Street,
London, S.W.1.
Tel; 01-222 6557

## Consulting Marine Engineers and Ship Surveyors

The increasingly heavy demands made upon the Shipping Industry in terms of specialised tonnage, and the increasing costs of ship

s

construction and maintenance, have made the employment of Consulting Marine Engineers and Ship Surveyors of paramount importance.

The services offered by the Consulting Marine Engineer and Ship Surveyor can be described broadly under three main headings:

(i)   *Ship and Engine Construction.* The Consultant will advise on and draw up plans, specifications and technical data to produce a ship of specialised design, size, category, or power, giving the greatest efficiency compatible with the needs of the Shipowner. He will act in liaison with the ship and engine builders during all stages of construction and during the guarantee period, to ensure that the terms of the contract are carried out.

(ii)  *Maintenance.* Routine maintenance is supervised by ship's personnel, but certain items (mainly those required to meet Board of Trade or Classification Society's periodical survey requirements) are frequently carried out under the additional supervision or advice of a Consultant to avoid delay and minimise cost.

(iii) *Contingency work.* The Consultant will advise Shipowners, Authorities, etc. in cases of damage (fire, collision, stranding, etc.) or abnormal stresses, malfunctioning of engines, equipment, etc. according to the limitations of the situation.

The Consulting Marine Engineer and Ship Surveyor will also advise on new techniques and developments, on the complex requirements of Classification Societies, on international and local safety requirements, on changes in conditions necessitated by Government and Union agreements, on changes in type, nature and stowage of cargo, and on shore installation developments. He will also advise on the sale and purchase of ships, lighters, yachts, etc.


Society of Consulting Marine Engineers and Ship Surveyors,
5 Fenchurch Street,
London, E.C.3.
Tel; 01-626 3135


**Dentists**

Dental disease, in one or other of its several forms, is the only disease which everyone must expect to suffer some time during his life. The treatment of this – the most common of illnesses – is the responsibility of the dental profession, but modern dental surgery covers a much wider field than the relief of suffering and the replacement of hopelessly diseased teeth, important though both these functions are.

Society is increasingly coming to recognise and demand the benefits to health and the sense of wellbeing to be gained from a well-cared for, functionally efficient and aesthetically pleasing dentition. So the dentist to-day has utilised his greater knowledge and extended his skills to give this service in a number of special directions.

Orthodontics, which literally translated means "the straightening of teeth", involves a study of the causes of deformities of the teeth and jaws in children and young people, and their correction. Advanced restorative techniques employ engineering principles on a minute scale and have been developed to a high degree of precision so that the cosmetic standards demanded, for example, by the television screen can be achieved. All this work can now be accomplished with the complete absence of pain and the minimum of discomfort, thanks to advances in the realm of anaesthesia and sedation, where dental surgeons have been prominent as pioneers for a hundred years.

Prevention must, however, be the ultimate objective of the healing professions and dentistry is no exception. By way of advice and prophylactic treatment, dentists have much to offer in this connection although the true origins of dental disease are not yet fully understood.

British Dental Association,
63 Wimpole Street,
London, W.1.
Tel; 01-935 0875

## Medical Practitioners

Medicine as a whole is directed to the overall care of the individual patient whether at home, at work or in hospital. But to achieve this the practice of medicine has evolved into a number of specialised branches. These divisions hold good both within the National Health Service and outside it.

*Preventive Medicine* is mainly the task of the Public Health Medical Officer who with his staff on the local health authority is responsible

S*

for a great variety of services such as immunization programmes, campaigns for accident prevention, running clinics for mothers and children, maintaining proper standards of public hygiene. Under his general direction work health visitors, home helps, public health inspectors, district nurses, midwives, special visitors for old people and mental welfare officers.

*General Practice* is always the first point of contact — save in some emergencies — between patient and doctor. The main tasks in general practice are diagnosis and treatment and it is the family doctor who is responsible for the continuing care of the patient in the community. He also plays a part in preventive medicine. When necessary the general practitioner is able to call upon other branches of medicine, as for instance when the patient needs specialised medical attention. It is he who arranges for a consultant opinion and/or admission to hospital.

The *Hospital Services'* role is again that of diagnosis and treatment under the care of a consultant — either as an inpatient for whom the consultant assumes responsibility or as an outpatient when responsibility remains with the family doctor. Hospital doctors specialise in specific sections of medicine, such as surgery, general medicine, anaesthetics, pathology, neurology and ophthalmology to name but a few.

The degree of specialisation is increasing as a result of the rapid progress in medical science. It is open to doctors in every branch of medicine to undertake research but a great deal must be carried out necessarily in a hospital environment. Those hospitals with medical schools attached play a particularly important role in medical research.

British Medical Association,
Tavistock Square,
London, W.C.1.
Tel; 01-387 4499

## Patent Agents

Patent Agents act for clients — individual inventors, companies and similar corporate bodies and associations — and for professional associates overseas, primarily in obtaining patents for inventions both in the United Kingdom and in foreign countries.

This involves the drafting of specifications, correspondence with the

Patent Offices concerned to overcome any statutory or technical objections raised by the examiners, and attendances at the Patent Offices for formal interviews and hearings.

In addition to these basic duties, Patent Agents make novelty investigations, file oppositions to competitors' patent applications and defend their own clients' patent applications against competitors' oppositions. They also advise clients on the validity and infringement of patents which are potential sources of litigation. When involved in litigation, they co-operate with barristers and solicitors; and some act as expert witnesses. This type of work is also often carried out in connection with foreign patents.

Some Patent Agents specialise in technical subjects, and many are employed on the staffs of industrial companies and Government Departments. Others are in private practice, acting on instructions from their clients.

In addition to handling patents, Patent Agents act similarly for clients in connection with registered designs and with trade marks, all connected with their clients' developments and activities. As with patents, there is a considerable proportion of the work involving overseas countries. Advice on the legal and commercial aspects of these matters is often requested by clients.


Chartered Institute of Patent Agents,
Staple Inn Buildings,
London, W.C.1.
Tel; 01-405 9450


**Pharmacists**

A pharmacist, that is, a Fellow or Member of the Pharmaceutical Society of Great Britain, will be found in charge of every chemist's shop and will give advice as mentioned below (usually without payment).

*Medical and Dental Prescriptions.* As the dispenser of prescriptions given by doctors and dentists, the pharmacist will ensure that the patient understands the instructions for dosage and use of the prescribed medicine. If a patient who is taking prescribed medicine needs advice on whether he may safely take some other preparation as well, the pharmacist will inform him whether the two are consistent or whether the second will duplicate or conflict with the first.

*Other Drugs.* Where there is no prescription the pharmacist will advise whether a preparation named by the customer is suitable for a given ailment or will recommend a suitable treatment. He may volunteer advice where a customer asks for a quantity of medicine which seems to be excessive, or asks for a particular preparation too frequently or over too long a period. He frequently has to correct misunderstandings about the uses or effects ot a particular preparation, sometimes caused by exaggerated advertising.

*Treatment.* The pharmacist will give first aid in emergency until a doctor can be seen, and will also advise on the treatment of minor ailments. He will advise that a doctor (or dentist) be consulted whenever this is necessary.

*General Advice.* The pharmacist will give general advice to customers whenever this is sought. He is often asked for this kind of help by the elderly and mothers of young children.


Pharmaceutical Society of Great Britain,
17 Bloomsbury Square,
London, W.C.1.
Tel; 01-405  8967



## Shipbrokers

The function of the shipbroker, reduced to its simplest terms, is to bring together the two parties concerned, namely the owner of the ship and the owner of the cargo; and the broker's income is derived from commission payable by the shipowner on completion and fulfilment of the contract.

In addition to fixing vessels, a most important part of a shipbroker's duty lies in acting as agent for the shipowner. As such, he is responsible for everything which may concern the vessel whilst she is in his port. His duties range from customs formalities and requirements to dealing with the crew; from arranging the loading and discharge of the vessel to dealing with collisions and the hundred and one other matters far too numerous to mention. His work as an agent will, at times, require him to be available at all hours of the day and night in order to render any service or assistance which may be necessary to the ship, her master and her owners.

Apart from agency work, which requires a high degree of skill and experience, shipbroking may be subdivided as follows:

(i)   *Owner's Broker.* He acts for the shipowner in finding a cargo for the vessel.

(ii)  *Chartering Agent.* He acts for the merchant seeking tonnage to carry his goods.

(iii) *Sale and Purchase Broker.* His concern is acting on behalf of the buyer or seller of ships and in bringing the two parties together.

(iv)  *Coasting Broker.* He deals with vessels, usually small, trading round the British coast and to and from ports on the Continent. Whereas the Deep Sea Broker will normally only act for the shipowner or the merchant, negotiating with a fellow broker for the other side, it often happens that the Coasting Broker will act for both parties.

(v)   *Tanker Broker.* Some shipbrokers make a speciality of dealing with tankers, which is a market of great importance.

(vi)  *Cabling Agents.* This again is a specialised business, where the broker keeps in touch with other markets of the world, as for instance New York, and where business is arranged (as the term implies) on the cables.

Institute of Chartered Shipbrokers,
25 Bury Street,
London, E.C.3.
Tel; 01-283 1361

## Solicitors

The main function of a solicitor in modern society is to give practical guidance to the public in the various transactions with which they are concerned during the course of their lives upon which the law, with its ever increasing complexity, impinges. The service afforded by solicitors thus extends far beyond the field of strict law and includes the giving of practical business advice based, not only on the legal position but also on the solicitor's knowledge and experience as a man of affairs.

The majority of solicitors in private practice in the smaller provincial towns are primarily engaged in conveyancing (the buying, selling. letting and mortgaging of houses, flats, farms or business premises). in acting for small family businesses, in making Wills, in obtaining probate of such Wills, in the winding up of estates of deceased persons, in the formation and administration of trusts and in conducting cases (both civil and criminal) for their clients before the County Courts and the Magistrates Courts. They also conduct cases before a wide range of Administrative Tribunals.

In the larger towns a number of solicitors in private practice tend to specialise in certain branches of the law such as company formation, reconstruction and amalgamation. There are also specialists in tax matters, in town and country planning, in trade marks, patents and designs, in insurance law, etc.

The overwhelming volume of a solicitor's work is preventive in its nature and directed towards keeping his client out of trouble rather than getting him out of it. Nevertheless by far the greatest part numerically of all Court advocacy throughout England and Wales is undertaken by solicitors because in the County Courts and in the Magistrates' Courts (in which over 90% of all the criminal cases brought before the Courts in England and Wales are heard and which also have civil jurisdiction to deal with certain matters such as the making of Separation Orders, between husband and wife and Orders for Maintenance of the wife and children) solicitors and barristers have an equal right of audience and in the bulk of these cases the solicitors act as the advocates. In cases which come before the Supreme Court, barristers have a sole right of audience; but even in these cases it is the solicitor who is responsible for all the preliminary work. Where, for example, there has been a road accident and there is a claim for damages for personal injury or for damage done to a vehicle, it is the solicitor who sees the client, takes a statement from him, interviews the witnesses and inspects the scene of the accident and if litigation becomes necessary, issues the Writ to start proceedings.


Law Society,
113 Chancery Lane,
London, W.C.2.
Tel; 01-242 1222


## Veterinary Surgeons

About two-thirds of the veterinary profession are in General Practice and provide a direct service to the public seeking treatment for sick animals or seeking protection for their animals against possible diseases. Veterinary practices in towns deal mostly with domestic animals kept as pets, while those in rural areas deal also with cattle, pigs, horses, sheep, goats, poultry, etc. The veterinary surgeon in general practice is as much concerned with the prevention of disease, particularly in flocks and herds, as with the treatment of individual animals. A veterinary practice may be run by a single veterinary surgeon, or may be a larger organisation managed by a principal with several qualified assistants, or a partnership. All practices have facilities for the diagnosis of disease and for medical and surgical treatment, and arrange for any necessary post-operative care and supervision.


Royal College of Veterinary Surgeons,
32 Belgrave Square,
London, S.W.1.
Tel; 01-235 4971

# INDEX